Politics and Ideology in Children's Literature

Marian Thérèse Keyes & Áine McGillicuddy

EDITORS

FOUR COURTS PRESS

Set in 10.5 pt on 12.5 pt Ehrhardt for
FOUR COURTS PRESS LTD
7 Malpas Street, Dublin 8, Ireland
www.fourcourtspress.ie
and in North America for
FOUR COURTS PRESS
c/o ISBS, 920 N.E. 58th Avenue, Suite 300, Portland, OR 97213.

A catalogue record for this title
is available from the British Library.

ISBN 978–1–84682–526–2

Printed and bound by
CPI Group (UK) Ltd, Croydon, CR0 4YY

Contents

Acknowledgments

Politics and ideology in children's literature is the seventh publication of the Irish Society for the Study of Children's Literature (ISSCL). The editors would like to thank the ISSCL's executive committee for their support and encouragement during the preparation of this volume for publication: the president, Anne Markey; the members of the committee: Ciara Ní Bhroin, Ríona Nic Congáil, Patricia Kennon, Nora Maguire, Julie Anne Stevens and past committee member, Beth Rodgers. We would also like to express our deep gratitude to the peer reviewers and members of the ISSCL editorial review board who provided such invaluable assistance on this volume: Matthew Grenby, Peter Hunt, Vanessa Joosen, Margaret Kelleher, Farah Mendlesohn, Emer O'Sullivan, Pat Pinsent and Mary Shine Thompson. The editors wish to acknowledge Dún Laoghaire-Rathdown County Council and the Faculty of Humanities and Social Sciences Book Publication Scheme at Dublin City University for providing financial aid towards the publication of this volume.

Sincere gratitude, also, to Martin Fanning and Meghan Donaldson from Four Courts Press for their assistance and encouragement, and to Marie-Louise Fitzpatrick for the wonderful cover image from her picturebook *I am I*.

Introduction: politics and ideology in children's literature

MARIAN THÉRÈSE KEYES & ÁINE McGILLICUDDY

'[C]hildren's literature and childhood do not exist outside ideology.'[1]

Children's literature, like literature for adults, is a product of its time and place and is shaped by the values and beliefs of those who write it. Indeed, there is a 'widespread acknowledgement that all texts are ideological and that those produced for children are especially so'.[2] Literature then is value-laden, to the extent that it can be argued that 'ideology is inescapable'.[3] The view that children's literature is deemed more ideological than literature intended for an adult readership, stems in large part from the perceived power imbalance in the relationship between adult and child. Such arguments put forward by Jacqueline Rose in her controversial work *The case of Peter Pan or the impossibility of children's literature*,[4] thirty years ago, that children's literature is never wholly free of this power imbalance, nor of adults' idealized perceptions of childhood, still resonate today. Adults, whether as authors, illustrators, publishers, teachers or parents, wield enormous power in the choice of what is written, published and selected for the child reader. Playing with the balance of power and the questioning of values and beliefs are central concerns in *Politics and ideology in children's literature,* the seventh edited collection of essays produced by the Irish Society for the Study of Children's Literature (ISSCL).[5]

---

1 Peter Hunt (ed.), *Children's literature: critical concepts in literary and cultural studies*, 3 (London, 2006), p. 2. 2 Ciara Ní Bhroin & Patricia Kennon (eds), *What do we tell the children? Critical essays on children's literature* (Newcastle upon Tyne, 2012), p. 1. 3 Hunt, *Children's literature*, 3, p. 3. 4 Jacqueline Rose, *The case of Peter Pan, or the impossibility of children's literature* (London, 1984). 5 The ISSCL is a research society that seeks to foster a multi-disciplinary approach to the study of literature for children and young adults in Ireland. Its publications are Celia Keenan & Mary Shine Thompson (eds), *Studies in children's literature, 1500–2000* (Dublin, 2005); Mary Shine Thompson & Celia Keenan (eds), *Treasure islands: studies in children's literature* (Dublin, 2006); Mary Shine Thompson & Valerie Coghlan (eds), *Divided worlds: studies in children's literature* (Dublin 2007); Mary Shine Thompson (ed.), *Young Irelands: studies in children's literature* (Dublin 2011); Ciara Ní Bhroin & Patricia Kennon (eds), *What do we tell the children? Critical essays on children's literature* (Newcastle upon Tyne, 2012); Nora Maguire & Beth Rodgers (eds), *Children's literature on the move: nations, translations, migrations* (Dublin 2013). Further information on the activities of the ISSCL is available at www.isscl.com.

In *Language and ideology in children's fiction*,[6] John Stephens contends that, 'the discourses of children's fiction are pervaded by ideological presuppositions, sometimes obtrusively and sometimes invisibly'.[7] His main concern is the relationship between ideology and language or how discourse, narrative processes and structures in children's literature transmit certain ideas and values. The quotation also posits that ideology is explicit, implicit or at times both, in children's fiction. Peter Hollindale refines notions of implicit and explicit ideology into conscious or overt ideology, passive or covert ideology and ideology that reflects not just an author's own conscious world view, but also his or her received assumptions and values from the environment in which they live and write.[8] Thus, ideological content can be transmitted in various ways in children's literature, at times not even deliberately on the part of the author.[9] From a variety of fresh perspectives, including ecocritical, biopolitical, cinematic and other comparative approaches, *Politics and ideology in children's literature* examines these implicit and explicit manifestations of ideology in children's literature, where the focus is on how children's literature can advocate or contest particular world views.

When Robert D. Sutherland states that 'the author's views are the author's politics'[10] he is more concerned with persuasive tactics in writing for children as opposed to political themes. He identifies three types of political ideology: the politics of advocacy, the politics of attack and the politics of assent. The first type is easy to recognize, where writers range from being openly didactic to using indoctrination in transmitting a particular moral or belief system. The politics of attack frequently adopt satire or negative object lessons as devices (punishment for behaviour perceived as wrong) to undermine beliefs or behaviour that run counter to the author's own views. This type of ideological message can be more difficult to recognize, particularly in works where the message is subtly portrayed. Finally, the politics of assent affirm ideologies already present in society and internalized, perhaps subconsciously by the author. This concurs with Stephens' opinion and that of Hollindale's (above) that '[i]deology [...] reflects beliefs and assumptions of which the author is, or may be, unaware'. [11] A discussion of ideological and political intent, used to persuade young readers to adopt certain values and to be shaped and socialized in particular ways, might suggest that the child reader is an empty vessel, passively receiving values transmitted by adults in an asymmetrical power relationship.

---

6 John Stephens, *Language and ideology in children's fiction* (London, 1992).   7 Ibid., pp 1–2.   8 Peter Hollindale, 'Ideology and the children's book', in Peter Hunt (ed.), *Children's literature: critical concepts in literary and cultural studies*, 3 (London, 2006), pp 101–19 at 119.   9 Hollindale perceives it as a truism that '[a] novel may be influential in ways its author did not anticipate or intend'. Ibid., p. 102.   10 Robert D. Sutherland, 'Hidden persuaders: political ideologies in literature for children', *Children's Literature in Education*, 16:3 (1985), 143–57 at 143.   11 Stephens, *Language and ideology*, p. 9; Hollindale, 'Ideology and the children's book', p. 102.

However, this is often far from the case. As Hollindale and others argue, it is not enough to acknowledge that ideology exists in children's literature. Adults, and children alike, must also be able to recognize, interpret and question it.[12] In other words, the child reader can be encouraged to think in a more critical manner, engage and act upon what they have read, even if this may not always be in the way the author had originally intended.

Children's literature therefore can also serve as a vehicle for social and political transformation, where the private and public spheres elide. The child reader can be challenged in his or her assumptions and in turn challenge adults and /or society's assumptions and beliefs. Children's literature offers the possibility to explore and promote new ideas that question, resist and undermine the status quo, just as much as it serves as a repository for encoded beliefs, prescribed doctrines or propaganda that support and reinforce this status quo. Both aspects underline the powerful potential of children's literature to shape and influence their readers and subsequently the society in which they live. Whether it is, as we shall see, a didactic tale chosen for a nineteenth-century annual for children or a twenty-first-century French picturebook, the central concern is to influence society for the better.

One of the distinct qualities of children's literature is that it is a genre that is both heavily monitored and tightly controlled for didactic purposes, yet also enjoys a greater freedom than literature for adults to be rebellious, illogical and irreverent. Kimberley Reynolds describes children's literature as 'a curious and paradoxical cultural space: a space that is simultaneously highly regulated and overlooked, orthodox and radical, didactic and subversive'.[13] This polemical description of children's literature mirrors that of attitudes to children themselves: children are controlled and socialized in preparation for their future roles as adults in the world; but can also be considered as naïve or somehow incomplete and therefore not always taken seriously. In her introduction to *Young Irelands*, Mary Shine Thompson describes childhood in the new Irish Republic as 'a metaphor for the emerging nation', where '[i]n every child is evident the possibility of improvement, growth and change [...] a ready symbol of progress and possibility, but also an affirmation of present inadequacy and imperfection'.[14] Such dichotomized views of childhood and fiction for children facilitate spaces in between for contestation and subversion and, as Reynolds describes it, ensures that the act of writing for young people can be an act 'replete with radical potential'.[15] Whatever the ideologi-

---

12 'Our priority in the world of children's books should not be to promote ideology but to understand it, and find ways of helping others to understand it, including the children themselves'. Hollindale, 'Ideology and the children's book', p. 108. See also Ní Bhroin & Kennon (eds), *What do we tell the children?*, p. 7.   13 Kimberley Reynolds, *Radical children's literature: future visions and aesthetic transformations in juvenile fiction* (London, 2007), p. 3.   14 Mary Shine Thompson (ed.), *Young Irelands: studies in children's literature*. Introduction, p. 11.   15 Reynolds, *Radical children's literature*, p. 1.

cal or political motivation, it can be agreed that fiction for children reveals the adult's 'impulse to intervene in the lives of children'.[16]

Children's literature therefore has the potential to subvert or promote particular political or ideological messages and it can transmit cultural or social values, often at critical junctures in history or in different social or geographical contexts. Thus, many of the studies in this book have a historical, political or social thrust. The essays in *Politics and ideology in children's literature* fall into four categories: ideology and subversion; utopias and dystopias; experiences of war and exile; and gender politics. Each of these sections includes original case studies, underpinned by diverse theoretical approaches that relate back to the leitmotifs of politics and ideology. These underlying twin themes are discussed in a variety of temporal and cultural contexts ranging from Victorian and Edwardian England to fascist European regimes and from mythical and modern Ireland to contemporary American and Canadian society. Many new voices, in addition to specialists from related disciplines, have joined established children's literature experts, to provide a wealth of important contributions to international scholarship in the field of children's literature.

Ideology and subversion are the main thematic considerations in the first section of the book, manifested in a range of theoretical approaches that deal with such varied topics as radical picturebooks, Beatrix Potter and ecocriticism, Aesop's fables and biopolitics and the subversive potential of Edward Lear's limericks.

Clémentine Beauvais' opening essay explores new approaches to analysing politically transformative children's literature. She identifies a split between children's books that encourage the child reader to take up political action on a local or microcosmic level and those that promote political action on a wider national or global stage at a macrocosmic level. Rather than dividing radical literature up thematically, she argues that important aspects of analysis can be lost if not discussed more holistically. To illustrate her thesis, her essay includes an analysis of two picturebooks that deal with the politically transformative at either end of this scale. The Spanish picturebook *¿Y yo qué puedo hacer?* (And what can I do?) is discussed for its microcosmic perspective, where the individual 'I' is rooted in existential angst but initiates political change by asking what he can do to connect with those around him. The second example, a French picturebook, *Révolution*, is explored as an example of change on a wider scale, where the focus is not just on the individual's ability to initiate change but on the individual as part of a wider group or community. Macrocosmic political change in children's literature is marked by the heritage of critical pedagogy and heterological power theories of the twentieth century and this jubilatory, radical form of politically transformative children's literature promotes a complete and systemic restructuration of socio-political con-

16 Stephens, *Language and ideology*, p. 8.

figurations through collective action. Here therefore, socio-political change is presented as something to strive for in an optimistic but realistic manner, influenced by theories of twentieth-century critical pedagogies. Beauvais, citing these and other well-known picturebooks, argues persuasively that radical children's literature needs to be approached from a different perspective, where the scope of politically transformative literature will enable us to comprehend, with greater clarity, the many diverse aspects of its radical potential.

Eithne O'Connell applies ecocritical theories to children's literature in an innovative study linking the life and work of Beatrix Potter to contemporary environmental research. Ecocriticism is concerned with the relationship between literature and the physical environment, often highlighting the fact that culture and the natural world are perceived as two separate domains, with culture prioritized to the detriment of nature and environmental concerns. Against this backdrop, Beatrix Potter's avoidance of overly sentimental depictions of nature and the animal kingdom is considered in tandem with her subtly subversive critical representation of British urban and rural culture and norms of her time. O'Connell draws, in particular, on the theories of Greta Gaard and her six boundary conditions for an ecopedagogy of children's environment literature.

Victoria de Rijke examines how biopolitics – a discipline which had its genesis in Michel Foucault's *The birth of biopolitics*[17] – can be applied to animal characters in children's literature. Animals feature in many tales for children and de Rijke demonstrates how fables, in particular, can be examined effectively through a biopolitical lens. Animals in fables are presented as cognizant human beings in the bodies of animals and, as such, they are political, a less than oblique reference to humans as political animals. De Rijke investigates the origins and adaptations of Aesop's fables over the centuries, the 'whitewashing' of the author for ideological reasons and the potential of fables to challenge accepted norms and mores in a radical way. She completes her study with an exploration of a selection of contemporary examples of playful political messages in books and film adaptations of books, using 'creaturely life' or animal characters which distil radical messages in a deceptively simple way. The often-unconscious relationship of children's literature to the symbolic order cracking under political pressure, using a series of fables and their 'creaturely life' posits the inherently subversive potential of this category of children's literature.

The relationship between ideology and subversion is pursued in quite another context in Olga Springer's essay, which explores Edward Lear's limericks, drawing on theories of the carnavalesque by Bakhtin, representations of the eccentric individual and the conflict between individual priorities and com-

17 Michel Senellart (ed.), *Michel Foucault, the birth of biopolitics. Lectures at the Collège de France, 1978–9* (Basingstoke, 2008). Trans. Graham Burchell.

munity expectations in conventional society. Bakhtin's dialogic theory, applied here to the interplay between text and image, highlights their open-ended meanings, which undermine explicit or reliable interpretations of the poems. Comparisons with Lear's contemporary John Stuart Mill on the ideologies of individualism and conformity in Victorian English society are emphasized throughout. Springer underlines the similar ideological content of their writings despite their diverse forms of expression. Reynolds points out that 'literary nonsense is precisely about the kind of wordplay that destabilizes meaning and so could be argued to be putting the self in jeopardy'.[18] In this light, the role of language (choice of adjectives, incoherency, nonsense) is identified by Springer as a subversive act reflecting the wider conflict between the interests of the individual and society.

Utopian and dystopian fiction – in particular the latter – is exceptionally popular at present, reflecting contemporary anxieties of young people. As Hollindale argues, 'authors can either transmit recommendations for an improved world reflecting not what it is but what (s)he hopes it can be or literature of warning about a corrupt world as the author *fears* it truly is or might be'.[19] The essays in this section respond to these concerns as they move between the emerging Irish Republic, Ireland's mythical past and contemporary Irish and Canadian societies and finally between a projected futuristic vision of the United States and echoes of its foundational past.

In the first essay in this section, it becomes apparent that novels are not always clearly polarized as either dystopian or utopian but can contain messages both of warning and recommendation. Anne Marie Herron's essay discusses the work of Irish author Eilís Dillon, who wrote for the future generation of young Irish, openly advocating 'a new role for the young as transmitters of nationalist ideology'.[20] Her stories, written mainly in the 1950s and 1960s, when Irish society was becoming increasingly modernized and commercialized, follow in the tradition of the Irish Literary Revival of the late nineteenth and early twentieth centuries, idealizing rural Ireland of a few decades previous as a symbol of untainted Irish identity and a repository of ancient wisdom. The recent past, in this sense, is presented in utopian terms. Herron highlights the didactic and political overtones of Dillon's fiction in her exhortations to the young to take pride in and learn from Ireland's past in order to build a positive Irish society. Nevertheless, more dystopian views of this past are also palpable, when Dillon warns her young readers to avoid romanticizing the Irish Republic's recent turbulent beginnings (of which the young Dillon and her family had direct experience) and to turn their back on violence. The flame of Irish nationalism and tradition, like the flame in the

18 Reynolds, 'Radical children's literature', p. 6.   19 Hollindale, 'Ideology and the children's book', p. 112.   20 Thompson, *Young Irelands*, Introduction, p. 11. Dillon was also the focus of the second book in the ISSCL series *Treasure islands* (2006).

hearths of those idealized rural Irish cottages, must be tended continuously, but also peacefully, to ensure an Ireland for future generations, which is devoid of the violence out of which it was born.

Mythical utopian visions of a past Ireland used as a cultural critique of the present are examined in Ciara Ní Bhroin's essay, which focuses on three fantasy novels set partially in contemporary Canada and Ireland and more predominantly in an imagined, mystical Irish past. Written by Irish-born, Canadian writer Orla Melling, Ní Bhroin demonstrates how Melling's fantasy fiction was inspired by her personal experiences as a returned emigrée to Ireland. Her work reveals the romantic wish-fulfilment of those returning to their land of origin where they experience displacement, dislocation and alienation. The idealized but also regressive images of Ireland accentuated in Melling's novels are presented as an escape from underlying tensions indicative of these difficulties of one's return to origins, to a modern but unfamiliar Ireland. Utopian images of a unified and mythical Ireland are promoted as a positive antidote to a more complex modern society in Canada but also as a message to modern day Ireland not to forget its traditions and ancient cultural heritage. Idealization of the past, issues of identity and recovery of origins are all central themes in this examination of utopian fantasy fiction.

In the final essay in this section, Susan Tan analyses a dystopian future rather than a utopian past, in her study of Suzanne Collins' *The hunger games* trilogy. The vision of the United States presented here is interpreted as a cautionary tale about contemporary values of modern-day American society. Tan examines notions of place and cultural memory in the trilogy through a variety of approaches, both textual and paratextual, and demonstrates how historical and geographical references create connections with and act as a critique of current society. Each district in the dystopian Panem relates to a distinct location in today's United States, creating an uncanny sense of both a familiar and unfamiliar place. The characteristics and activities in some of the districts in this dystopian totalitarian society are shown to allude to historical moments of violence in the United States, which jar with official (hi)stories of founding America's utopian past. The absence of historical memory, chillingly reminiscent of the aims of a Big Brother regime to alter and eradicate history, is presented in this essay as a highly troubled vision of national identity. Dystopian literature is used here to explore and target underlying current crises and ideological concerns, to warn against the dangers of forgetting and, as Tan concludes, to alert readers to the impossibility of ever escaping the evils of history.

'War and exile', the third section of this volume, explores through a variety of strategies, more overtly political topics in particular historical contexts. These essays underline how literature for children shapes attitudes to war, can explicitly serve as a vehicle for propaganda but also implicitly promote pacifism and tolerance as well as encourage empathy in depicting childhood experiences of political exile. In particular, the first two of the three essays in this section echo Reynold's view that, '[i]t is not accidental that at decisive moments in social history children have been at the centre of ideological activity and that writing for children has been put into the service of those who are trying to disseminate new world views, values and social models'.[21]

Elizabeth Galway's essay exemplifies this overtly ideological approach as she examines how a select range of children's literature during the First World War promoted propagandistic and often conflicting images of the child and were used to influence young readers in their attitudes to militarism, pacifism and gender politics. Galway demonstrates how such messages are especially contradictory during wartime, revealing conflicting ideological opinions. Taking examples from First World War British and American periodicals for young readers, Galway identifies depictions of the child in various guises at this significant moment in history. Images of the child as victim, used to promote in some instances the absurdity of war, but more often used to garner support for the war cause are contrasted with images of the child actively contributing to the war effort in a variety of ways. Galway highlights how these latter images are quite pervasive, where children are depicted as resourceful and valiant, both on and off the battlefield. War is presented to the child as a liberating activity, bringing with it adventure and autonomy. Galway draws attention to politically gendered images of childhood, such as girls fighting the enemy or nursing the war wounded in more unconventional and newly reconfigured female roles. Distinctly more pacifist images of children in the American context are also analyzed, where the child is perceived to be key in reconstructing the future. The contrast between the destruction of European youth, with its images of child victims and soldiers, and the promotion of an intact American youth, full of energy and vigour, at a further remove from the battlefields, is emphasized. This younger American generation symbolizes hope as the world's future thinkers and leaders. Such examples of contrasting images of the child all serve to highlight the multi-layered and complex ideological functions at play in some examples of First World War literature for children.

Jessica D'Eath's treatment of fascist children's literature of the interwar period in Italy is a reminder of arguments by Thompson and Reynolds that not all children's texts promote liberal values.[22] Certainly the texts discussed here, like those in the previous essay, are noteworthy examples of children's literature that has fallen out of favour as society's attitudes and political regimes change. Nevertheless, such literature offers valuable insights into particular political and historical contexts. In her study, D'Eath examines a body

21 Reynolds, *Radical children's literature*, p. 2.   22 Keenan & Thompson (eds), *Studies in children's literature, 1500–2000*; Reynolds, *Radical children's literature*.

of children's propaganda novels written in the 1930s, recalling and glorifying the violent but often controversial acts of the 1920s grassroots movement of fascist squad members or *Squadrista*. She demonstrates how these revisionist writings of the 1930s, to promote the image of squad members as gallant fascists, were markedly absent from Italian popular culture of the 1920s, when many of these squads were at the height of their power. As such, the novels are a conscious attempt to rehabilitate the squad's aims and activities into the official narrative of the fascist regime a decade later in the 1930s. D'Eath explains that given the negative perceptions of the squads amongst the adult population of Mussolini's Italy, who remembered and were possibly the victims of their actions, children were considered the ideal target audience for these revised accounts. The violent acts of the squads were not omitted from stories for children but, as D'Eath points out, contextualized in a different manner, where depictions of violence were acceptable as long as they adhered to a certain 'ethical' code. In the aftermath of the First World War, D'Eath highlights how the squad members are also presented as guardians of the memory of the First World War and its veterans. The aim was to foster patriotic sentiment in Italy's young generation in preparation for future war. Such novels are an obvious example of how children's literature can be used effectively as a tool of propaganda to embed particular ideas in a generation of young readers.

Áine McGillicuddy's essay explores issues of identity around growing up in exile against the backdrop of another fascist context: Nazi Germany, the Second World War and its aftermath. Her study examines German-born, British author Judith Kerr's fictionalized autobiography, a trilogy entitled, *Out of the Hitler time*. Kerr, under the guise of her alter ego and protagonist, 9-year-old Anna, recalls her experiences as a Jewish child refugee, fleeing Nazi Germany with her family when Hitler came to power in 1933. Much of the examination of a childhood in exile in this essay focuses on the first book in this trilogy, *When Hitler stole Pink Rabbit*. The physical and psychological shifts in migrating from one country to another, and from one cultural and linguistic space to another are explored in terms of their effect on Anna and her family. References are also made to Kerr as author and illustrator of children's classics, such as *The tiger who came to tea* and her *Mog the cat* series, within the context of the lasting effects of upheaval and exile experienced as a child. Representations of contrasting images of German and individual identity, as well as those of the other cultures encountered and described in Kerr's works, are also examined, where it is argued that the trilogy implicitly teaches valuable lessons about the trauma of political rupture and encourages empathy in the child reader for the plight of refugees in other more contemporary contexts.

'Gender politics' is the title of the final section in this collection and covers a variety of contexts, spanning from nineteenth-century England and Ireland to twenty-first-century France and contemporary American society.

Even more varied are the materials used to explore the theme of gender politics, ranging from an examination of the role of paratexts in gender formation, to film adaptations of a fairytale to a discussion of rape myths in popular teen fiction.

The use of the paratext in a selection of nineteenth-century publications by Anna Maria Hall is the focus of Marian Thérèse Keyes' essay. Texts are rarely presented in an unadorned state without such elements as bindings, frontispieces, prefaces and advertisements. These paratextual elements can function persuasively, in an openly didactic manner, playing into what Sutherland describes as '[t]he overt didacticism of much Victorian children's literature [...] exhortations to religious piety, right conduct and good manners'.[23] In other words, it is a literature that exemplifies Sutherland's notion of the politics of advocacy. In the first section of her essay, Keyes examines three portraits of Hall that highlight the ideological power of the frontispiece authorial portrait. These portraits are loaded with gendered significance, demonstrating to readers how the author conformed to and embodied Victorian values of family duty, hard work and female virtue. In the second part of the essay, Keyes analyses a range of paratextual elements in *The Juvenile Forget-Me-Not* (1829–37). As the editor of this popular annual for children, Hall was well placed to control such elements, harnessing them to reinforce the didactic content of her publications for children.

French film director Catherine Breillat's 2009 adaptation of the *Bluebeard* tale is examined by Brigitte Le Juez against the backdrop of a discussion ranging from its folk tale origins to Charles Perrault's literary fairy tale version and the many subsequent adaptations, particularly by feminist writers. Le Juez discusses the cinematic aspects of Breillat's version of *Bluebeard*, arguing that it brings a fresh perspective to the development of the female protagonist by a film director, renowned for her many, often controversial, films, that centre on young female protagonists. Female empowerment is shown to be at the heart of Breillat's film, reflecting changing perceptions of gender roles over the last century and how this most unconventional of fairy tales is constantly revised and revitalized. Nonetheless, Le Juez also reminds us in her conclusion that, despite the female protagonist's successful struggle for survival, continued preoccupation and fascination with this tale reveal the persistent failure of society to address issues of abuse of young women to the present day.

Ambiguous messages about gender roles and myths about rape and sexuality in popular teenage and vampire literature are the thematic concerns in the final essay of this collection. Marion Rana examines the eroticization and trivialization of sexual violence in contemporary popular teenage fiction and demonstrates how it is justified by its authors through different plot devices.

23 Sutherland, 'Hidden persuaders', 144.

Sexual violence is shown to be a recurring topic in young adult literature. Some works deal with this topic openly to contribute and stimulate debate in public on sexual violence, but Rana is concerned with those that present sexual violence as unproblematic, variously reinterpreting it as passion or reassigning responsibility to the victim. Different rape myths put forward to justify sexual violence against women are examined by Rana, using the framework of six categorizations outlined by theorist Martha Burt. Rana then analyzes works such as *Girl, 15, charming but insane*, *Twilight* and *Vampire diaries* for their use of such rape myths. Rana's study also highlights another issue, one that has been raised by Reynolds: that of the uncritical reader, who, in consuming certain types of popular teenage fiction, can assume that such representations of gender roles are the norm.[24] Rana advocates that young readers need to be alert to recognize how they can be manipulated through these ideologically-charged discourses.

Through a variety of critical perspectives on historical and contemporary texts, *Politics and ideology in children's literature* highlights conflicts between individualism and the desires and expectations of the community, extending to troubled visions of national identity and indeed global power. There is no doubt that politics and ideology play a central role in children's literature, either implicitly or explicitly and the essays in this book highlight how adult ideologies can imbue children with powerful philosophical mindsets.

24 See chapter 4 of Reynolds, *Radical children's literature*, pp 68–87.

Little tweaks and fundamental changes: two aspects of sociopolitical transformation in children's literature

CLÉMENTINE BEAUVAIS

So-called 'radical' books for young readers, whether they follow Philip Nel and Julia Mickenberg's political definition[1] or Kimberley Reynolds' wider one,[2] do not constitute a monolithic corpus. Beyond being difficult to categorize – one country's radicalism may be its neighbour's mainstream – and easily outdated, this type of children's literature, when studied, is often divided up thematically. 'Green', 'Marxist', 'antiracist', 'queer': though helpful for some purposes, such terminology artificially fragments the corpus into a jigsaw puzzle of political bibliotherapy, each piece catering to a different malady of contemporary society. It prominently betrays a critical tendency to draw further dividing lines between sociopolitical struggles at the level of literary analysis, the better to reassert the relevance of such books only to their chosen injustices. It finally tucks into easily handled packages, by baptizing them 'feminist' or 'alterglobalist', a wealth of vibrant perspectives expressing themselves through endless play on the possibilities of the children's book. Metacritically speaking, it is, in short, a treatment of political radicalism in literature that innocuously segments its objects of study to weaken their powers, and remains impervious to their aesthetic variations.

I call for the fluid, controversial, commonly disagreed-upon, ever-changing corpus of texts that we might name politically 'radical' or 'transformative' children's literature to be analysed transversally. If *Princess Smartypants*[3] never meets *Click, clack, moo! Cows that type*[4] in scholarly writing due to their articulating different 'struggles', we are missing out on essential reflection on the use of humour and repetition in radical children's literature. Conversely, throwing Armin Greder's *The island*[5] alongside Shaun Tan's *The arrival*[6] on grounds of similar subject matter risks drowning the

1 Julia Mickenberg & Philip Nel, *Tales for little rebels: a collection of radical children's literature* (New York, 2008). 2 Kimberley Reynolds, *Radical children's literature: future visions and aesthetic transformations in juvenile fiction* (London, 2007). 3 Babette Cole, *Princess Smartypants* (London, 1986). 4 Doreen Cronin & Betsy Lewin, *Click, clack, moo! Cows that type* (New York, 2000). 5 Armin Greder, *The island* (Sydney, 2007). 6 Shaun

many formal and aesthetic divergences that make the former a chilling thought experiment in political theory and the latter an intimate and lyrical tale of contestation.

In this essay, I propose to reflect on politically transformative children's books according to a line of enquiry that, I believe, has the capacity to enhance our understanding of the different conceptions of change and political theories underlying this type of literature.[7] This is, namely, a consideration of the *scope* of the social and political transformation encouraged by the works, regardless of their subject matter. Between books that present and promote local, gradual changes to sociopolitical configurations and those that advocate complete restructuring of whole 'worlds', subtle non-thematic distinctions can be articulated. The former type, as we shall see, is characterized by an existentialist form of reflection, typically precipitated by an epiphany, and entailing for the characters and for the reader a consideration of absolute responsibility for the world. But this endeavour finds its limitations in itself, and the necessarily restricted scope of the change accompanies a reflection on the restricted scope of human action. The latter type, on the other hand, is celebratory and jubilatory. It delights in pinpointing, idealistically, the endless potential of humanity to bring about modifications to the world, and particularly that of children exposed to its educational ideals. Aligned with the critical pedagogy of the twentieth century (itself derived from Marxism), these books glorify the figure of what I call the mighty child, and only find their limitations in the eye of the less optimistic reader.

To this duality corresponds a dual conception of the child as gazed upon by the adult. In the former, the child is glorified *as child* for being a vector of absolute change: condensing, as a figure, adult desires for newness, it will by necessity transform the world – it contains its action, in other words, within its intention. In the latter, the child, though it is still a partly numinous and meaningful figure, is glorified *as person* – symbolizing, through the failure of intention, the 'nothingness coiled in the heart of being – like a worm' that Sartre placed as the centre of existential vertigo.[8] Nowhere, perhaps, is this distinction more clearly articulated than in politically transformative children's literature; however, I would like to make it clear that I do not claim that it is limited to this type of book. Though politically transformative children's lit-

Tan, *The arrival* (New York, 2005).   **7** This project draws heavily on my doctoral research, which investigates the exchange of power(s) between adult and child in what I call politically transformative children's literature – a political subcategory of Reynolds' 'radical' children's books. My corpus of international picturebooks has been gathered according to this stipulative definition: they are books which encourage the child reader to question the social and political configurations of the world, and optionally entice him or her to modify them in the future.   **8** Jean-Paul Sartre, *Being and nothingness*, trans. H.E. Barnes (London, 1958).

erature offers a convenient package for observing this phenomenon, I maintain that more conventional examples of children's books articulate a similar distinction, and that by grasping it through the means of 'radical' stories, we can enhance our comprehension of the more mainstream ones.

LITTLE TWEAKS TO THE WORLD: TRANSFORMATIVE CHILDREN'S LITERATURE AND THE EXISTENTIALIST CONDITION

> I emerge alone and in anguish confronting the unique and original project which constitutes my being; all the barriers, all the guard rails collapse, nihilated by the consciousness of my freedom [...] I have to realize the meaning of the world and of my essence; I make my decision concerning them – without justification and without excuse.[9]

As a Sartrian reading of children's texts that advocate sociopolitical change on a microscopic scale reveals, the child figures in such texts may be addressed as transformative agents without being sanguinely endowed with idealistic adult desires for the future. Instead, the texts can be seen as equipping the child with both responsibility for the world and the resulting anguish to witness its limitations. Pedagogically speaking, it is, of course, an undeniably paradoxical position, which envisages the child as *project* rather than as object of the adult's gaze, but still requires the didactic discourse in order to be activated. Gazed at by the angst-ridden adult, and made to experience an existential epiphany in turn, the child is thrown into the world with new freedom, but new anguish also: and it is from this highly ambiguous sense of empowerment that sociopolitical change is brought about in these deceptively optimistic children's books.

An exploration of an example of such children's books – Jesus Cisneros and José Campanari's *¿Y yo qué puedo hacer?*[10] [And what can I do?] illustrates how, from absolute negativity, these picturebooks infused with existential anguish substitute the 'super-child' of much radical children's literature with an epiphanic understanding of one's responsibility for the world, in all its greatness and with all its flaws. A decidedly didactic picturebook, *¿Y yo qué puedo hacer?* offers a clear line of action for social changes on the scale of the city, and a critique of the individualistic and solipsistic tendencies engendered by consent for the sociopolitical status quo.

In this contemplative urban tale, the protagonist, Señor Equis (Spanish for 'Mr X'), lives alone with an unnamed dog. Señor Equis is extremely sensitive

---

9 Ibid., p. 63.   10 José Campanari, ill. Jesus Cisneros, *¿Y yo qué puedo hacer?* (Pontevedra, 2008). Publication has not been translated into English to date.

to the world around him, of which he gets, a presumably distorted view, through his reading of newspapers at breakfast. Sad news 'gives him the chills from his big toe to the tip of his nostril',[11] and his body becomes *literally* charged with concerns – represented, in a typically postmodern fashion, through the use of newspaper cuttings. He is plagued by a constant question: 'And what can *I* do?'. It is only when he finally voices this question out loud that people start answering it, and Equis discovers how he can help, at a local level, his neighbours and passers-by. As Equis' engagement with the world increases, so does the space devoted to visual material on the page. The vast emptiness of Equis' solitary life slowly evolves towards the last people-filled doublespread.

Equis lives in 'one of these cities full of people'[12] but with no collective glue. His semi-accidental fall into action, when he lets slip the question 'And what can I do?', has an exponential effect, as he gradually finds more to *do* in the city. Like Equis, readers are invited by the verbal and the visual text to perceive themselves as responsible agents. But the picturebook insists that it all begins on a microcosmic, individual scale, with the realization that *I* is the basic entity from which all world-constructions derive. The question that forms the title of the book is revealing: since '¿qué puedo hacer?' would suffice to ask 'What can I do?', the redundant 'y' (and) and 'yo' (I) double the insistence on the active subject. However, despite the subject enhancement, this question illustrates the inextricable engagement of this *I* with the world in the form of the active verb 'to do', presenting 'I' as both a lonely, singular entity, and as a participant in world-creation – the value-builder.

Señor Equis is the existentialist individual, at the heart of the nausea-inducing tension between meaning and meaninglessness. He is Mr X, the meaningless Everyman, an inexcusable, baseless basis for his own actions. But he is also, in the narrative, the spotlighted one: the focus for all action – there would be no story without Señor Equis. He is at once absolutely ordinary and absolutely irreplaceable: he is, the story tells the reader, just like you in the world; no one else can be you, but you are chillingly surrounded with the 'nothingnesses' (what Sartre calls *négatités*) of what you can sense you are not and what you will one day – albeit unimaginably – cease to be. It is very revealing that the way in which Equis acquires authenticity is by asking a question. The existentialist epiphany derives from the individual's status as questioner of being and finder of nothingness. The value-building dimension and the instability of this act are highlighted in the picturebook, which encourages the child reader to voice questions out into the unpredictable world – even though the answers might pull them far out of their comfort zone.

11 Ibid., unpaginated, Clementine Beauvais' translation. 12 Ibid.

But whatever Señor Equis might do, loneliness, anguish and concern about the world and one's meaningful role in it are an ineluctable part of maturing. Being a transformative agent – acting authentically by understanding that one's actions involve the whole of humanity – entails feeling the shortcomings of the world. The world, or so the picturebook tells us, is an essentially unknowable and untrustworthy mess in which we attempt, sometimes vainly, to detect patterns. By forming Equis' body out of newspaper cuttings, additionally printed backwards, Cisneros (the illustrator), deconstructs the meaning pieced together by narrative. In so doing, he questions the validity of the information displayed within the picturebook itself. It is beyond narrative that a solution is to be found; not in the tidy order of print, but in accidental slips of the tongue and considerations of what is not. The picturebook inscribes the temporary resolution of Equis' anguish in a malleable, self-originating sense of agency. Equis can never know the world and make it fully his; what his body takes of the world – words printed backwards, cut and pasted – are just shreds of knowledge, resulting from a consciousness throwing itself blindly into existence. This recomposed knowledge also triggers destructive interrogations. As Señor Equis' 'And what can I do?' is still 'inside' him, it actively blocks his senses: 'But the question/ covers his eyes/ lodges itself inside his nose/ enters his ears/ and Señor Equis/ cannot see or smell or hear [...]'.[13]

But finally the question settles for his tongue, and the next morning, as he opens the window: 'he can see the clear sky, smell the flowers on his neighbour's balcony, hear the song of the birds'. Just then the question finally escapes his mouth and is immediately answered by his neighbour on the third floor. This incident marks the sudden encounter of two subjectivities, ending the solipsistic period that surrounds Equis' first steps into the existentialist condition. In this new development, Equis' anguished mind gives birth to a question about his role in the world, and because of this he finds himself immediately clashing with another subjectivity.

This encounter of subjectivities gradually becomes a systematic event in Equis' life and the picturebook ends by welcoming it in all its unpredictability: 'But he knows that every time the question leaves his mouth, someone will answer it.' The accompanying picture shows Equis and his dog walking through a doublespread filled with all kinds of people. His size on the page, compared to earlier spreads, has decreased: he is now fully aware of his own existence, of the dynamic nature of his actions to construct values and his own essence, and of the importance of others in this process. But there is no clue that his previous encounters have led to any close relationships – he is still alone, his body language remains meditative. The child reader is left with a bittersweet ending: that one, in order to act

13 Ibid.

authentically, has to build oneself and one's values from nothing, to clash against other subjectivities and create meaning out of these encounters; but that this is no guarantee of ever finding an ultimate meaning in these relationships. The picturebook's repetitive structure hints at the Sisyphus-like nature of such an existence. If there is no justification for it, there is no direct consolation either and it gains and loses meaning with no teleology other than the one which it creates for itself.

This is not to say, however, that such stories are *hopeless* or validate a meaningless portrayal of life. If that were so, they would not be truly trans-formative, as they would turn active engagement with the world into a super-fluous expression of personal whim. The narrative, on the contrary, defines hope for future changes in society, as stemming from a primary transforma-tion of destructive feelings into constructive decisions at the level of the indi-vidual. These decisions, the picturebook tells us, have recognisable repercussions on the workings of the city and on the human community. In other words, they are political. It is by turning anguish into meaning-making and value-building in one's own life that a sociopolitical programme of change can be designed. This is the defining element of the *hope* of the adult of politically transformative children's literature: hope is the feeling that one's authentic conduct may lead to the materialization of one's created values on a wider sociopolitical scale. Nothing can be counted upon other than the notion that one is doing as much as one can to act as authentically as possi-ble, realizing the extent of one's freedom and using it to create transforma-tive social and political values.

REVOLUTIONARY CHANGES: THE CREATION OF A CRITICAL MASS

On the other end of the spectrum of radical children's literature lies the politically transformative children's book that advocates change on a macrocosmic scale – the city, the nation, even the world – relying, in this process, on addressing not the individual but the multitude. Or, perhaps, the individual *as part of* the multitude: following the philosophical heritage of Paulo Freire,[14] the founder and proponent of critical pedagogy. The role of the educational text is here to generate and galvanize a critical mass, capable of confronting the established order. Anguish in the face of nothingness, a highly individualistic and solipsistic phenomenon, is here erased by the focus on the common struggle. Such books often display a teleological conception of sociopolitical change, which provides both a cause to strive for and a

---

14 Paulo Freire, *Pedagogy of the oppressed*, trans. M.B. Ramos (New York, 2003).

strategic way of fulfilling its potential. They are concerned with immanence, latency, potency: what the world could be and should be, who could enact the necessary changes, and the politically committed text becomes the mediator and generator of the answers to these questions. However, as Joe Kincheloe[15] points out, critical pedagogy is anti-Cartesian and anti-positivist in nature: the concern is not to present sociopolitical change as monolithic and ready-made, but rather to display a form of 'critical hope'[16] that the students, turned into *mighty* questioners and problem-posers, will actively feed into.

Such books therefore, reintegrate the concept of utopia within the educational endeavour, insofar as they subsume a general optimism for improvement within a communitarian effort triggered and encouraged through education. However, this utopian imagination is not a naïve or unrealistic one: it has its roots firmly anchored in the present and the political. In this they join David Halpin's[17] concept of utopia and hope in education. Reintegrating hope at the core of the educational endeavour, Halpin distinguishes between two types of hope: absolute hope, often dependent on naïve faith and bound to cause despair when it is inevitably left unrealized; and ultimate hope, an 'aimed'[18] form of utopian thinking whereby one refuses fatalism and turns to transformative action without abandoning one's critical awareness of the limitations of one's project. I would argue that in the case of children's books concerned with macrocosmic, radical change, limitations are often overcome by the books' resort to narrative and visual strategies aiming to redistribute, and therefore multiply, the different areas of potency of the transformative agents.

This is nowhere more visible than in the ample corpus of picturebooks depicting revolution or rebellion against an oppressive state. A common point between these books is that they are often composed of a mixture of fictional and non-fictional elements, so as to provide the child reader not only with allegories or illustrations of revolutionary struggles but also with the historical, social and cultural keys to decode them, thus adding to the fine-tuning of their 'critical consciousness', a crucial factor in Freire's writings. I will examine an outstanding example of one such picturebook, *Révolution*,[19] by the renowned French artist Sara. Almost wordless (here and there, words such as 'Prisoner!' or 'Oooh!' appear on the pages like graphic rather than linguistic elements), the picturebook displays Sara's usual technique of torn paper, with only two colours (red and black) on white pages. The storyline can be summarized briefly as an account of a revolutionary crowd who, fighting against an oppressive army state, find hope and metaphorical guidance in the sacrifi-

15 Joe L. Kincheloe, *Critical pedagogy* (New York, 2004).   16 Ibid., p. 72.   17 David Halpin, *Hope and education: the role of the utopian imagination* (London, 2003).   18 Ibid., p. 17.   19 Sara, *Révolution* (Chennai, 2008).

cial figure of one of their members. The exact events occurring in the picturebook are unclear, dreamlike and purposefully left open to interpretation. Following the imprisonment of one nameless member of the crowd, the lion on the revolutionary flag escapes from the standard, frees the prisoner and the lion and the ex-prisoner both reintegrate the flag in the re-energized crowd. Counterbalancing the cryptic message of the picturebook, is a long postface by its Indian editor, who links the atemporal, uchronic fable to specific events of revolution in France, China and Latin America, before concluding:

> This book gestures towards diverse histories and events, but the power of what it represents is not exhausted by any of them. The red lion in the flag continues to beckon towards the future, even as it recalls past resistance and martyrdom.[20]

The alliance of informative text, with, or alongside the story of the picturebook, besides being a common device in such books, enables the young reader to be doubly interpelated: first via the imagination, and second (or in parallel) in his or her sociopolitical consciousness. In other words, the pedagogical agenda of such books is at least partly marked with a belief that the young reader must be addressed both as an emotional and as a rational agent in order for his or her transformative potential to be fulfilled. To become part of the critical mass against the established order, such literature tells us, it is necessary to understand the problem both vicariously and critically. Whether such an endeavour is excessively didactic or, on the contrary, equips the reader with intellectual tools to evaluate the situation remains to be evaluated; I would argue that such questions are very much subsumable into considerations of quality rather than genre or theme.

Recurring motifs of books that place such ultimate hope in the child as future member of a critical mass, are facelessness and namelessness. Picturebooks that focus on microscopic change, tend to focus, of necessity, on the individual. Conversely, the individual tends to merge into a crowd of equals in picturebooks that advocate revolution or collective resistance. The only visual difference between the young prisoner of Sara's *Révolution* and the other revolutionaries is a red bandana. The primary effect of this mass anonymity is that individual concerns (of an existential nature and beyond) are occulted or transferred to considerations of the common effort. Psychological depth, though not completely nonexistent, gives place to breadth of action. The child reader is thus not addressed as the unique, angst-ridden creator of his or her own existence but as a highly intersubjective player bound to the interests and dreams of the rest of the crowd.

20 V. Geetha, 'Revolution and memory', in Sara, *Révolution*, unpaginated.

A sense of balance must be found, however, in order not to depersonalize this representation of the common struggle completely. Sara's artwork in *Révolution* aptly plays on various degrees of focus to attract the reader's attention to the iconic figure of the resistant on one page and zoom back onto the crowd in the next. This very cinematographic approach to picturebook art leads to a constant readjustment of the reader's viewpoint from individual to mass and from symbol to person, creating a sense of fluidity between the real and the imagined, the critical and the emotional, in one's encounter with the concept of revolution and transformative action. Erasing the limits between, on the one hand, individuality and community, and on the other hand between the iconic and the tangible, the storylines and the artwork blend into the ideal of revolution, the fragments of personal and interpersonal hopes and actions which constitute it. Despite these flagrantly postmodern undertones, the representation of revolution remains idealistic, forcefully optimistic, even sublime; if there are obstacles to it, such as imprisonment or even death, they feed into it afterwards to reaffirm its objectives and reactivate ultimate hope. This vision of revolution is cyclical, if not eternal: its objective is its transmission as much as it is the transformation of the external world. The educational ideal of generational improvement is ubiquitous: the fallen fighter becomes the next generation's symbol. From this historicist perspective, radical children's literature participates fully in the constant progress of society toward equality and freedom.

These picturebooks, whether or not situated in a particular nation (as indeed they often are), delineate an 'imaginary homeland', to take Salman Rushdie's expression,[21] which is perfectible and in permanent reconfiguration – and one which depends on the critical army of the people to realize its potential. Relying on the multitude of child readers to achieve this goal, they transmit an ideal of growth and maturation towards adulthood as a series of sometimes violent reconstructions of one's project in accordance with or against others. The child, as a citizen-in-becoming, sees its physical and intellectual maturation paralleled with the maturation of the people. The revolutionary impulse becomes naturalized, integrated within the developmental process of the child's growth. The educative mission of the picturebook returns to the etymological sense of the word *education*, 'to make something come out of', teasing out the 'natural' impulse to rebel, contest and transform which the changing body of the child contains.

These picturebooks, though they do not necessarily eclipse the uncertainty of the revolutionary struggle, are celebratory odes to childhood as endowed with *time to act*. By investing the child as body and as symbol with the hopes of transformative action, they sublimate the time left of the group of citizens-to-be that children represent. Contrary to the books that focus on the faulty

21 Salman Rushdie, *Imaginary homelands* (London, 1991).

individual as modifier of the world motivated by anguish, and therefore as a unique person plagued by their existential condition, picturebooks which advocate change on a macrocosmic level focus on the mighty child: the child able to decode, critique, act and interact. The ideology is idealistic insofar as it is optimistic and infused with symbol; the revolutionary movements certainly acquire a mythical dimension.

But if the ultimate hope knows no bounds, the picturebooks certainly do. As always, it is difficult to evaluate whether the right balance can ever be found, in such occurrences of critical pedagogy, between spurring learners into action and forcing them into it; between activating their critical judgement and giving them, inadvertently or not, oppressive lines of reasoning. Within the current paradigm of children's literature criticism, which tends to detect the normalization of adult values and the ostracism of childhood in many aspects of the children's book as such, it is often easy to interpret these books as equally indoctrinatory or authoritarian as the regimes they claim to want to overthrow. The wide variety of such picturebooks, however, has to be noted; and I would argue in favour of a case-by-case approach to such categories, so as not to dismiss in one large sweep a highly variegated spectrum of discursive, aesthetic, thematic and ideological approaches to the question of macrocosmic sociopolitical change.

CONCLUSION: TWO IDEOLOGIES OF CHANGE, TWO LEVELS OF IMPLICATION

Reducing politically committed books to their superficial messages of sociopolitical transformation runs the risk of obliterating the major differences in the address to, and the implication of the reader by, the text and the ideology. The scope and degree of perfection of the change enacted, imply different conceptions of the role of the individual in the world, with external and internal limitations, and with or without an awareness of them. Their educational projects are therefore different. While one appeals to the anguish-ridden freedom of the individual and seeks to trigger motivation for change through the realization of one's potential (despite the certainty of ultimate annihilation), the second plunges the reader into the jubilatory spectacle of anti-authoritarian action, merging the individual into the collective and the symbolic into the real. Emerging from the melancholic realization of one's freedom, microcosmic change in politically committed picturebooks is above all an address to the individual as eternally alone and yet compelled to project herself or himself into the world. Macrocosmic change, optimistic and future-bound, springs from an inherent faith in the perfectibility of the world and of the child in it, an emotional and intellectual agent whose growth mirrors the longed-for evolution of society. These picturebooks, in short, do not occupy the same aesthetic, ideological and pedagogical territory, and it is through an analysis of their subtleties and peculiarities that we will achieve a better vision of the extraordinarily varied corpus under the umbrella-term of 'radical' literature for children.

Ecocriticism, ecopedagogy and the life and works of Beatrix Potter

EITHNE O'CONNELL

INTRODUCTION

My initial exposure to environmental issues could perhaps be traced back to September 1962 when, at the age of five, I received my first Beatrix Potter book, *The tale of the Flopsy Bunnies*.[1] The book, with its cautionary text and wonderfully realistic rabbit illustrations, moved me beyond the more simplistic representations of animals and the natural world, which had characterized most of my early read-aloud books, and alerted me to the fact that animals have good cause to fear humans. But that date is significant for another, not entirely unrelated reason. September 1962 was also the original publication date of *Silent spring*,[2] the ground-breaking bestseller by American biologist and social critic, Rachel Carson. She critiqued the damage caused by the reckless use of DDT to the natural environment and the whole food chain – affecting insects, birds and, ultimately, humans. The book is credited with bringing about the US ban in 1972 on agricultural use of DDT, a victory that came too late for Carson, who had died of cancer in 1964, aged just 56. *Silent spring* is seen as marking the beginning of the environmental movement and, as such, is a key text in ecocritical studies. In 1965, my mother acquired a paperback copy and I can still recall how she introduced me to its contents by citing the post-apocalyptic fable of the first chapter:

> There was a strange stillness. The birds, for example – where had they gone? [...] The feeding stations in the backyards were deserted. The few birds seen anywhere were moribund; they trembled violently and could not fly. It was a spring without voices. On the mornings that had once throbbed with the dawn chorus [...] there was now no sound; only silence lay over the fields and woods and marsh [...] No witchcraft, no enemy action had silenced the rebirth of new life in this stricken world. The people had done it themselves.[3]

Some years ago, while conducting research on Potter, I discovered that one of her biographers, Linda Lear,[4] had coincidentally also written an acclaimed

---

1 Beatrix Potter, *The tale of the Flopsy Bunnies* (London, 1909). 2 Rachel Carson, *Silent spring* (London, 1965). 3 Ibid., p. 22. 4 See Linda Lear, *Rachel Carson: witness for*

biography of Carson. Reminded of how these two pioneering environmental-
ists had both exerted a strong influence on me at a young age, I started to
investigate ecocriticism and ecopedagogy with enthusiasm and curiosity.

ECOCRITICISM: AN OVERVIEW

Ecocriticism is a relatively new interdisciplinary approach to literary studies
that can be traced back officially to 1978, when the term first appeared in an
essay by the American critic, William Rueckert, entitled 'Literature and ecology: an experiment in ecocriticism'.[5] Although it was influenced by the environmental movements of the 1970s, it was slow to get off the ground as an
area of literary criticism, really only starting to attract serious academic attention in the 1990s, with the publication in the United States of key texts such
as *The environmental imagination: Thoreau, nature writing, and the formation of
American culture* in 1995[6] and *The ecocriticism reader: landmarks in literary ecology*[7] a year later. Since then, the field has developed in a number of directions
and moved beyond its initial confines of academia in the United States and
the United Kingdom.

While its focus was initially adult literature, ecocriticism has also been
applied to other literary fields, ranging from environmental texts to children's
literature.[8] The case for linking ecocriticism and literature for children owes
much to pioneering research by Harrison et al.,[9] which highlighted the extent
to which attitudes to the environment are traditionally shaped by childhood
experiences, as well as to the work of others such as Ward[10] on the role of
children's reading in the formation of these attitudes. A more recent publication draws attention to what Louv[11] identifies as a kind of nature deficit disorder in growing numbers of urban children, who do not play much, if at all,
in the outdoors and have not developed a necessary empathetic attachment to
nature, due to lack of exposure to the environment around them. Although
ecocriticism has only rather belatedly been applied to works for children, it is

nature (New York, 1997) and Linda Lear, *Beatrix Potter: the extraordinary life of a
Victorian genius* (London, 2008).   **5** William Rueckert, 'Literature and ecology: an experiment in ecocriticism', *Iowa Review*, 9:1 (1978), 71–86.   **6** Lawrence Buell, *The environmental imagination: Thoreau, nature writing, and the formation of American culture*
(Cambridge, MA, 1995).   **7** Cheryll Glotfelty & Harold Fromm (eds), *The ecocriticism
reader: landmarks in literary ecology* (Athens, GA, 1996).   **8** One of the first works linking
ecocriticism to children's literature was Sidney Dobrin and Kenneth Byron Kidd (eds),
Wild things: children's culture and ecocriticism (Detroit, 2004).   **9** Carolyn M. Harrison et
al., 'Recreation 2000: views of the country from the city', *Landscape Research*, 11:2 (1986),
19–24.   **10** Colin Ward, 'The child in the city', *Society*, 15:4 (1978), 84–91.   **11** Richard
Louv, *Last child in the woods: saving our children from nature deficit disorder* (Chapel Hill,
NC, 2006).

certainly highly appropriate that these texts should also be subjected to such scrutiny. Jonathan Levin argues that most people who adopt this interdisciplinary approach to the study of nature, environment, and culture 'put a premium on thinking about how representations of nature, as well as humans' various modes of cultural mediation with the natural world, contribute to contemporary environmental crises and shape the response to them'.[12]

As early as the 1970s, the case had been made by Joseph Meeker[13] that the predominance granted to the world of culture over the natural world lay at the heart of environmental crises. This insight raised, and continues to raise, the question of how a general societal willingness to accept the superiority of culture over nature has been persistently communicated in contemporary western societies. This, in turn, inevitably leads to the need to investigate the role played by authors of children's literature in the process of transmission, from one generation to the next, of attitudes and practices in relation to the fragile natural world in which we live and on which we all ultimately depend. A much-quoted early definition of ecocriticism is simply 'the study of the relationship between literature and the physical environment'.[14] Simon C. Estok[15] expands on this, explaining that what makes this field of study distinctive is 'the ethical standard it takes, its commitment to the natural world as an important thing rather than simply as an object of thematic study, and [...] its commitment to making connections'.[16] Ecocriticism's specific critique is based, according to Heise, on modernity's erroneous and damaging presumption:

> [t]o know the natural world scientifically, to manipulate it technologically and exploit it economically, and thereby ultimately to create a human sphere apart from it in a historical process that is usually labeled 'progress'. This domination strips nature of any value other than as a material resource and commodity and leads to a gradual destruction that may in the end deprive humanity of its basis for subsistence. Such domination empties human life of the significance it had derived from living in and with nature and alienates individuals and communities from their rootedness in place.[17]

This traditional western view of man's dominion over animals and nature dates back at least to the Old Testament and is rarely challenged in the classics of Anglophone children's literature. For Michael P. Branch and Scott Slovic,[18] ecocriticism describes scholarship that is concerned with the envi-

12 Jonathan Levin, 'Beyond nature? Recent work in ecocriticism', *Contemporary Literature*, 43:1 (2002), 171.   13 Joseph Meeker, *The comedy of survival: studies in literary ecology* (New York, 1974).   14 Glotfelty, *The ecocriticism reader*, p. xxxi.   15 Simon C. Estok, 'A report card on ecocriticism', *AUMLA*, 96 (2001), 220–38.   16 Ibid., 220.   17 Ursula K. Heise, 'The hitchhiker's guide to ecocriticism', *PMLA*, 121:2 (2006), 507.   18 Michael

ronmental implications of literary texts and these implications are crucial from a pedagogical perspective, given that adult attitudes to the natural world and the environment are largely formed in childhood. However, the environmental implications of many much-loved children's stories are not necessarily easy to discern. While animals and the natural world have traditionally featured frequently in children's literature, these have often been used merely as tropes representing humans and society respectively,[19] rather than addressing the real complexity of relationships between humans, animals and the natural world.

BEATRIX POTTER: AN ECOCRITICAL EXEMPLAR

An enduring exception to the paradigms of dominion and domination can be found in the works of Beatrix Potter, the Victorian/Edwardian English writer and illustrator of books for children. Potter (1866–1943) was born into a wealthy Unitarian family in London,[20] but generations of her family had strong roots in the Lancashire countryside. She spent long annual holidays as a child in the countryside and, in later life, she became a significant landowner in the Lake District, buying her first small farm in 1905.[21] It is worth noting that Unitarians in the Victorian period were among the first to embrace Darwin's evolutionary theories and, indeed, Darwin himself was a member of that faith community. An appreciation of evolutionary links between humans and other animals may well have informed Potter's attitude to, and interest in, all living things from an early age. Coincidentally, a number of other figures, who have attracted the attention of ecocritics, such as Ralph Waldo Emerson, Charles Dickens, Samuel Taylor Coleridge and more recently, the architect Frank Lloyd Wright, were also Unitarians.

What is impressive about Potter's texts and illustrations for children is that they do not replicate the long tradition of anthropomorphic animal characters that stretches all the way back to early texts such as Aesop's fables. Potter's animal stories tend to provide a more complex, dynamic representation of humans, animals and the environment. Thus, while she certainly presents many animals with at least some human characteristics and attire, other depictions of animal behaviour and the natural environment offer the child reader an authentic representation of life, with all its attendant dangers, including the stark threat of imminent death. In Potter's classic story about Peter Rabbit,

P. Branch & Scott Slovic, 'Introduction: surveying the emergence of ecocriticism' in M.P. Branch & S. Slovic (eds), *The ISLE reader: ecocriticism, 1993–2003* (Athens, GA, 2003), pp xiii–xxiii. **19** Classic examples from the English canon of children's literature include the works of Rudyard Kipling, Kenneth Grahame, A.A. Milne and Arthur Ransome. **20** Margaret Lane, *The tale of Beatrix Potter: a biography* (London, 1946), p. 1. **21** Susan Denyer, *At home with Beatrix Potter* (London, 2009), p. 26.

Peter's mother warns her offspring against venturing into Mr McGregor's garden, lest they should meet with the same fate as their father, who ended up as an ingredient in one of Mrs McGregor's pies.[22] Even more direct is the story about the adventures of Squirrel Nutkin and his friends, where text and illustration leave the reader in no doubt as to the very real mortal danger posed by a sinister, predatory owl.[23] In the former example, animals face a threat from humans but in the latter, another animal is the source of anxiety and terror. Since Potter's stories offer a particular alternative take on humans, animals and the environment in Victorian/Edwardian Britain, they have much to offer contemporary ecocriticism, as understood by Loretta Johnston:

> [a] field of literary study that addresses how humans relate to non-human nature or the environment in literature [...] So when subjected to ecocriticism, literature of all periods and places – not only ecocentric or environmental literature or nature writing, but all literature – is viewed in terms of place, setting, and/or environment, all of which have taken on richer meaning.[24]

SECOND WAVE ECOCRITICISM: BEATRIX POTTER'S ECOCENTRIC AND SOCIOCENTRIC PERSPECTIVES

Although ecocriticism, like most political, religious or social causes, started out with a simple agenda, namely 'to save the environment',[25] it now endeavours to make connections between this goal and other societal issues. Kate Rigby[26] states:

> [e]cocritics [...] are concerned to revalue the more-than-human natural world, to which some texts and cultural traditions invite us to attend. In this way, ecocriticism has a vital contribution to make to the wider project of Green Studies, which, in Laurence Coupe's words, 'debates "Nature" in order to defend nature' (Coupe 2000, 5). For many ecocritics, moreover, the defense of nature is vitally interconnected with the pursuit of social justice.[27]

This concern for social justice has been identified by Buell[28] as a particular characteristic of what he sees as second-wave ecocriticism, with first-wave

---

22 Beatrix Potter, *The tale of Peter Rabbit* (London, 1902), p. 11.   **23** Beatrix Potter, *The tale of Squirrel Nutkin* (London, 1903).   **24** Loretta Johnston, 'Greening the library: the fundamentals and future of ecocriticism', *CHOICE* (2009), 7–14 at 7.   **25** Ibid., 14.   **26** Kate Rigby, 'Ecocriticism' in J. Wolfreys (ed.), *Introducing criticism at the 21st century* (Edinburgh, 2002), pp 151–78.   **27** Ibid., p. 154.   **28** Lawrence Buell, 'Ecocriticism: some emerging trends', *Qui Parle*, Spring/Summer, 19:2 (2011), 87–115.

ecocriticism primarily associated with nature writing, deep ecology and scientific areas such as environmental biology and geology. By contrast, second-wave ecocriticism adopts a more complex perspective on the long history of environmentalism itself, moving beyond the first-wave, *ecocentric* focus on countryside and wilderness to a more *sociocentric* perspective which also engages with urban and industrial environments and their transformation. Thus, second-wave ecocriticism is not confined to the natural sciences and nature literature but rather also includes film, television, theatre, architecture etc. within its scope. Buell[29] points out that first-wave ecocritics (almost exclusively either North American or English), with their naïve, romantic, nature-based approach, characteristically chose to focus on the life and work of Anglophone literary figures such as the English countryside poet, John Clare, or Henry David Thoreau, the American nature writer. Second-wave ecocritics are more likely to be drawn to writers such as nineteenth-century novelist, Charles Dickens, or for that matter, twentieth-century environmentalist, Rachel Carson, attracted by their more socially and/or politically aware, activist lives, as well as their literary content and style. Thus, activist second-wave criticism, while still concerned with issues such as environmental pollution, more consciously engages with questions of social justice as seen above, and is increasingly committed to marginalized groups and minorities (as well as their literatures), both in the developed world and elsewhere. On the question of social justice, Rigby points out that ecocriticism 'differs from other forms of political critique in one important respect: namely, as a form of advocacy for an other, which is felt to be unable to speak for itself'.[30]

Beatrix Potter, by her life and works, provides useful examples of the kind of ecocentric and sociocentric advocacy that typically characterizes activist second-wave ecocriticism. These will be explored in more detail below but suffice to observe that, as an educated, monied, upper-middle-class woman, Potter continually spoke up for the environment like many a first-wave ecocritic. She was well positioned to do so, having studied flora and fauna to an advanced level, both in nature and for long hours in the Museum of Natural History and the Victoria and Albert Museum. Indeed, such was her competence as a naturalist, that her work on the germination of mould spores[31] was presented to the Linnean Society in 1897. The fact that she was not, as a woman, allowed to present it in person, no doubt contributed to her capacity, like many second-wave activists, to make the necessary connections between the lack of advocacy for the natural world and the inability, for example, of poorly educated, rural families (especially women and children), to speak up for themselves. While she could not be considered a feminist by contemporary standards, given that she did not support the suffragettes,[32] Potter, like most

29 Ibid., 95.   30 Rigby, 'Ecocriticism', p. 163.   31 Lear, *Beatrix Potter*, p. 117.   32 Lear, *Beatrix Potter*, pp 233, 491.

Unitarians, was nevertheless remarkable for her day in that she was in favour of higher education for women. Moreover, there is plenty of evidence to show how alert she was to the important potential contribution women could make in rural communities in areas such as nursing or farming life.[33] She campaigned effectively for improved healthcare and had a letter published in the *Times* advocating the employment of women on the land.[34] Indeed, she proved as good as her word, taking on a woman to work on her farm during wartime.

ECOPEDAGOGY AND CHILDREN'S LITERATURE: OVERVIEW

Relatively new areas of focus to have emerged within ecocriticism include ecocomposition and ecofeminism. The former aims to investigate how rhetoric and language have been used to define humans and our relationship with nature[35] and suggests that conventional approaches to identity, drawing on categories such as race, gender or class, have failed to understand that who we are is also profoundly influenced 'by our relationships with particular locations and environments'.[36] Thus ecocomposition, as Gaard[37] would have it, tries to look at writing from a more holistic and dynamic perspective, namely one that moves beyond the purely personal or social to include considerations of multiple relationships between humans, non-humans and the environment and how these affect the writer and the reader as well as the actual process of writing. It has considerable pedagogic potential as it encourages citizens to reflect on social differences and make connections between social and economic injustices, on the one hand, and the denigration of the environment on the other, in the hope that they will rethink relationships between humans and nature, ultimately developing more respect for all forms of biodiversity.

Ecocomposition's linking of perspectives on environmental issues to various forms of social injustice has contributed to the emergence of ecofeminist literary criticism which also makes fundamental connections between social and environmental problems:

> Beginning with the recognition that the position and treatment of women, animals, and nature are not separable, ecofeminists make connections among not just sexism, speciesism, and the oppression of nature but also other forms of social injustice – racism, classism, het-

33 J. Taylor et al., *Beatrix Potter (1866–1943): the artist and her world* (London, 1988), p. 29.   34 Lear, *Beatrix Potter*, pp 272–3.   35 Sidney I. Dobrin & Christian R. Weisser, 'Breaking ground in ecocomposition: exploring relationships between discourse and environment', *College English*, 654:5 (2002), 566–89.   36 Ibid., 567.   37 Greta Gaard, 'Children's environmental literature: from ecocriticism to ecopedagogy', *Neohelicon*, 36:2 (2009), 321–34.

erosexism, ageism, ableism, and colonialism – as part of Western culture's assault on nature.[38]

Activists working in ecocriticism in relation to children, drawing on ecocomposition and ecofeminism, have emphasized the need to link theory and practice and to develop civic engagement as a fundamental component of the ecocritical classroom experience and gradually since the 1990s, ecocritical pedagogy has started to be applied to the critical reading and teaching of children's environmental literature. With a view to addressing the ecopedagogical imperative, Gaard proposes 'six boundary conditions for an ecopedagogy of children's environment literature',[39] which are summarized briefly here before being linked to examples from the life and works of Potter:

1   Praxis or putting theory into practice, for example, by recycling materials in classroom.
2   Teaching *about* the social and natural environment, for example, by using texts that raise issues and possible responses to them.
3   Teaching *in* the social and natural environment, for example, taking children out into the streets and countryside and exposing them to cultural diversity and nonhuman animals.
4   Teaching *through* the social and natural environment, for example, involving experiential learning and civic engagement with social and environmental justice, health and sustainability.
5   Teaching the connections of sustainability, for example, the interdependence of social justice/environmental health and of human and nonhuman species.
6   Urgency, for example, communicating the need for understanding, commitment and action to achieve personal and sociopolitical change for the betterment of all life on the planet.

ECOPEDAGOGY AND BEATRIX POTTER'S LIFE AND WORKS

The first of these boundary conditions is concerned with putting ecocritical theory into practice in the classroom and other learning environments. Introducing not just Potter's storybooks, but also details of her life and conservation work to provide an ecopedagogical context for the stories could prove fruitful here, not least because it is easy to demonstrate how the author brought her environmental awareness and concerns to bear on the publication of her works. Even in her initial contacts with her London publisher, Warne & Co., she specified that she wanted her books to be produced at affordable

38 Ibid., 323.   39 Ibid., 332–4.

prices. Moreover, they were to appear as small books, suitable for little hands, with sturdy covers so that they would last. Flimsier productions might have increased sales, and thereby profits, over the decades but simplicity, practicality and durability were ecological values by which Potter set great store throughout her life. Her production values provide a useful, practical illustration for children of the principle of responsible environmental sustainability in action.

The second boundary condition is concerned with teaching and learning *about* the environment, for example, by using texts (whether factual or fictional) to raise and discuss issues with children relating to the social and natural world. With careful guidance, close scrutiny of the scientifically accurate representations of flora and fauna in Potter's works could have the important ecopedagogical effect of stimulating children to engage with the nonhuman life in their surroundings. It could help them to develop interest in and respect for the natural environment, while the anthropomorphically presented animals could encourage children to identify and empathize with other living creatures in a non-hierarchical way, potentially contributing to a shift in attitudes towards the environment and ecological issues in the younger generation. In addition, Potter's illustrations of the built environment can encourage children to observe architectural interiors and exteriors more closely, noting differences not only between urban and rural practices but also between lifestyles in other societies, periods and climates and their architectural expression.

Background biographical detail on Potter could be provided concerning the relative loneliness of her childhood and the absence of contemporary playmates which contributed to her need to develop a menagerie of frogs, newts, lizards, mice, bats, birds, guinea pigs, hedgehogs, and of course, rabbits. After all, it was because she kept them as pets, observing them closely, that she developed the skills necessary to be able to draw them with such accuracy.[40] Debate could be stimulated about the fact that although Potter cared for her animals, she seems to have been remarkably unsentimental about the lives of some of her charges, even from a very young age. Indeed, she is said to have boiled frogs in order to study their skeletons and to have dissected newts so as to examine them more closely under a microscope.[41] The fact that, finding her brother's bats difficult to keep when he went to boarding school, Potter decided to chloroform one before recording it in great anatomical detail in her sketches[42] could provide an appropriate lead in to such issues as the testing of pharmaceuticals on animals and the practice of dissection in anatomy classes.

While it would be easy to read accounts of Potter's scientific experiments as indications of innate cruelty or indifference to the suffering of animals, it

40 Lear, *Beatrix Potter*, p. 71.   41 Taylor, *Beatrix Potter*, p. 7.   42 Lear, *Beatrix Potter*, p. 71.

is more likely that she was simply influenced as a child by the contemporary attitudes and behaviour she observed in adult naturalists she met within the family circle. This could provide a possible opening to a discussion of how attitudes to animals and nature may vary or change over time and across cultures as well as between children/adults and/or males/females and urban/rural dwellers. In the case of Potter, there can be little doubt that from her youth to old age, she had a rather matter-of-fact attitude to the natural cycle of life and death. This could prove quite a revelation, particularly to urban children, who may never have been exposed to the practical realities of animal husbandry as part of farm life. A passage in one of her biographies explains that in later life, her farm workers were well aware that she would have 'everything possible done for a sick animal on any one of her farms, so long as there was a chance of recovery, but once that point was passed she was quite matter-of-fact and unsentimental'.[43] Children, who have lost a pet, may be able to relate at least in part to the author on this issue but to others, it may come as a thought-provoking shock that can also be worked through productively in an ecopedagogical context.

It could be pointed out to children that Potter's personal pragmatism is clearly discernible in many of her children's stories which integrate mortal danger and the reality of death in a matter-of-fact way. While she kept animals as pets on occasion, Potter was not one to spare children from the fact that humans eat animals and animals prey upon each other. A classroom discussion about the ethics of vegetarianism and responsible animal welfare could be encouraged after explaining that, at the time of the First World War, when Britain was subject to rationing, Potter wrote to a boy informing him that her hen, Semolina, had hatched two chicks called Tapioca and Sago. 'We have eaten Sago [...] it was rather dreadful and the stuffing disagreed with my conscience [...] I have a lot of rabbits [...] Old Benjamin and Cottontail are pets, but I'm afraid we do have rabbit pies of the young ones'.[44] Details such as this could help alert children to such issues as food shortages in times of war and crisis and/or natural disaster.

The third boundary condition relates to ecopedagogy *in* the social and natural environment, for example, getting children out onto the streets and into the countryside so that they can learn about cultural diversity and nature by dint of being and experiencing. After studying Potter's stories and her observations on nature and diversity, children could be inspired and motivated by the author's own practical commitment to helping young people to engage with and relate to the natural environment as evidenced by the fact she regularly accommodated the Girl Guides and sometimes the Boy Scouts,[45] who camped on her lands. She delighted in the opportunity it gave them to be out of doors and close to nature.

43 Ibid., p. 422.   44 Ibid., p. 292.   45 Ibid., pp 307, 382.

The fourth boundary condition relates to teaching and learning *through* the social and natural environment, for example, through experiential learning and civic engagement with social and environmental justice, health and sustainability issues. Potter was genuinely concerned about the welfare of her local community, especially in relation to issues of rural health and employment as evidenced, for example, by her efforts to have a District Nursing Association established in her Lake District area of Hawkshead in 1919.[46] Traditional rural health problems, exacerbated by a shortage of doctors and distance from hospitals, were made even worse by the hardships of the First World War, followed soon after by the influenza pandemic of 1918. Elderly people and mothers in childbirth often died unnecessarily due to lack of care and child mortality rates were unacceptably high. Realizing that poor healthcare, rising unemployment and a general lack of rural infrastructure could lead to a detrimental migration from country to town, Potter worked tirelessly to improve local conditions, for example, organizing a committee and raising funds until her area finally was granted a nurse. This is a practical example that can be used to teach children not just about activism but also about varying standards in relation to health provision in different places and at different times and to alert them to the value of individual and community campaigning to effect changes to the status quo.

The fifth boundary condition suggested by Gaard concerns the connections of sustainability such as the interdependence of social justice and environmental health, and of human and nonhuman species. In this regard, Potter provides a fine example of what is popularly known as the power of one, that is, what a single individual can achieve through a lifetime of ecological commitment and engagement. Although reared as a Londoner, once she started to buy land from the proceeds of her first publications, Potter took to country life seriously and as early as 1906, she began to stock rare endangered breeds of Herdwick sheep and Fell ponies.[47] However, her commitment to the countryside went beyond good animal husbandry and farming practices, important though these were in themselves. She understood the links of sustainability between the people who farmed the land, the livestock they kept and the land itself. Thus her approach was holistic and coherent in that she consistently made social and environmental connections, showing considerable concern not just for her tenant farmers, their welfare and the welfare of their livestock, but also for the integrity of their holdings, their vernacular dwellings, the farm estates to which they belonged and, thus, the Lake District as a whole. These principles of coherent connectedness could easily be enacted in educational situations through thoughtful approaches to such practices as the careful disposal of lunchtime waste to create compost for use in the school garden. Children will learn the value of responsible behaviour

46 Taylor, *Beatrix Potter*, p. 187.   47 Denyer, *At home with Beatrix Potter*, p. 124.

which is not simply worthy in itself but can also be a source of pleasure, bringing practical benefits to humans, wildlife and the environment.

The sixth and final boundary condition relates to the urgent need to develop understanding, commitment and action so as to improve the environment in the broadest sense of the word through personal and sociopolitical endeavour. Potter's conservation interests were far reaching and, working closely with the National Trust,[48] she did much to preserve such varied and distinctive features of the Lake District as the local houses and cottages, stone walls, forests and lake shores. In addition to being primarily a steward or custodian of the countryside, she also became something of a conservation activist. In 1912, when the peace and tranquillity of Windermere Lake[49] was threatened with plans to introduce hydroplanes, she became involved in a campaign to prevent this happening.

Even when she had more-or-less withdrawn from her career as an author, she continued to be active on conservation issues, and she sold drawings to raise funds to protect the threatened Windermere shoreline. Her success as a writer and her substantial inheritance upon the death of her father enabled her to continue to acquire land in the Lake District from 1905 right through the second half of her life. Her acquisitions included a substantial sheep farm known as Troutbeck Park, which extended over almost 2,000 acres. To this, she added a further 5,000 acres, seven years later when she purchased Monk Coniston. By investing in these extensive properties,[50] she actively contributed to the sustainability of rural life in the region, preventing the break-up of large estates and thereby helping to secure the future of hill-country farms and the small communities who worked them. In 1937 she decided that the management of her largest farm should be handed over to the National Trust and at the time of her death in 1943 at the age of 77, she was able to leave some 4,000 acres, incorporating many fell farms to the Trust to be held for the nation in perpetuity.[51] Taking their cue from Potter, teachers could find numerous ways to educate their students about civic awareness and personal accountability leading to a sense of individual and group empowerment around environmental issues such as recycling and energy usage.

CONCLUSION

From an ecocritical perspective, Beatrix Potter was ahead of her time, both in terms of environmental awareness and activism and in terms of the content and production of her books. Thus, both her life and works provide invalu-

48 Shelagh J. Squire, 'Valuing countryside: reflections on Beatrix Potter tourism', *Area* (1993), 5–10 at 6–7. 49 Taylor, *Beatrix Potter*, p. 171. 50 Denyer, *At home with Beatrix Potter*, pp 26, 30, 120, 126. 51 Ibid., p. 8.

able material from an ecopedagogical prospective. Her storytelling methodology and her choice of a low child's perspective in many of her illustrations also represents a concrete example of a non-hierarchical, respectful attitude to her readers. Moreover, rather than opting for sentimental depictions of animal characters, her drawings offer anatomical accuracy, revealing the physical wonders of the natural world rather than some fantastical realm. From a narratological perspective, there is ample variety in the manner in which Potter's animals either parallel humans or are true to their own nature. Thus some are presented realistically in their natural state, as is the trout in the tale about the frog, Jeremy Fisher.[52] At other times, animals may transition from animal to human behaviour as in the story of the two mice, Tom Thumb and Hunca Munca.[53] Elsewhere, the characterization of the animals is quite anthropomorphic from the outset in that they wear (at least some) clothes. Benjamin and Flopsy Bunny[54] are such examples and they behave like responsible adults. However, while their offspring act as human children might, the young rabbits are also partially true to their animal nature in that none of them wear clothes.

This shifting representation of animals within Potter's stories can assist children to consider real animals in their natural state with greater empathy. Potter's approach is important in that it is somewhat at variance with the traditional Judaeo-Christian view of animals as at the service of humankind, frequently exploited without due regard for long-term consequences. Potter's innovative views on animals and environmental and social activism may have taken root during her Unitarian upbringing. This point finds a useful parallel in the suggestion that Rachel Carson's environmental and social critique may, at least in part, be attributed to her Presbyterian background. Both authors reflected in their writings, and in diverse ways, the mainstream Protestant thinking of their respective eras, a way of thinking that promoted and cultivated personal action to right the wrongs of society.[55]

While representative of her time and place, Potter seemed to embrace the essence of the North American Indian proverb and latter-day Green mantra: 'We do not inherit the earth from our ancestors, we borrow it from our children' and managed in text and illustration to convey a serious sense of wonder and respect for the natural world. In harmony with the desiderata of contemporary ecopedagogy, Potter's writings, which combine economic prose, juxtaposed with simple but very accurate illustrations, encourage personal readings and interpretations, as well as supporting reflective adult/child dialogue. Her subversive elements encourage children to think for themselves

---

52 Beatrix Potter, *The tale of Mr Jeremy Fisher* (London, 1906). 53 Beatrix Potter, *The tale of Two Bad Mice* (London, 1904). 54 Potter, *Flopsy Bunnies* (London, 1909). 55 www.nytimes.com/2012/09/23/magazine/how-silent-spring-ignited-the-environmental-movement.html?pagewanted=all&_r=0, accessed 10 Feb. 2014.

and develop critical attitudes to existing social and environmental norms. Potter tended to avoid Victorian/Edwardian moralizing although many stories have clear didactic content such as her tale of Tom Kitten who goes roaming in a rat-infested house and nearly comes to a grisly end.[56] Finally, in line with the approach of second-wave ecocritics, she exposes her readers to a view of the natural world which emphasizes relatedness, a world where misfortune, injustice, loss, danger and death are presented quite matter-of-factly, but where responsible choice and individual and collective agency clearly also have a part to play and are shown to contribute to more desirable outcomes.

---

56 Beatrix Potter, *The tale of Samuel Whiskers* (London, 1908).

'Creaturely life': biopolitical intensity in selected children's fables

VICTORIA DE RIJKE

In Maurice Sendak's seminal picturebook, *Where the wild things are* (1963), the child Max leaves the constraints of home in his wolf costume to seek out and face his wild things. The American critic Hal Foster, writing on 'creaturely life', suggests that:

> [p]erhaps it is a question less of where the wild things are – we have names for those spaces, which we project inward or outward as the unconscious or the other – than *when* they appear. Potentially this is right now, or whenever the symbolic order cracks under political pressure. This is not necessarily a psychotic moment, or even a romantic one; it can be, as it is with Max, an intense imagining, via the creaturely, of new social links.[1]

In this article, reviewing the publication of Jacques Derrida's last seminar series, *The beast and the sovereign* (2009), Foster explores Eric Santner's use of the term 'creaturely life', as 'life abandoned to the state of exception/emergency [...] on the threshold where life takes on its specific biopolitical intensity, where it assumes the cringed posture of the creature'. Santner refers to these moments of intensity as 'fissures or caesuras in the space of meaning'[2] where power can be resisted or re-imagined; moments of creativity and criticality.

Animals are not, by nature, secondary entities in children's literature. As Claude Levi-Strauss maintains, 'Animals are good to think with'.[3] In fable, they stand for us; *as us*. This essay aims to explore 'creaturely life' in relation to the 'creativity and criticality' of the fable genre and what I will argue for is its special relationship to biopolitical intensity; an (often unconscious) relationship of children's literature to the symbolic order cracking under political pressure. Citing a number of classic and contemporary works of children's literature and culminating in a work of animation, I will explore how particular

1 H. Foster, 'I am the decider', *London Review of Books*, 3:6 (17 Mar. 2011), 32.   2 Ibid., Eric Santner, quoted in same article, 31.   3 C. Levi-Strauss, 'The totemic illusion' in Linda Kalof and Amy Fitzgerald (eds), *The animals reader: the essential classic and contemporary writings* (Oxford, 2007), pp 251–61.

fables, suggestive of class struggle and revolution, may be smoothed over or radicalized in children's literature.

As Foster acknowledges, 'when' is a crucial factor in relation to any political reading of literary texts. A socio-historical analysis of various publications of Aesop's tales can exemplify some of the worst 'whitewashes' in terms of illustrations or texts, contrasted with more recent examples, all illustrating – via text and image – that inherent creativity and criticality demanded of materialist readings of children's literature and culture. Seth Lerer[4] has skillfully explored the fable's tradition across centuries of western cultures with Aesop, arguably the West's first exponent of the form, via Caxton's fifteenth-century and Godwin's nineteenth-century collections, exemplifying both the genre's potential for radical moral challenge and, perhaps, certain gaps. Aesop's untimely death[5] and his subsequent depiction or ideological 'whitewash' in children's literature as an old white man's moral tales rather than a young disabled black slave's political propaganda is the most grave of these fissures.[6]

French philosopher Michel Foucault's lectures from 1978 to 1979 entitled 'The birth of biopolitics' explored neo-liberalist economy and government. In fact, although the term has since become well-worn, Foucault does not really define it in his lectures, reminding us that only when we know what this governmental regime called liberalism was, will we be able to grasp what biopolitics is. For him, the term refers to that which 'brought life and its mechanisms into the realm of explicit calculations and made knowledge-power an agent of transformation of human life'. According to Foucault, biopolitics marks the threshold of modernity as it places corporal life at the centre of political order. In his interpretation, there is a close relationship between the constitution of a capitalist society and the birth of biopolitics:

> Society's control over individuals was accomplished not only through consciousness or ideology but also in the body and with the body. For capitalist society, it was biopolitics, the biological, the corporal, that mattered more than anything else.[7]

Aware that a long philosophical connection between human life and animals gave shape to biopower, Foucault states 'modern man is an animal whose politics places his existence as a living being in question'.[8] Foucault's series of lectures did not, strictly speaking, mark the birth of the term biopolitics. Liesen

---

4 Seth Lerer, *Children's literature: a reader's history from Aesop to Harry Potter* (Chicago, 2008). 5 Several accounts suggest that Aesop was sentenced to death for recounting fables that were deemed insulting and he was forced to jump from a cliff to his untimely death. 6 Lerer, *Children's literature*, pp 32, 51. 7 M. Foucault, *The birth of biopolitics: lectures at the Collège de France, 1978–1979* (New York, 2008). 8 M. Foucault, *History of sexuality vol. 1: the will to knowledge* (London, 1978), p. 143.

and Walsh describe how it was used in the first half of the twentieth century in relation to state control of life and race, most prominently in the writings of National Socialists in Germany.[9] Later, taken up as a useful term for the analysis of political structures and processes, drawing from research into the biology of behavior, socio-biological ideas and evolutionary theory,[10] its earlier sense refers to the welfare of all forms of life and how they are moved by one another; or, put another way, biologically orientated politics. In fable we deal with the idea of the individual at intellectual and at species level, with the minds of thinking, speaking humans and the bodies of animals. And the human is, by nature, a political animal.

In the context of this essay, 'fable' will mean prose, verse or animation featuring animals, mythical creatures, plants, inanimate objects or forces of nature that are given human qualities, all of which illustrate a moral lesson, perhaps expressed in a pithy maxim, such as 'slow and steady wins the race'. Fable's key trope is action in the face of impending doom or in response to the constancy of danger that lies in wait for us all, especially the over-confident. Fables offer violent retribution, trouncing, reprisals, reversals of fortune in a style featuring simple, witty wordplay, occasionally in vernacular, slang or dialect. Its form is everyday, plain, humble and realistic.

AESOP AS EXEMPLAR

There is a vast scholarship on Aesop's publishing history, not least in critical works on children's literature, notably Grenby[11] and Lerer. Such scholars provide evidence that present-day collections are frequently the result of many tales: Greek and Latin verse or Jewish commentaries from the first century, ninth-century Oriental sources, Syriac from the eleventh century and Phaedrus' first-century Latin version. Interpretations and translations abound. Aesop's fables have been adapted for feudal, medieval, clerical, educational use; in fact, the fable form is also part of worldwide acculturation. One example to illustrate the case is that of Portuguese missionaries, arriving in Japan at the end of the sixteenth century, who introduced the Fables as *Esopo no fabulas*, *c.*1593. This was soon followed by a complete Japanese translation entitled *Isopo monogatari*. This Western work survived into later publication after the expulsion of Westerners from Japan, since by that time the figure of Aesop had been acculturated and presented as if he were Japanese. Fables are never politically neutral.[12]

9 Laurette T. Liesen & Mary B. Walsh, 'The competing meanings of "biopolitics" in political science: biological and postmodern approaches to politics', *Politics and the Life Sciences*, 31:1 (2012), 2–15.   10 Ira H. Carmen, 'Biopolitics: the newest synthesis?', *Genetica*, 99:3 (1997), 173–84.   11 Matthew Grenby, *Children's literature: Edinburgh critical guides to literature* (Edinburgh, 2008).   12 Annabel Patterson, *Fables of power: Aesopian writing and political history* (Durham, 1991), pp 140–3.

In European publishing terms, the first attempt at an exhaustive edition was made by Heinrich Steinhöwel in his *Esopus*, published *c.*1476; William Caxton's of 1484 being the first edition for children in English. William Godwin's *Fables, ancient and modern* of 1805 is surely one of the most traditional in didactic prose addressed to the child, whilst at the same time the most radical in illustration, with William Mulready's storyteller (presumably Aesop) depicted as unequivocally black. In his preface to the *Fables*, Godwin lectures the child in a somewhat patronizing manner: '[f]or fear of mistakes. Beasts and birds do not talk English [...] [whilst] it is not always necessary that a story may be true [...] a lie is what naughty folks say'.[13] Apparently, Walter Scott's word for Godwin's work of this time was 'twaddling' and the opportunity for fables to challenge aristocratic privilege or political and social injustice seemed quite lost. Far from the anarchic circles of London in the 1790s, now writing under the pseudonym Edward Baldwin (since his real name was tinged with disreputable political positions), perhaps Godwin had lost his nerve. This form of 'selling out', when representing fable to children, seemed to set a precedent for an unending series of illustrated and picture-book versions of Aesop as twaddle tales.

A multitude of revised Aesop's fables from original sources were illustrated by classic illustrators such as Ernest Griset (1844–1907), Walter Crane (1884–1915) and Arthur Rackham (1867–1939). A collection of tales selected and introduced by G.K. Chesterton, originally published in 1912 and reissued in 2010, points out a few blunt facts about Aesop, as a Phyrgian philosophical slave, 'if he lived at all' and that fables differ from fairy tales in that they are fundamentally phenomenological:

> [e]verything is itself and speaks for itself. The wolf will always be wolfish; the fox will always be foxy, [...] all the animal forces drive like inanimate forces, like great rivers or growing trees. It is the limit and the loss of all such things that they cannot be anything but themselves.[14]

Rackham did not picture Aesop himself, but the animal and plant characters invariably perform the role of storyteller: in many illustrations they are publicly speaking, privately whispering, confiding; always listening. Everything has life, even usually inanimate objects. Rackham's illustration to the tale 'The Blackamoor' is thought to refer to Aesop's own experience of racism. It shows a severe old man taking a vicious-looking scrubbing brush to the back of a little black boy who stands in a saucer. The eye is drawn along diagonal lines from

13 William Godwin, *Fables, ancient and modern: adapted for the use of children* (Richmond, 1818), pp 13–14.   14 G.K. Chesterton, 'Introduction to Aesop's fables', *The Project Gutenberg eBook of Aesop's fables* (1912), http://www.gutenberg.org/files/11339/11339–h/11339–h.htm, accessed 28 Jan. 2014.

the urn in the bottom right corner, past the small bar of white soap, along the brickwork and stripes on the rug, to the bucket of water. The material reality of the stone urn, flagstone floor, wooden bucket and large metal saucer suggest there is no running away from this event. Such domestic objects are not usually sinister, and it would just be an old man washing a child but for our knowledge that he is to be washed white, and Nature (in this sense) surely cannot be altered without harm. The little boy's hands are clasped and his eyes turned up, as if in prayer. Is this the 'cringed posture of the creature' Foster described as the moment of biopolitical intensity? There is a terrible kind of tenderness in Rackham's attention to *physical* detail in both figures, from fingers to toes: the similarities of their skinny limbs and long, bony toes, the differences of skin colour and the few thin strands of comb-over on the old man's bald head contrasted with the thick black curls on the child. It is shockingly pitiful and funny, all at once. Perhaps after all this *is* Rackham's picture of Aesop: the old man exemplifying white Greek (moral) authority, the boy, black inferiority through slavery; the injustice of their difference enacted in tableau. The tale 'Washing the Ethiopian/Blackamoor white', attributed to Aesop, suggests the metaphor of the political whitewash and is a very old phenomenon with a powerful emblematic and proverbial history.

In many collections, Aesop's own story is omitted, glossed over, or liter-ally painted white, as is his beard in John Harris and Calef Brown's pop-up version.[15] Given that he never grew to old age, why is Aesop so often pre-sented as a white old man in a robe and white beard? If the fables were orig-inally told as a form of resistance using risky humour to expose uncomfortable truths, this surely heightens the savage irony in the plethora of publications continuing to omit Aesop's true identity and life history? We might hope that twenty-first-century versions owe some honesty of depiction to centuries of scholarship on the facts of Aesop's case and it is certainly the case with South African artist Piet Grobler's 2011 illustrations to Beverley Naidoo's collection *Aesop's fables*.[16] Piet depicts him as an Afro-haired brown-skinned man in tribal dress, sitting up a tree surrounded by the animals of his stories. Warmly toned, humorous illustrations interspersed throughout the book evoke characteristically African art forms such as elongated, dynamic figures, meticulous animal depiction and decorative patterning.

Yet it is not just about depictions of Aesop the man. One of the key rea-sons for the popularity and success of Aesop's fables must be their textual simplicity: lending themselves to translation across languages, notably regional dialects (such as Creole), as a means to assert regional specificity against cen-tralism and monolingualism. For example, the large number of translations of the fables found in French and Belgian dialects is largely attributed to these

15 John Harris, ill. Calef Brown, *Aesop's fables* (Los Angeles, 2005). 16 B. Naidoo, ill. Piet Grobler, *Aesop's fables* (London, 2011).

regions' need to sustain their own languages. As part of the oral tradition, fables require a distinctive, *politicized* voice (as patois or slang forms are), such as François Marbot's 1869 parody of La Fontaine's fables *Les bambous*[17] in Creole patois for the French Caribbeans, or Paul Terry's *Farmer Al Falfa* series of cartoons based on Aesop's fables substituting moral issues for urban gags[18] or Addison Hibbard's *Aesop in negro dialect* (1926).[19] The key to a successful translation of Aesop must be where the noisy politics of creaturely life is not suppressed in favour of generalized, anodyne moralizing. Helen Ward's collection *Unwitting wisdom* (2004) has on its copyright page: 'To Aesop and all tellers of moral tales, who, despite a monumentally ineffective history, still gently try to point the human race in a better direction'.[20] Ward uses perspective and size relativity to expose political inequalities, such as the vulnerability of the small and less powerful. Like Rackham, Ward's illustrations are full of creaturely life drawn in exquisite detail, and unlike many other versions, the text is kept at an absolute minimum to the point of epigram. The tale of 'The ant and the grasshopper' is condensed to the line 'A time to dance: in which a cricket learns about work the hard way'.[21]

ANIMAL METAPHOR

If end-of-century literature typically rejects liberal democracy, features cynicism with tradition and suggests new beginnings, Paul & Marc Rosenthal's *Yo Aesop! Get a load of these fables* offers quirky twists on well-worn fables, such as 'Bad hare day' where two turtles race but the winner is a wolf inside a turtle suit.[22] Jon Scieszka and Lane Smith's *Squids will be squids: fresh morals, beastly tales* also fits the description.[23] Its zany collages and anarchic text on topics such as parental control, homework and TV, are a kind of punk counterculture response to traditional fable forms. Interestingly, it is one of the few collections that depicts Aesop – albeit in politically incorrect form, as a large-lipped, ugly, knock-kneed, hunch-backed cripple. On a page mockingly headed 'Serious Historica', the text quips: 'Aesop is the guy most famous for telling Fables. Though he wasn't the first [...] or the best looking'. And at the end of the book, a warning: 'If you're planning to write Fables, don't forget to change people into animals and avoid places with high cliffs'.[24]

17 François Marbot, *Les bambous: fables de la Fontaine, travesties en patois Créole*, in Creole patois (1846); new ed. (Martinique, 1869), http://gallica.bnf.fr/ark:/1248/bpt6k54261407, accessed 17 Oct. 2012.   18 Paul Terry, *Farmer Al Falfa* (Fables Studios Inc., 1921–9). 19 Addison Hibbard, 'Aesop in negro dialect' in J.L. Miller (ed.), *Accented America: the cultural politics of multilingual modernism* (Oxford, 2011).   20 Helen Ward, *Unwitting wisdom: an anthology of Aesop's fables* (San Francisco, 2004).   21 Ibid.   22 P. Rosenthal, ill. M. Rosenthal, *Yo, Aesop! Get a load of these fables* (New York, 1998).   23 J. Scieszka, ill. L. Smith, *Squids will be squids: fresh morals, beastly tales* (London, 1998).   24 Ibid.

In her study on metamorphosis, Maria Lassén-Seger noted that animal imagery and the child/animal connection has been used for centuries in western culture to connote the instinctual or uncivilized in contrast to the rational or civilized. These may be 'non-pejorative' or exploitative metaphorical uses of animal characters, and when they feature the metamorphosis of human into animal, they can signal Kafkaesque 'unpleasurable' reflection of questionable human morality.[25] Anthony Browne's *Piggybook* functions precisely in this category.[26] *Piggybook* questions the morality of male sexism and oppression in a household where all the domestic labour is left to the wife and mother, as indicated by the series of images of a faceless housewife at work, washed out in dull sepia. When she decides to leave, household objects hint at pig-forms: wallpaper, doorknobs, lamps, crockery, while the males of the household, living in filth, gradually turn into pigs, reduced to snuffling on the floor for scraps. The males become ideologically and culturally charged phenomena once they become pigs, literalizing the label 'male chauvinist pigs'.

Yet, in overtly fable form, the use of animals inverts the politics of civilized morality as held by humans. Roald Dahl's character, Mr Fox, continues to outwit and steal from three farmers we know to be villains: 'Boggis and Bunce and Bean, one short, one fat, one lean. These horrible crooks, so different in looks, were nonetheless equally mean'.[27] A highly political animal, leading an organized collective of 'underground' countryside animals to victory, losing his tail in the struggle, Mr Fox does not reflect a political discourse, he *embodies* it.

Comic tales of proletarian political consciousness are part of children's literature in late capitalism. Doreen Cronin and Betsy Lewin's award-winning picturebook *Click, clack, moo: cows that type* depicts cows, who, on finding a typewriter in their barn, write increasingly demanding letters to Farmer Brown for better living conditions.[28] Likewise, the duck in their *Duck for President*,[29] does well in elections with the promise 'I'm a duck, not a politician!' but ends up back on the farm since running the country was hard work; in fact, 'no fun at all'. These picturebooks point to the central ironies of biopolitical modes of government, where liberal, rational goals should be possible (all creatures being equal, a duck might run for President), failing in the face of political realities. But the earlier, multiple award-winning British fable, *Farmer Duck*, by Martin Waddell and Helen Oxenbury goes furthest.[30] On Amazon, the book is either loved or loathed and a sample American reviewer who gave it five stars states:

25 M. Lassén-Seger, *Adventures into otherness: child metamorphs in late twentieth-century children's literature* (Åbo, 2006). 26 A. Browne, *Piggybook* (London, 1996). 27 R. Dahl, *Fantastic Mr Fox* (London, 1970). 28 D. Cronin, ill. B. Lewin, *Click, clack, moo! Cows that type* (New York, 2000). 29 D. Cronin, ill. B. Lewin, *Duck for President* (New York, 2004). 30 M. Waddell, ill. H. Oxenbury, *Farmer Duck* (London, 1995).

I've had university faculty tell me that it's the Communist Manifesto for kids (the centrality of labour, organization, and consciousness), that it's a Trotskyist text (the role of the Duck at the end) and that it's a classic of feminism (the multiple voices considered to fashion the uprising). It's a classic, from whatever interpretation, because it's full of joy, resistance, and hope.[31]

Another reviewer, giving it no stars, denounces it as 'Terrible! A perfect fit for the socialist/communist propaganda tag'.[32] In Britain, the book is used extensively in schools, perhaps with a conscious nod back to George Orwell and the fact that Waddell himself calls it *Animal Farm* for 5-year-olds, or because of Oxenbury's evocative watercolours of the English countryside, or because of the rhythms of language and onomatopoeia. Leon Trotsky would probably have approved of *Fantastic Mr Fox*, *Piggybook*, and *Farmer Duck* as, in *Literature and revolution,* he asserts: 'During the period of revolution, only that literature which promotes the consolidation of the workers in their struggle against the exploiters is necessary and progressive'.[33] The animals do overthrow the farmer and take over the farm. But what of Oxenbury's last ironic image of 'their' farm, free of the oppressor, in which Duck stands high above the others on a hay-piled cart, appearing to hand out the orders? Is Duck to become Stalin to the Farmer's Lenin? Trotsky continues:

> Revolutionary literature cannot but be imbued with a spirit of social hatred, which is a creative historic factor in an epoch of proletarian dictatorship ... Literature and art will be tuned to a different key.[34]

'Social hatred' or any kind of rage against the machine is a rare thing in children's literature. The literature referred to here has neither been produced under dictatorship nor revolution but under conditions of privilege, falling short of what Noam Chomsky calls 'radical democracy'.[35] Perhaps the range of institutions and practices that name what the child is in our culture (educationalists, psychologists, parents, publishers, etc.) has, to a worrying extent, set the key for an *unradicalized* tune which writers and artists sing to, if they wish to make a living. For example, why does no one die in the struggle in *Fantastic Mr Fox*, *Farmer Duck* or *Click, clack, moo*? Are any political struggles worth the fight really without loss?

Nigerian novelist Chinua Achebe, in his essay 'What has literature got to do with it?',[36] refers to animal fables about class division and privilege and the

31 http://www.amazon.com/Farmer-Duck-Martin-Waddell/product-reviews/076362425X, accessed 15 Oct. 2012. 32 Ibid. 33 L. Trotsky, *Literature and revolution* (1925; Chicago, 2005), p. 188. 34 Ibid. 35 N. Chomsky interview with John Nichols, 'Radical democracy', *Capital Times*, 3 Mar. 1997. 36 C. Achebe, 'What has literature got to do with it'

seeds of revolution they contain, arguing that they often carry the suggestion of the dissolution of an incompetent oligarchy. The Grimm tale *The mouse, the bird and the sausage* (1812) plays ironically with this premise, in what has to be the shortest and grimmest of Grimm tales, depicting class struggle, division and privilege:

> Once upon a time, the Mouse, the Bird and the Sausage lived happily together. The Bird brought home wood from the forest; the Mouse delivered water & made the cooking fire; and the Sausage cooks. One day, other birds make fun of the Bird, saying that it is doing the hardest work. Next day, the Bird suggests they switch roles and refuses to go to the forest. The Mouse and the Sausage oppose the idea at first, but in the end, they give in. The Bird can bring home the water, the Mouse cook, and the Sausage go to the forest to collect wood. The Sausage leaves to gather wood in the forest early in the morning but it meets a dog and does not come home again. The Mouse tries to cook. It imitates the Sausage, rolling himself in the pot to mix and season the food. However, the Mouse cannot stand the heat and dies. The Bird panics and in order to put out the fire, goes to the well to get some water. It leans too far over and falls into the well. The Bird cannot get back out and drowns. The end.[37]

This reads more like a fable than a fairy tale, but what is its didactic message? Is the moral imperative a call to maintaining the status quo? Or is it a savagely ironic insight into life as merely capital; the impact of politics on all aspects of life and survival; how certain change cannot be borne, and under that ghastly moment of biopolitical intensity, the symbolic order of creaturely life cracks and fails? Corporeal reality dictates terms in this fable. Birds are not 'made' to carry water, mice cannot withstand heat and it is a surreal absurdity to imagine a sausage collecting sticks. Unusually defeatist in tone, this fable suggests that true equality of opportunity is not possible. Foster's 'new social links' cannot be forged and in this revolution, no one survives.

TWENTY-FIRST-CENTURY BIOPOLITICAL FABLE

However, as defined by Marxists Michael Hardt and Antonio Negri, biopolitics can carry positive meanings. In an era of postmodern neo-capitalism, what constitutes life can no longer be reduced to forms of reproduction or simplistic

in his *Hopes and impediments: selected essays* (New York, 1990).   37 Jacob & Wilhelm Grimm, 'The mouse, the bird and the sausage', *Grimms' fairy tales* (*Kinder und Hausmärchen*), no. 23 (1812), Victoria de Rijke's translation.

working processes. They argue that life in the twenty-first century is vital in its plurality, and yet, at the same time, they might be describing *The mouse, the bird and the sausage*. 'Now we are speaking of the connection between the power of life and its political organization. The political, the social, the economic, and the vital here all dwell together.'[38] For them, anti-capitalist insurrection can use life as a weapon, such as the flight from power, or running away. It can be a moment of insurgency. Children understand running away. It can be a playful, tactical biopolitics. In that moment, the individual and the body are in action, running towards something else. Making biopolitical connections is an exciting possibility for twenty-first-century children's literature, in all the manifestations and new forms it may take.

Wes Anderson's animated version of Roald Dahl's *Fantastic Mr Fox*[39] contains a scene that is important in this context. Anderson shows Mr Fox and his gang making their escape – their flight from power – on a motorbike in bandit hats and goggles, portrayed as humorous anthropomorphic characters in a modern fable. Suddenly we see a shaggy black shape high on a snowy crag, looking down on the cartoon creatures. This wild beast recalls older fairy tales, where the wolf was a living danger, both as a real animal and a mythic creature. Mr Fox puts up goggles and hat and addresses the wolf, asking 'Where do you come from?', pointing to it, naming it *Canis lupus*, and himself *Vulpes vulpes* before admitting to the others, 'I don't think he speaks Latin or English'. As he points, the eye follows the fox's arm in his russet-coloured suit to the wolf on the rock wearing nothing but his own black shaggy coat, panting. In the cultural phenomenology of late modernity, the gang of animals' tiny woollen bandit hats, hand-knitted using micro-needles and the fox's tight-fitting corduroy suit made out of scraps of fabric from one of Anderson's own suits connects the social, physical bodies of animal and human. 'I have a phobia of wolves!' Mr Fox calls out, and, gazing at the creature stiffening up proudly at that, his eyes well with tears. Mr Fox then raises his fist in a salute of solidarity that the wolf returns before he runs away. The other animals drive off on their bike and a high-speed train passes in the other direction.

None of this action exists in any form in Dahl's book; it is purely Anderson's invention. He points – as Mr Fox points – to the futility of cultural classification (Latin terms), natural hierarchies of the food chain (phobia) and nature-culture bound together in shared, political consciousness (salute). Animal scientist George Page states: 'the more a species needs to be conscious, the more it is conscious. Either that or it becomes extinct'.[40]

As the director of the film, Anderson had to resist suggestions to cut this scene as it bears no relation to the rest of the narrative. 'That scene is why

38 M. Hardt & A. Negri, *Empire* (London, 2000), pp 405–6.   39 W. Anderson (dir.), *Fantastic Mr Fox* (Los Angeles, 2009).   40 G. Page, *The singing gorilla: understanding animal intelligence* (London, 1999), p. 100.

I'm making the movie,'[41] he insisted. Animation critic, Paul Wells, supports the seriousness of such creative sensibility:

> Animated animals can also be understood as anthropomorphic phe-
> nomena foregrounding the acute sensibility of the animator in prompt-
> ing visions of animality and advancing a view of phenomenological
> performance in animal animation as a model of philosophical inquiry.[42]

This attention to detail in Anderson's animation expresses something of the biopolitical friction of what has been termed 'rewilding'. Through engagement with the biophilosophies of Gilles Deleuze and Donna Haraway's recent work on companion species, animal specialists now 'cautiously affirm the potential of a biopolitics of rewilding for the flourishing of nonhuman difference.'[43] Anderson's mini-fable explores that 'fissure in the space of meaning', or what John Berger in his essay *Why look at animals?*[44] calls 'unspeaking companion-ship'; animals as *the* relational metaphor, placed in a receding past – once threatening now threatened. 'What a beautiful creature', says the cartoon Mr Fox, as if celluloid self-aware. 'Wish him luck, boys'. The animated film po-rtrays a real animal even though it is of course a cartoon like the others. Drawn somewhat differently to Mr Fox and his friends, the wolf exists in an altered reality, calling to mind Berger's description of animals in zoos as 'living monu-ments to their own disappearance'.[45] The scene also evokes Giorgio Agamben's distinction of bare life (*zoé*) and political existence (*bíos*); between natural existence (such as the wolf inhabits in the wild) and constructed existence (puppet creatures dressed in human clothes acting out a work of children's literature).[46] Audiences read the wolf as organic, raw material; the fox as genetic.

Without wanting to over-read an incidental moment in a cartoon, the scene calls up a key philosophical twenty-first-century challenge for all of us (particularly for the young), namely, that life and death no longer necessarily exist in the natural rhythms of the organic body, since it can be stored in biobanks and cultivated artificially. Do the possibilities of re-animation even offer immortality? If the wolf does become extinct, could we simply rebuild the species genetically? In this new context, biopolitics requires radical re-thinking. Such deep reading is made possible by several moments of biopo-litical intensity in the creaturely life of Anderson's animation like this

---

41 Wes Anderson interviewed by Joe Utichi, 'Wes Anderson talks Darjeeling Limited and Mr Fox', *Rotten Tomatoes*, 22 Nov. 2007. 42 P. Wells, *The animated bestiary: animals, cartoons and culture* (London, 2009), p. 175. 43 C. Driessen & J. Lorimer, 'Biopolitics' in *Wild experiments: new natures for the Anthropocene*, http://wildexperiments.com/biopoli-tics, accessed 10 Mar. 2013. 44 J. Berger, 'Why look at animals?' in G. Dyer (ed.), *Selected essays* (London, 2001), p. 261. 45 Ibid., p. 272. 46 G. Agamben, *Homo Sacer: sovereign power and bare life* (Stanford, 1998).

encounter with the wolf, as it slows the pace, focuses political thinking. It is charged with an anxious wonder.

As Paul Wells and others have argued, the animal animation plays out our foibles as a satiric form par excellence.[47] Anderson's animation seems marked by spontaneity of spirit. The director sent acted-out scenes by iphone from Paris to London while the animation team deliberately employed what are now (in the context of computer generated imagery) slow, old-fashioned forms (using miniature hand-crafted creatures and stop-motion) juxtaposing the techniques. Sound came from real contexts, recording voices in situ rather than in a studio: 'We went out in a forest, [...] went in an attic, [...] went in a stable. We went underground for some things. There was a great spontaneity in the recordings because of that'.[48] The speaking part actors lived on a farm while shooting, and the actor Bill Murray offered to pretend to 'be the wolf' to give the dialogue for that scene something real to relate to, so:

> [h]e ran, ran, ran, ran really far away until he was tiny. And he turned around and actually became the wolf, like he, it's almost as if he embodied the wolf. And he acted it out for us, and it was so inspiring and so beautiful. And Wes actually took out his camera phone, filmed it, and then sent that footage to the animators to base the wolf on Bill Murray, so Bill Murray is the uncredited wolf in this movie.[49]

The cinematic use of close-ups for the Fox party and distance shots for the wolf offer a visual statement about the simultaneous proximity and distance of animals, with the added irony that the *embodiment* of animality was actually provided by a human actor. The success of that scene stems from the spontaneity and great care in its making; an intense imagining resulting in its special intensity. Trotsky warns us to beware those writers who 'sing the old feelings over again with slightly new words',[50] but the political, the social, the economic, and the vital can all dwell together when new versions of familiar stories work like 'old wine in new bottles'.[51] Tales can retain their original power yet still surprise. Fables for children throw open the political possibilities of becoming a free, autonomous subject, in the face of a dangerous world where freedom carries responsibilities and risks. They offer the promise of biopolitical insurgency. The best children's literature can boil highly complex political ideas down to their essence; their fastest form. Running – not as escape, but as Bill Murray ran to embody and animate the wolf, in the spirit of pure play and solidarity, 'Run, run, fast as you can, you can't catch me, I'm the gingerbread man!' – *towards* the risk is fable's tactical biopolitics.

47 P. Wells, *The animated bestiary*, pp 65, 95.   **48** W. Anderson interview by Joe Utichi, 22 Nov. 2007.   **49** Jason Schwartzman, interviewed by Lance Carter, *The Daily Actor*, 23 Nov. 2009.   **50** Trotsky, *Literature*, p. 131.   **51** A. Carter, 'Notes from the front line' in M. Wandor (ed.), *On gender and writing* (London, 1983), p. 69.

'That imprudent Old Person of Chili': individual and They in Edward Lear's limericks

OLGA SPRINGER

The eccentrics of Edward Lear's limericks are famous.[1] From the first line of each poem, even prescribed by its very form ('There was an/a [...]'), it is clear that an individual character stands at its centre, often in some interaction with a group of other persons ('They'),[2] who sometimes criticize and punish the eccentrics for their unconventional behaviour and sometimes help, warn or ignore them. A typical example is the limerick of the old person of Deal, whose 'otherness' arouses Their curiosity:

> There was an old person of Deal,
> Who in walking, used only his heel;
> When they said, 'Tell us why?' – He made no reply;
> That mysterious old person of Deal.[3]

This essay analyzes the portrayal of the individual in Lear's limericks, in light of the relationship between the eccentric individual, whose behaviour often remains inexplicable, as in the example above, and the community (mostly represented by Them and sometimes by the speaker of the poem). The poems will be discussed as part of a discourse on the individual's role in society (focusing on John Stuart Mill's notion of individuality) and as contributions to the critique of conventional views of individuality.[4]

---

1 Lear published two series of limericks: the first came out in final form in 1861 (it was an expanded version of his *Book of nonsense* of 1846, which he originally wrote for the Earl of Derby's grandchildren – the Earl was Lear's patron); the second appeared in *More nonsense* (1872), see T. Byrom, *Nonsense and wonder: the poems and cartoons of Edward Lear* (New York, 1977), p. 51. 2 In line with other commentators on Lear, I have used capital spelling ('They', 'Them', 'Their') when referring to the characters described by that pronoun in the limericks. 3 H. Jackson, *The complete nonsense of Edward Lear* (London, 1965), p. 199. The formatting, i.e., capitalizations and number of lines, follows the one employed by Jackson. Where other sources have been used, I have followed their respective formatting. 4 Lear himself uttered a caveat concerning the (especially political) interpretation of his limericks: 'The critics are very silly to see politics in such bosh: not but that bosh requires a good deal of care, for it is a sine qua non in writing for children to keep what they have to read perfectly clear & bright, & incapable of any meaning but one of sheer nonsense'. (*Selected letters*, p. 228; quoted in J. Rieder, 'Edward Lear's limericks: the function of children's

Lear's limericks create a world of their own, populated by characters like the old person of Deal, who seem to represent the essence of individualism: although the reader obtains hardly any information about him, the protagonist has quite a marked 'character'. He refuses to explain his behaviour, thus becoming 'mysterious' to the speaker of the poem. He resembles many other limerick characters, who insist on following their own inclinations as opposed to doing things in a customary way (in this case employing an uncommon part of the foot for walking), to Their astonishment or irritation. The characters' comic individual traits, however, are diluted by the serial form in which the limericks are published, potentially blurring the various personas and their behaviour in the reader's mind (unless one considers the rhyme as a phonetic guide to remembering that, for example, the old person of Deal was the one who always walked on his heel). However, considering the number of limericks, there is bound to be confusion.

While it is doubtful that John Stuart Mill had in mind poems like Lear's when he tried to formulate his idea of poetry in his essay 'What is poetry?', the limericks' individuals' unconcern for the opinion of their fellow men and their eccentricity suggests a likeness to poets as Mill describes them: '[t]he persons, and the nations, who commonly excel in poetry, are those whose character and tastes render them least dependent upon the applause, or sympathy, or concurrence of the world in general'.[5] His views on the individual and his/her place in 'the world in general' as expressed in the third chapter of 'On liberty' (1859), 'Of individuality as one of the elements of well-being', will be discussed as a contemporary foil to the representations found in the limericks. Mill argues in favour of encouraging uncustomary behaviour in 'exceptional individuals' in order to benefit society as a whole.[6] He defines individuality as the tendency to question the decisions and choices of the majority. The ideal individual does not unthinkingly adopt customs, but stands out by forming and upholding his own opinion and by translating this opinion into action. Observing that mass opinion was becoming the dominant power in British society, Mill writes:

> It is in these circumstances most especially that exceptional individuals, instead of being deterred, should be encouraged in acting differ-

---

nonsense poetry', *Children's Literature*, 26 (1998), 47–61 at 47.) Carolyn Wells writes that '[b]oth Lear and Carroll suffered from the undiscerning critics who persisted in seeing in their nonsense a hidden meaning, a cynical, political, or other intent, veiled under the apparent foolery'. (C. Wells (ed.), *A nonsense anthology* (New York, 1902), p. xxviii.) Despite these valid points against examining the limericks with contemporary political thought like John Stuart Mill's in mind, the results that are yielded by such readings are worthwhile.   5 J.S. Mill, 'What is poetry?' in L. Trilling and H. Bloom (eds), *Victorian prose and poetry* (New York, 1973), p. 81.   6 J.S. Mill, 'On liberty: of individuality as one of the elements of well-being' in L. Trilling and H. Bloom (eds), *Victorian prose and poetry* (New York, 1973), p. 92.

ently from the mass. In other times there was no advantage in their doing so, unless they acted not only differently, but better. In this age, the mere example of nonconformity, the mere refusal to bend the knee to custom, is itself a service. Precisely because the tyranny of opinion is such as to make eccentricity a reproach, it is desirable, in order to break through that tyranny, that people should be eccentric.[7]

It could be argued that They represent Mill's notion of mass opinion, simply because They always figure in the anonymous plural[8] and because They tend to censor and attempt to restrict the individual's unconventional behaviour. Mill's writings and the limericks both reflect on the role of the eccentric individual in society, although they obviously approach it in a different spirit and format. Nevertheless, Mill's assertion that the deviation from customary behaviour should be cultivated for its own sake (which is somewhat retracted in the rest of the chapter) mirrors the fact that the limerick characters' behaviour often remains unexplained.

The limericks have both a narrative element and a 'dramatic' quality,[9] which unfolds in the interaction between individual and Them. The poems are constructed in a way that makes it difficult to discern which of the characters represent 'proper' behaviour. The narrative nature of the limericks introduces the question of focalization and voice. Who is speaking/who is seeing in the little stories the poems tell? At least in the first volume of poems, it initially seems that the 'old Derry down Derry' will provide an orientation as to the author figure (and speaker?) of the limericks:

> There was an old Derry down Derry,
> Who loved to see little folks merry;
> So he made them a book, and with laughter they shook,
> At the fun of that Derry down Derry![10]

Lear constructs an alter ego or narrator for himself and a 'frame narrative' for his limericks in this introductory poem on the title page of the volume. John Rieder, referring to the illustration accompanying the poem, points out the ambiguity of the relationship between the old Derry down Derry and the children around him.[11] He interprets the cover page as a possible refutation of social roles and emphasizes the ambiguity of the image: '[t]he point is not that it is one way or the other, but that both possibilities are offered. The

---

7 Ibid.   8 At least this is the case in the text portion of the limerick; in the image They are paradoxically sometimes represented by a single figure.   9 Byrom, *Nonsense and wonder*, p. 50.   10 For the title page of the third edition of *A book of nonsense* (1861, first edition 1846), see http://www.nonsenselit.org/Lear/BoN/, accessed 13 January 2014.   11 Source: http://www.nonsenselit.org/Lear/BoN/index.html, accessed 15 October 2012.

adult's authority is neither protected nor abdicated, but rather suspended, at least for as long as the fun continues'.[12] The drawing raises many questions about the poem. Is the author really about to hand his book over to the children – or does he take it back from them? His hand is still/already on the book. It is unclear who is in charge in the scene. Is it really the only adult, clearly standing out by his size and his position in the foreground? Or are the dominant ones the children, outnumbering him and keeping a firm hold on the book?

The group on the right, throwing up their arms and jumping, anticipate the bird-like appearance of some of the limerick characters. Has reading the limericks made their own eccentricity apparent? The feet of the group on the left are mostly touching the ground, while the old Derry down Derry has lifted one leg in a jumping movement, and even the other one is hanging in the air. In the background, one of the little readers is standing on his head. Have the limericks inspired him to look at the world and its familiar hierarchies upside down?[13]

We have now arrived at the subversive potential of the limericks. This potential is primarily realized in the interplay of text and image, or in the ambiguity of the speaker's voice. The latter point is illustrated by the limerick of the Old Person of Chili:

> There was an Old Person of Chili,
> Whose conduct was painful and silly,
> He sate on the stairs, eating apples and pears,
> That imprudent Old Person of Chili.[14]

The humour of the limerick stems from the discrepancy between the speaker's harsh judgment and the old person's harmless behaviour. Three adjectives are used to condemn the protagonist: 'painful', 'silly' and 'imprudent'. The second line is remarkable for combining three different registers of decreasing formality: from 'conduct', fairly formal, via the neutral 'painful', to the more colloquial 'silly' (the triad even vaguely evokes the steps the figure is sitting on). It almost seems as though the speaker is looking for a poignant expression to 'accuse' the old man, but instead he ends on 'silly', anticipating the anticlimax of the rather ordinary activity of eating apples and pears. The limerick thus not only questions the standards of behaviour implied here, but also the authority of the speaker's judgment. However,

---

12 Rieder, 'Edward Lear's limericks', p. 49.   13 This implied reversal of hierarchies (seeing that which is usually the lowest uppermost) is characteristic of Bakhtin's notion of the carnivalesque in literature. M. Bakhtin, *Problems of Dostoevsky's poetics*, ed. and trans. Caryl Emerson, *Theory and History of Literature*, 8 (Minneapolis, 1984).   14 Jackson, *Complete nonsense*, p. 6.

when the reader takes a look at the picture, the final 'imprudent' still ringing in his ears, he finds the seemingly unfitting adjective confirmed in the character's roguish, even sly expression, throwing apples and pears about him. The image thus confirms the poem's judgment, and 'eating apples and pears', an activity certainly familiar to young and old readers of the limericks, is suddenly turned into an eccentric undertaking.

The notion of the carnivalesque, as defined and analysed by Mikhail Bakhtin, illustrates the subversive potential of the limericks: '[t]he laws, prohibitions, and restrictions that determine the structure and order of ordinary, that is non carnival, life are suspended during carnival: what is suspended first of all is hierarchical structure [...]'.[15] Bakhtin underlines the 'joyful relativity characteristic of a carnival sense of the world', which is opposed to 'rationality, [...] singular meaning, [...] dogmatism'.[16] The limericks, especially in the relationship of text and image, thus retain an openness of meaning and undermine the notion of a stable truth which provides unambivalent answers.

Another limerick, 'There was an Old Man with a gong', illustrates Their punitive measures in response to eccentric behaviour, at least in the text.[17] The picture does not show the Old Man's demise (They smash him after his persistent use of the gong), but rather an indefinite number of Them (Lear here uses his 'accordion' technique of drawing) clapping for his unconcerned performance. It is meaningful that the Old Man's eyes are closed, showing his indifference to Their opinion, and even to the fatal consequence of his insistence on playing his instrument, bringing to mind once more Mill's thoughts about poets and their special role in society:

> That mankind are not infallible; that their truths, for the most part, are only half-truths; that unity of opinion, unless resulting from the fullest and freest comparison of opposite opinions, is not desirable, and diversity not an evil, but a good, until mankind are much more capable than at present of recognizing all sides of the truth, are principles applicable to men's modes of action not less than to their opinions.[18]

The accordion audience represents such a mass opinion, whether they smash or applaud the Old Man. They and he occupy different levels in the picture: They are firmly rooted on a considerably lower plane, while the Old Man has risen higher up before his gong. In fact, Their reactions in many limericks illustrate Mill's credo: 'But the evil is that individual spontaneity is hardly

---

15 Bakhtin, *Problems*, p. 123.   16 Ibid., p. 107. Bakhtin is contrasting the serio-comical literary genres with others.   17 'There was an Old Man with a gong, / Who bumped at it all the day long; /But they called out, "O law! You're a horrid old bore!" / So they smashed that Old Man with a gong.' (Jackson, *Complete nonsense*, p. 6.)   18 Mill, 'On liberty', p. 84.

recognized by the common modes of thinking as having any intrinsic worth, or deserving any regard on its own account'.[19]

The juxtaposition of Mill's thoughts on individuality and its representation in Lear's limericks is not to imply that there is a political intent behind the limericks. Rather, the linking of the two texts is supposed to illuminate the significance of the limericks for the topics of the time. The limericks are a playground of meaning, in which different scenarios may be explored without devastation about the occasionally fatal consequences.[20] The reason for this openness is the relationship between poem and picture: the drawings often tell a different story than the texts do, in the manner of a discussion about the meaning of the limerick between these two 'interlocutors'. The interplay between them creates an openness, whose purpose is not to be resolved, but to persist. Despite the shortness of the text, there is not just one voice, but a plurality of voices, and the meaning(s) of the limerick come into being in the dialogic, serial exchange between speaker and Them, image and text. [21]

Several critics have commented on the discrepancy between poem and picture in the limericks. Thomas Byrom has compiled an extensive collection of examples of this phenomenon in *Nonsense and wonder: the poems and cartoons of Edward Lear* (1977). The conclusion he draws is that '[t]he motive of the discrepancies is to make life look strange and more joyful'.[22] In the context of individuality, the discrepancy between image and text reminds the reader of the plurality of voices involved in recounting the characters' respective stories and underlines the peculiar 'self-will' of limerick language. One of many examples is 'There was an Old Man of Peru', whose wife bakes him in the stove 'by mistake'.[23] The picture, however, shows said wife in the act of pushing her husband into the oven on a dish, gleefully pointing at him in his distress. Their difference in stature is moreover remarkable: the wife is of gigantic proportions compared to her diminutive husband, whose legs are helplessly flailing about. Her face has distinctly apish features.[24] The discrepancy between image and text can be read as a refutation of a final answer to the question of what com-

---

19 Ibid.   **20** Ann Colley points this out in her essay 'Edward Lear's limericks and the reversals of nonsense': '[...] because Lear releases his subjects from the burden of time and memory, the limericks are unoccupied by tragedy', *Victorian Poetry*, 26:3 (1988), 285–99 at 291.   **21** The term dialogic is used in allusion to Bakhtin's notion of the same name: 'The dialogic means of seeking truth is counterposed to *official* monologism, which pretends to *possess* a *ready-made truth*, and it is also counterposed to the naive self-confidence of those people who think that they know something, that is, who think that they possess certain truths' (Bakhtin, *Problems*, p. 110).   **22** Byrom, *Nonsense and wonder*, p. 138.   **23** 'There was an Old Man of Peru, / Who watched his wife making a stew; / But once by mistake, in a stove she did bake, / That unfortunate Man of Peru.' (Jackson, *Complete nonsense*, p. 28.)   **24** This trait can be found in several of the limericks, especially in the characters called Them. Another ape is featured in 'There was an Old Person of Buda' (Jackson, *Complete nonsense*, p. 14), which is discussed below.

prises the authoritative version of events. In the dialogic interaction of both limerick elements, the Old Man's wife pushes him into the oven by mistake and on purpose at the same time.

Susan Stewart has described the language of nonsense writing as 'language lifted out of context, language turning on itself [...] language made hermetic, opaque [...]'.[25] Referring to the Stewart quote, Rieder points out the playfulness of Lear's limericks, in which signifier and signified are not necessarily of the same value, and interprets this as the insulation of the artistic event from its social context. This seems like a contradiction to the notion that the limericks illustrate the relationship between individual and society, but both readings can coexist when the independence of the signifier from a static signified is read as a symbol of the isolation of some of the characters. In this sense, the sometimes puzzling language underlines the characters' and the speaker's eccentricity.

Language therefore plays a central role in the exploration of the notion of individuality in the limericks. In their brevity, the limericks both invite and refute interpretation.[26] Language appears like a character itself in the poems, in possession of an individual being (Mill's praise of 'self-will'[27] comes to mind): self-sufficient, obstinate and playful, especially in the use of the final adjective. The adjective in the last line of the limerick plays an important role in expressing eccentricity. Ann Colley remarks about two of the limericks that Lear read before he started composing them himself that they represent a more or less logical sequence from one event to another.[28] She continues:

> Both verses set up a logical sequence of events which Lear's limericks subvert by only pretending to move forward from cause to effect. The originality of Lear's verse is that the last line, by repeating the first, undermines the progressive movement of the 1823 models. The memory of the model, however, is available, but displaced to throw over all the expectations of a connected sequence.[29]

Colley moreover emphasizes the eccentricity of the final adjectives: 'Being larger, longer, and having a rougher texture than the words around them, each

---

25 S. Stewart, *Nonsense: aspects of intertextuality in folklore and literature* (Baltimore, 1979), p. 3. Quoted in Rieder, 'Edward Lear's limericks', 49.   26 John Rieder even defines this as an essential characteristic of literary and artistic nonsense in general: it invites multiple interpretations and at the same time refutes attempts at making sense of it ('Edward Lear's limericks', 47).   27 Mill, 'On liberty', p. 88.   28 The construction of the last line indicates a significant difference between Lear's and earlier limericks (Colley, 'Reversals of nonsense', p. 293). One of the two 1823 examples of conventional limericks discussed by Colley is this one: 'There was a sick man of Tobago, / Liv'd long on rice gruel and sago; / But at last to his bliss, / The physician said this – / "To a roast leg of mutton you may go."' (ibid.)   29 Ibid.

is distinctive'.[30] Sometimes the adjective is a neologism but more often it is a word whose meaning cannot easily be 'appropriated' by an interpretation:

> There was an Old Man of Peru
> Who never knew what he should do;
> So he tore off his hair, and behaved like a bear,
> That intrinsic Old Man of Peru.[31]

The effect of this adjective is certainly one of puzzlement and fascination. How can a person be intrinsic? But also: how does one behave like a bear? The drawing does not help much with these questions; the old man is sitting rather unspectacularly on a chair and only his face and short limbs have faint traces of a bear-likeness. The adjective promises 'to justify and combine the disparate elements of the entire verse'[32] – but instead of offering a 'dénouement' or clue at interpretation, it frustrates attempts at explaining the limerick. The gesture of the adjective illustrates the eccentricity of the language itself (or of the speaker using it), since it does not bear any relation to the poem's content. Rather, it seems to mimic a child having learned a new word and now using this word in creative, rather subjective ways.

If one takes the meaning of 'intrinsic' to be '[b]elonging to the thing in itself, or by its very nature; inherent, essential, proper; "of its own"',[33] the adjective suggests a link to a thought expressed by John Stuart Mill in 'On liberty': '[a] person whose desires and impulses are his own – are the expression of his own nature as it has been developed by his own culture – is said to have a character'.[34] The limerick of the Old Man of Peru, especially with regard to the final adjective, reads like a parody of this definition of character. The adjective can moreover be applied to the limericks in general (in conjunction with a person, it sounds quite odd), which present parodies of conventional logic. T.S. Eliot described nonsense writing as parody in 1942: Lear's 'non-sense is not vacuity of sense: it is a parody of sense, and that is the sense of it'.[35] Lear was clearly interested in the adjective 'intrinsic', since he first used it in another limerick, which he was to change in the published version:

> There was an old man of Cape Horn,
> Who wished he had never been born;
> He sate on a chair, and behaved like a bear,
> That intrinsic old man of Cape Horn.

Herman W. Liebert interprets the adjective in this version as '[a]dmirably precise: it describes perfectly the old man's "capacity for work in virtue of

---

30 Ibid., p. 294.   31 Jackson, *Complete nonsense*, p. 12.   32 Colley, 'Reversals of nonsense', p. 294.   33 *Oxford English dictionary*, 'intrinsic', 3a.   34 Mill, 'On liberty', p. 87. 35 J. Gantar, *The pleasure of fools*, p. 62.

actual condition, without any supply of energy from without'".³⁶ Lear later changed the adjective to 'dolorous', maybe following the man's facial expression in the drawing.

Another interesting adjective that undermines the conventions of limerick communication is 'incipient' in 'There was an Old Man at a casement'.³⁷ Read with the meaning of '[b]eginning; commencing; coming into, or in an early' stage of, existence; in an initial stage'³⁸ in mind, the reader struggles to make sense of the word. However, when taking into account its obsolete homophone 'insipient' ('[v]oid of wisdom; unwise, foolish.? Obs. Now mostly, or wholly, disused to avoid confusion with *incipient*'),³⁹ the adjective actually describes the Old Man's obstinacy, and the drawing, in which he is in fact beginning to fall.

The interplay of language and image in Lear's 'nonsense' lends itself to reflecting on the relationship between eccentric individual and society and contributes to the dialogic nature of the limericks. As we have seen, the ambiguities arising from the text-image discrepancies question the existence of a final interpretation. Close reading of some limericks will illustrate the observations made so far:

> There was an Old Person of Buda,
> Whose conduct grew ruder and ruder;
> Till at last, with a hammer, they silenced his clamour,
> By smashing that Person of Buda.⁴⁰

The reader does not learn what his 'conduct' has been, only that it has become too rude to be tolerated. The drawing, however, calls this account into question: the Old Person of Buda, perching on one foot with arms stretched behind like wings and a round, birdlike belly, small and harmless-looking, is approached by his gigantic hammer-wielding opponent, who strongly resembles an ape. The apelike appearance evokes Mill's assertion that a real individual lacks the 'apelike [faculty] of imitation'⁴¹ and prefers to do things in his own fashion instead of following the repetitive patterns of customary behaviour. Visually, this finds an interesting expression in the 'accordion' drawings representing a great number of persons and underlining their 'uniformity'⁴² (see earlier discussion of 'There was an Old Man with a gong').

---

36 H.W. Liebert, *Lear in the original: drawings and limericks by Edward Lear for his book of nonsense* (New York, 1975), p. 70 (qtd. in J. Gantar, *The pleasure of fools: essays in the ethics of laughter* (Québec, 2005), p. 62). 37 Jackson, *Complete nonsense*, p. 55. 'There was an Old Man at a casement, / Who held up his hands in amazement; / When they said, "Sir! You'll fall!" he replied, "Not at all!" / That incipient Old Man at a casement.' 38 *Oxford English dictionary*, 'incipient', A.1. 39 *OED*, 'insipient', A. 40 Jackson, *Complete nonsense*, p. 14. 41 Mill, 'On liberty', p. 86. 42 'It is not by wearing down into uniformity all that

The limericks seem to parody and to take to the extreme Mill's notion of individual freedom:

> As it is useful that while mankind are imperfect there should be different opinions, so it is that there should be different experiments of living; that free scope should be given to varieties of character, short of injury to others; and that the worth of different modes of life should be proved practically, when anyone thinks fit to try them.[43]

In this context, the limericks might be read as such 'experiments of living', but they seem to be taking the experiment to another level insofar as they (ambivalently) show the outcome of individual modes of living.

Returning to the Old Person of Buda, things are not as univocal as they seem: first, the Old Person has not been smashed yet (as the text declares), and Their gesture does not indicate that he will be anytime soon. The hammer is not held firmly and with its head in an upright position, but in a manner suggesting a curious or even caressing approach rather than a fatal blow. The meaning of the limerick thus oscillates between a fatal and a more fortuitous outcome for the old person.

Mill pleads for exercising each person's understanding in deciding which customs to follow and to what extent.[44] Concerning the role of desires and impulses, he writes:

> Desires and impulses are as much a part of a perfect human being, as beliefs and restraints: and strong impulses are only perilous when not properly balanced [...] Strong impulses are but another name for energy. Energy may be turned to bad uses; but more good may always be made of an energetic nature than of an indolent and impassive one.[45]

While Lear's limericks are not concerned with the moral aspect of the use of energy, they do display a lot of literal energy: characters dance ('There was an Old Person of Ischia';[46] 'There was an Old Man of Whitehaven'),[47] rush

---

is individual in themselves, but by cultivating it and calling it forth, within the limits imposed by the rights and interests of others, that human beings become a noble and beautiful object of contemplation;' (Mill, 'On liberty', p. 89) and 'People think genius a fine thing if it enables a man to write an exciting poem, or paint a picture. But in its true sense, that of originality in thought and action, though no one says that it is not a thing to be admired, nearly all, at heart, think that they can do very well without it. [...] Originality is the one thing which unoriginal minds cannot feel the use of' (Mill, 'On liberty', pp 90f.). Lear often transfers the very unoriginality of the majority into his drawings by making Them look like indifferent copies of each other.   43 Mill, 'On liberty', p. 84. Mill then emphasizes that this freedom to experiment can only be granted when it does not affect others.   44 Ibid., p. 92.
45 Ibid., pp 86f.   46 Jackson, *Complete nonsense*, p. 9.   47 Ibid., p. 39.

about ('There was an Old Man on a hill';[48] 'There was an Old Man of Corfu'),[49] climb ('There was an Old Man of Dundee'),[50] make noise ('There was an Old Man with a gong') and scream ('There was a Young Lady of Russia').[51] Many of Lear's protagonists follow their eccentric desires and impulses, like the Old Man of the Coast, who sits on a post, or the Old Person of Bangor, who angrily tears off his boots and only eats roots.[52] Evidently, the characters' activities are nothing like what Mill has in mind – but the limericks do show some conceptual parallels with Mill's ideas of individuality, even if they turn their earnestness upside down.

Mill's main point of criticism of contemporary British society is that conformity is the first and foremost principle according to which people make choices – both in their private and public existence:

> Thus the mind itself is bowed to the yoke: even in what people do for pleasure, conformity is the first thing thought of; they like in crowds; they exercise choice only among things commonly done: peculiarity of taste, eccentricity of conduct, are shunned equally with crimes: until by dint of not following their own nature, they have no nature to follow: their human capacities are withered and starved: they become incapable of any strong wishes or native pleasures, and are generally without either opinions or feelings of home growth, or properly their own.[53]

In the absoluteness of their choices and wishes, the characters of the limericks exist on account of their 'unreasonable', uncompromising individuality, in a carnivalesque joyful relativity. The motivations of their actions are often obscure, which might even make it easier to sympathize with them. They simply exist, mostly without providing explanations of their choices and desires – one of many examples is 'There was an old person of Wilts, /Who constantly walked upon stilts'. Read in the serial manner in which the limericks are presented, the scenarios they feature resemble a series of experiments on individuality. They are indeed carnivalesque in their nature: '[c]arnival is the place for working out, in a concretely sensuous, half-real and half-play-acted form, *a new mode of interrelationship between individuals*, counterposed to the all-powerful socio-hierarchical relationships of noncarnival life'.[54] This effect is reinforced by the fact that some of the limericks end in violence and death in the text, but hardly ever in the image. As Byrom points out, even the Old Person of Tartary[55] is not shown in death, but still has the energy to

48 Ibid., p. 4.   49 Ibid., p. 32.   50 Ibid., p. 35.   51 Ibid., p. 48.   52 Ibid., p. 44.   53 Mill, 'On liberty', pp 87f.   54 Bakhtin, *Problems*, p. 123.   55 'There was an Old Person of Tartary, / Who divided his jugular artery; / But he screeched to his wife, and she said, "Oh, my life! / Your death will be felt by all Tartary!"' (Jackson, *Complete nonsense*, p. 50).

raise his head to look at his wife, and the knife does not touch him. Death is never an actual event, even if it is the fate of some of the characters in the limericks.[56] Moreover, the sheer number and sequence of limericks suggest that the protagonists' eccentric behaviour continues almost endlessly.

The pleonastically named representatives of the community, 'They', always seem to be the same, but eventually They are as capricious in their judgments as the characters are in their activities and desires. Sometimes They punish, sometimes They do not, but there is almost always a form of censure or admonition imposed by Them, even if it remains verbal. In the second volume of limericks, however, They become more peaceful, especially towards the character of the old man.[57] The earlier limericks appear anti-authoritarian and anti-conformist, with the reader's sympathies on the side of the protagonists rather than the anonymous Them.

Byrom comments on the themes of the limericks: '[b]ut the experiences which they [the limericks] reduce, with such bold dispatch, to absurdity are central to the human condition, at least as Victorians felt it – alienation, social and spiritual dislocation, loss of trust and belief; […]'.[58] '[L]oss of trust and belief' might be summarized under the notion of doubt or undertainty – sentiments featured explicitly in three of the limericks. A prominent example is the old Man of th'Abruzzi:

> There was an old Man of th'Abruzzi,
> So blind that he couldn't his foot see;
> When they said, 'That's your toe,' he replied, 'Is it so?'
> That doubtful old Man of th'Abruzzi.[59]

The uncertainty occurs in the verbal and physical interaction with Them. Lear's eccentrics insist on exercising their own judgments, but without necessarily arriving at a 'productive' conclusion. The old Man prefers to rely on his own impressions – which are doubtful per se because he is blind. His doubtfulness does not allow him to accept others' observations without confirming their statement through his own sensory impressions (which is impossible). The limerick of the old Man of th'Abruzzi appears as a parody of Mill's liberal thought as he expresses it here:[60]

---

56 Byrom, *Nonsense and wonder*, p. 127.   57 Byrom has pointed this out (*Nonsense and wonder*, p. 92).   58 Ibid., p. 150.   59 Jackson, *Complete nonsense*, p. 27.   60 The following limerick, published in the 1872 volume *More nonsense, pictures, rhymes, botany, etc.*, makes customary behaviour an explicit topic: 'There was an old person of Shoreham, / Whose habits were marked by decorum; / He bought an Umbrella, and sate in the cellar, / Which pleased all the people of Shoreham' (Jackson, *Complete nonsense*, p. 184). The notion of 'decorum' is parodied in the limerick: the old person simply hides himself away, which apparently finds favour in the eyes of his fellow citizens. If it is a sign of propriety to be invisible, then the old person has succeeded.

> The human faculties of perception, judgment, discriminative feeling, mental activity, and even moral preference are exercised only by being used. The faculties are called into no exercise by doing a thing merely because others do it, no more than by believing a thing only because others believe it.[61]

Mill writes this in the context of customs, which he claims to be useful, but not beyond improvement through change. That is why he advocates the exercise of the human faculties rather than accepting customs without further thought. The old Man refuses to believe 'a thing only because others believe it' – although it is a matter of immediate importance only to himself and nobody else (which does not keep Them from interfering, however). He insists on relying on his own (probably inaccurate) perception. Since the old Man is both blind and will not accept anybody else's perception, all that remains is doubt. Mill can be characterized as an advocate of doubt, as far as re-thinking and questioning customary behaviour on the basis of commonsense is concerned. He argues against the mindless acceptance of customs for their own sake, and the old Man takes this maxim to extremes. Likewise, the Old Lady of Prague shows doubt concerning exterior appearances:

> There was an Old Lady of Prague,
> Whose language was horribly vague;
> When they said, 'Are these caps?' she answered, 'Perhaps!'
> That oracular Lady of Prague.[62]

In this case, however, the uncertainty does not arise from an inability to determine the facts, but a communicative decision, as the adjectives 'vague' and 'oracular' imply. The examples moreover show a difference in 'focalization': in the Abruzzi limerick, the adjective 'doubtful' might either refer to the old Man's character (in the sense of questionable) perceived through Their eyes, or to his state of mind (doubting) as perceived by himself; in the second one, it is clearly spoken from Their point of view, perceiving the Old Lady's answer as an oracle. The Old Lady's refusal to give a definitive answer might be interpreted as her refusal to conform or to play along with the communicative games of society: the picture makes it very clear that the articles of clothing They offer to the Old Lady are indeed caps – the obvious does not require her confirmation.

Another example illustrates the further rejection of conventional communication by the old Person of Burton:

> There was an old Person of Burton,
> Whose answers were rather uncertain;

61 Mill, 'On liberty', pp 85f.   62 Jackson, *Complete nonsense*, p. 54.

When they said, 'How d'ye do?' he replied, 'Who are you?'
That distressing old person of Burton.[63]

Instead of politely answering the question by echoing it or by a brief reply, he calls into question the whole communicative situation by denying acquaintance with Them. The drawing gives more insight into his reasons for doing so, since 'They' are represented by just one female person, reaching out her arms with an expression of stupid contentment. The old Person of Burton, however, maintains his distance by leaning stiffly backwards on his toes with an indignant expression on his face. The adjective of the last line is clearly spoken with Their point of view in mind, although They are not even pictured (except for one of Their representatives, the old Person's would-be acquaintance – or even would-be wife?). The humour of the limerick does not only derive from the discrepancy of text and image: the text portrays the protagonist's behaviour as a habit, while the image shows the reader one particular instance of his reticence, putting it into a romantic context. Even within the limerick itself, at least two voices seem to be present: the first three lines are spoken in an emphatically neutral tone of understatement ('rather uncertain'), which seems to parody the polite language of a social encounter of the kind pictured. The fourth line, then, introduces the evaluative adjective 'distressing'. They are implicitly presented as spectators of the scene (as the readers are at this moment), feeling distressed by the old Person's lack of protocol.

Further considering the question of identity which is raised by the old person of Burton, the young lady in blue presents another voice in Lear's doubtful canon. This time, it is the protagonist herself who directly addresses Them:

> There was a young lady in blue,
> Who said, 'Is it you? Is it you?'
> When they said, 'Yes, it is,' – She replied only, 'Whizz!'
> That ungracious young lady in blue.[64]

The urgency with which the young lady repeats her question stands in contrast to her reaction to the affirmative answer – an unimpressed sibilant sound. After the revelation of her interlocutor's identity, the young lady loses interest. Her question moreover implies that she already has a certain person in mind, since she does not ask 'Who are you?' Maybe the problem is a referential one and the 'you' of the young lady and that of Them is not identical. The irresolvable doubt which is so dominant in the limericks just examined is part and parcel of the respective character's identity. Taking the young lady's point, some conversations are better left incomplete.

63 Ibid., p. 55.   64 Ibid., p. 163.

The exuberant individuality of Lear's characters stands in parodic contrast to the fear Mill expresses in his writings: '[b]ut society has now fairly got the better of individuality; and the danger which threatens human nature is not the excess, but the deficiency, of personal impulses and preferences'.[65] Society still has its representation in the censoring, but also applauding presence of Them and in the final adjective, so the individual's freedom mostly remains relative. The controlling framework cannot be eluded, although it is undermined by the ambiguities of language and those inherent in the text–image relationships. Nevertheless, the language and the 'plots' of the limericks express and embrace a special kind of freedom, which gives them their singular charm. It is a freedom without purpose or aim, and, consistently, its exercise leads only to ambivalent results – but certainly to the reader's delight.

65 Mill, 'On liberty', p. 87.

'Don't let the fire go out': echoes of the past, aspirations for the future in the teenage novels of Eilís Dillon

ANNE MARIE HERRON

Don't let the fire go out [...] That fire hasn't gone out in a hundred years.[1]

As the author of more than fifty books for both adults and children, across a number of genres, Eilís Dillon (1920–94) was one of Ireland's most prolific twentieth-century writers. Dillon was foundational in terms of her success, in that most of the thirty-seven books she wrote for children were published internationally and were translated into a variety of sixteen languages.[2] Over the course of a long career, she was reviewed in a wide range of publications and became an established and popular writer for children of all age groups.[3] Posthumously, scholarly attention, most notably from Dunbar,[4] Rahn,[5] Ní Bhroin[6] and Watson,[7] has focused, in the main, on her body of work aimed at a teenage readership. Dillon is remembered, in particular, for this collection of fifteen books, all but two of which were written between the years 1952 and 1969. These novels, also the focus of this essay, echo the sentiments of earlier writers, including J.M. Synge (1871–1909), for whom Dillon held a deep admiration.[8] They also demonstrate Dillon's inimitable merging of entertainment and didacticism, as well as her personal aspirations for a new generation of Irish citizens, derived from her own background and experience.

In keeping with the belief that literature is never independent of the social, political and economic tensions that pertain at the time of writing, Dillon's work exposes her acute awareness of the prevailing conditions in Ireland from

---

1 Eilís Dillon, *A herd of deer* (London, 1969), p. 106. 2 Anne Marie Herron, 'The published works of Eilís Dillon: editions and translations' (2010) http://research.dho.ie/dillon/index.html. 3 Eilís Dillon, National Library of Ireland, MS Collection, Dillon Papers, No. 41, 33,338–43, 'Press Cuttings'. 4 Robert Dunbar, 'Rarely pure and never simple: the world of Irish children's literature', *The Lion and the Unicorn*, 21:3 (Dec. 1997), 309–21. 5 Suzanne Rahn, 'Inishrone is our island', *The Lion and the Unicorn*, 21:3 (Dec. 1997), 347–68. 6 Ciara Ní Bhroin, 'Forging national identity: the adventure stories of Eilís Dillon' in Mary Shine Thompson & Celia Keenan (eds), *Treasure islands: studies in children's literature* (Dublin, 2006). 7 Nancy Watson, *The politics and poetics of Irish children's literature* (Dublin, 2009). 8 Dillon, NLI, 33318, 'The western writer'.

the early twentieth century onwards. With a deep consciousness of the long shadows cast by the 1916 Rising, the War of Independence and the ensuing Civil War, she was anxious to celebrate the country's eventual social and economic growth and recovery in the 1950s and 60s and to contrast this renaissance with what had gone before. Immensely proud of the development of Ireland's prosperity and culture,[9] Dillon creates young protagonists who, although products of a troubled past, are model citizens who will encourage her readers to cope, in their turn, with this new, progressive Irish republic.

Her stories, set on the west coast of Ireland and its neighbouring islands, take place in an indefinable past, probably in the late 1920s, 30s or 40s; a period when the author had developed an enduring affinity with the landscape and its inhabitants. It was also an era when remnants of an older Ireland – an 'Irish Ireland' – adhering to traditional values, still remained but which, by the time Dillon was writing about it, had largely disappeared.[10] Following in the tradition of the Literary Revival of the early twentieth century that had created and maintained an image of rural Ireland as an ideal linked to the political vision of Irish nationalism, Dillon engaged in her own aristocratization of the peasant population.

Writing for both Irish and international audiences, she presented a renewed sense of Irishness at a time when people were distanced from their roots through emigration and urbanization. Dillon echoed Synge's portrayal of the island people and their isolated offshore communities as being uniquely uncontaminated by modernity and commercialism.[11] She perpetuated the notion that the islanders were repositories of culture, wisdom and the best of Irish language and tradition; facets of Ireland that were much less visible in urban areas. Her characters, 'members of a lost aristocracy', through a form of 'racial memory', manage to maintain vestiges of their former greatness, behave with innate nobility and gentility, are attuned to the land of their forebears and have a deep awareness of Ireland's past.[12] In this rural environment, the people – poor and hard working – battle on a daily basis with nature and the ever-changing moods of the sea, untainted by materialism, bureaucracy and snobbery; features that Dillon disliked among the emerging urban middle classes. The older members of these communities, with a strong sense of responsibility to their people, are ideally placed to dispense deep and sustaining ancient wisdom and to transmit significant values to the younger islanders. Meanwhile, Dillon's protagonists, generally boys of about fourteen

9 Dillon, NLI, 33323, 'Forty years of freedom'.   10 'Irish Ireland' is a generic term for the forms of cultural nationalism from the 1890s onwards, as articulated by D.P. Moran in 'The philosophy of Irish Ireland', *New Ireland Review* (1 Sept. 1900).   11 J.M. Synge, 'The Aran Islands' (1907) in A. Arrowsmith (ed.), *The complete works of J.M. Synge: plays, prose and poetry* (Hertfordshire, 2008).   12 Dillon, NLI, 33337, 'Irish books for the Irish library'.

years of age, growing up in these cohesive settings, engage in sea voyages, become involved in local intrigue, solve mysteries and find solutions – all the time growing in physical and mental strength and learning the courage and tenacity expected of them as they approach manhood. By the end of these novels, their adventures have led them towards a physical, moral and social coming of age.

From the late nineteenth century onwards, a need had been articulated for what Fr Stephen J. Brown described as 'strongly national' material specifically for Irish boys, stories that could compete with British adventure narratives and their symbols of Empire.[13] Dillon, writing a generation later, sought to fill this still-largely vacant niche for authentic popular literature written by Irish writers for Irish boys. She appears to have taken this notion quite literally as her characters are predominantly male, although she defended this choice as based on the fact that the extra freedom afforded to boys than to girls allowed them to engage more easily in outdoor adventures. Consequently, her novels were regularly reviewed internationally as 'books for boys'. Turning for inspiration to Pádraic Colum's tale *The king of Ireland's son* (1916), which she saw as 'the prototype for all such stories in mixing and blending all the traditional elements in a masterly way',[14] Dillon created her own version of the genre, while simultaneously adhering to many of the motifs of British adventure stories. With echoes of the Irish heroic warrior blended into the more relevant search for a post-independence national identity, she tailored her stories within a distinctively Irish context to impart convictions that suited the Irish situation.

While her novels dealt with adventure, they aimed to engender confidence in Irish children – a feature that Dillon felt was lacking in the Irish personality but was an essential characteristic for national progress. But this maturation is greatly enabled by the boys' capacity to embrace the literal and symbolic values of hearth and home that Dillon uses so strongly and to good effect, if somewhat repetitively, in her stories.

Given the physical dependence on it within the small rural cottages, the fire in the hearth, as Dillon describes it, is understood initially for its practical and comforting role and allows the writer to present an idealized version of the traditional way of life. The directive referred to in the title of this essay, to keep the fire alight, was a warning by an older family member to a younger person, to be mindful of what was really important to survival. The ritual, and indeed 'the art', of keeping the fire going was part of daily life for the older people who had years of experience in all aspects of its creation; the

13 Stephen J. Brown, 'Irish fiction for boys', *Studies: An Irish Quarterly Review, Irish Province of the Society of Jesus*, 7:28 (Dec. 1918), 665–70.   14 Dillon, 'Literature in a rural background', 14th Loughborough International Conference on Children's Literature, Trinity College Dublin, Proceedings (1981).

cutting and drying of the turf, the placing of 'an odd number' of turf sods to get the fire to 'draw' properly[15] and the stoking of the embers from the previous day. The undying flame gave continuity from night into day, from season into season, from year to year and from one generation to the next.

In winter and summer alike, the turf fire, the only source of heating in the small-windowed houses, was life sustaining in preparing the staple diet of potatoes, the steaming soda bread and the endless cups of tea shared with neighbours.[16] Dillon repeatedly romanticizes her fireside scenes, often from the perspective of outsiders who envy the peaceful life inside. With reminders of Synge's hyperbolic descriptions of island kitchens as 'full of beauty and distinction',[17] Dillon extols a similar 'beautiful warm scene'. Young Michael in *The lost island* longingly describes a house of happiness and welcome; the water gurgling and laughing around the potatoes in the pot and the 'firelight dancing on the lustreware and rosy cups on the dresser'.[18] However, this almost opulent description is at odds with the reality of the life Dillon had witnessed as a child living in Barna, Co. Galway, in the 1920s. There, as she outlines in an autobiographical work *Inside Ireland*, families were trying to scrape a living from 'the bitter boggy soil'[19] while living in 'germ ridden cottages' that would have been 'dismally damp' 'but for the great turf fires that were kept burning always', protecting them from even greater misery.[20] But Dillon, ever anxious 'not to harrow children's feelings too much',[21] carefully omits descriptions of this severe poverty, preferring to focus on the positive, and, in particular, on the kindness that these gentle people extended to others. Wishing to pass on this good example to her readers, she repeatedly notes that even for the poorest in the community, the 'laws of hospitality' were obeyed.[22] Based on the belief that 'every stranger is sent by God',[23] the smoke trailing up from the chimney indicated a house with a welcome for neighbours and strangers alike, a place where a passerby would get a meal and some warmth and shelter from the wind outside. Once indoors, the extent of the generosity to come was measured by the size of the fire.

Smoke from the chimney was also a symbol of survival, an outward sign of life, of a house still inhabited, while its absence was a source of shame and of extreme poverty or meant that people had died from old age, illness or famine, or indeed, had been evicted. Synge had, in his time, also recognized the importance of the fireside, having witnessed the 'supreme catastrophe' of a woman driven through eviction from the 'hearth she had brooded on for thirty years'. He explained that in that world of consistent wild rains and

15 Dillon, NLI, 33337, 'Irish books'.   16 Dillon, *The San Sebastian* (London, 1953), p. 18.   17 Synge, 'The Aran Islands' (1907), p. 317.   18 Dillon, *The lost island* (London, 1965), p. 16.   19 Dillon, NLI, 33318, 'The western writer'.   20 Dillon, *Inside Ireland* (London, 1982), p. 114.   21 Dillon, NLI, 33337, 'Irish books'.   22 Dillon, *The singing cave* (London, 1959), p. 95.   23 Dillon, *The fort of gold* (New York, 1961), p. 103.

mists, the warm chimney corners 'grow into the consciousness of each family in a way it is not easy to understand in more civilized places'.[24] Dillon gave similar significance to the hearth and regularly reminds the reader of emigrants growing homesick when remembering the smell of the turf fire – the very essence of home and family.

But Dillon's stories depart from mere cultural imagery when she allows the flame to take on a very intentional presence as a symbol of Irish nationalism; a sign of the unflagging spirit of the Irish and as a useful vehicle for motivating patriotic action among the ordinary people. While the fireside innocently allowed neighbours to gather in the evenings for ballad singing, storytelling and for 'long slow leisurely talks',[25] it also facilitated the promulgation of nationalist thought and ideology. Dillon's young male characters speak of how they have witnessed the eyes of the old men dancing with excitement as they told stories of hiding from the enemy in the bogs, of daring escapes and of close encounters with their foe. These stories encourage the youngsters to believe in the efforts of their forebears and to keep elements of the Irish fighting spirit alive.[26] However, Dillon also consistently includes warnings about the negative connotations of misguided action. For example, in *The house on the shore*, the island men become over-enthused in an act of retaliation against a local Anglo-Irish landlord on the mainland and burn down his home, narrowly avoiding killing the inhabitant. In a lesson to her readers, the men in this story are ultimately ashamed of their actions and are upbraided by their more sensible womenfolk for their violent behaviour.[27] Dillon's message is that extenuating circumstances can lead intelligent people to adopt violent methods at certain times in history.

However, she also underlines the foolishness of some of the dogged and intransigent characters who, by recalling the glory days of fighting, continue to live in the past. Indeed, the futility of the struggle is summed up by the character James Hernon, who states 'Our whole war is madness [...] Our ammunition is mostly songs and ballads about the heroes of other days'.[28] The moral is explicit; the romantic aspirations of the past cannot lead to success in a new Ireland, although the determined spirit of the fighters can be applied in a positive way if directed towards peace. In *A herd of deer*, the reader is told that clinging to old ideas would result in 'rivers of blood' flowing through the kitchen. The character, Patsy, in a thinly veiled reference to the Anglo-Irish treaty of 1921, reminds the reader that 'Threats and guns are not needed. That was decided. We all agreed'.[29]

Dillon's didactic intent is most evident in her overtly nationalist novel *The seals*. Set during the War of Independence of 1921, the book forms a com-

24 Synge, 'The Aran Islands' (1907), p. 345.   25 Dillon, *The seals* (London, 1968), p. 21.
26 Dillon, *A herd of deer*, p. 45.   27 Dillon, *The house on the shore* (London, 1955), p. 204.
28 Dillon, *The seals*, p. 39.   29 Dillon, *A herd of deer*, p. 64, p. 101.

mentary on Ireland's military struggle and the need for eventual reconciliation. The writer again provides some justification for the violence by describing the Black and Tan soldiers as 'desperadoes' known for 'torturing, killing
and raiding'[30] and thereby leaving the people with no option but to resist.
Revisiting her fire motif, Dillon describes how, in order to divert the soldiers
and put them off the scent of a nationalist fighter on the run, the woman of
the house invites the soldiers in, lights up the fire, cooks a meal for them
over the flame and entices them to remain in its warmth, where they relax
and join in a few songs. The fire colludes by enabling her to distract the soldiers and deceive them. Singing in the Irish language, which the English soldiers do not understand, allows her to give instructions to the two visiting
young boys to warn the rebel of the dangers in the area and thereby save his
life. But while such simple trickery is seen as worthy, Dillon, ever in didactic mode, is nonetheless careful to point out that Ireland must move forward
when the fighting is done. Although the newly independent Ireland will be
tainted by what went before, it will be necessary to erase old habits in order
to progress. In a symbolic gesture, when the soldiers leave the cottage, the
young boy, feeling that the 'ghosts of the men were still there',[31] helps to
clear the table and wipe it clean. Old animosities would similarly have to be
laid aside, if not forgotten, as nothing would be achieved by looking back to
the horror and trauma of the past.

With hindsight, *The seals* has particular relevance, since its publication in
1969 coincided with a sensitive period in Irish political life with Northern
Ireland on the brink of its descent into violence. Nonetheless, it seems anom-
alous that more than half a century after the literary revival and the 1916
rebellion, Dillon was still perpetuating an outdated view of the peasantry and
promulgating nationalist ideals, albeit tempered with a need for pacifism.

The rationale for her approach, however, can be found within her family
background, through which she absorbed strong nationalist and patriotic
values. Dillon was descended, through her father's family, the Dillons, and
her mother's family, the Plunketts, from settlers who had arrived in Ireland
at the time of the Norman conquest in the twelfth century. Both sets of
ancestors had, through the centuries, played major roles in religious, military,
political and cultural developments in Ireland. Among them were politicians,
clerics, political leaders and military nationalists, all, in one way or another,
guardians themselves of that flame of Irish nationalism and all of whom had
demonstrated their patriotic virtues in various ways. The Dillons had excelled
in the military arena, with Dillon regiments, following the flight of the Wild
Geese,[32] having 'fought in every country in Europe and in their colonies,

---

30 Dillon, *The seals*, p. 15.   **31** Ibid., p. 111.   **32** This was a term generally used in Irish
history to refer to Irish soldiers who left to serve in European armies in the sixteenth, seventeenth and eighteenth centuries. It was specifically used in relation to the departure of

many of them dying on foreign battlefields'.[33] Other Dillons played key roles in Irish political life into the late twentieth century.

Even more significant for Eilís Dillon was the fact that her mother's brother, Joseph Mary Plunkett, was executed as a result of his leadership role in the 1916 Rising, while her grandfather, Count George Noble Plunkett, acted as an emissary for the Irish Republican Brotherhood at that time and in 1919 had addressed the first meeting of Dáil Éireann. Dillon's mother Geraldine Plunkett and her father Thomas Dillon had also supported the nationalist cause in 1916, had played roles in the War of Independence and were both imprisoned for their efforts. Dillon, born in 1920 at a time of political dissent, and, traumatized by early memories, was well aware of the aftermath of the Rising and the divisive effects of the Civil War. Her parents, reacting to the turmoil they had experienced, raised their children to believe that it was only through unity and reconciliation that the institutions of the new independent state could be established. Dillon was greatly influenced by her father's almost 'fanatical desire' to achieve an industrialized post-independent Ireland, in which 'self confidence would replace the dispirited attitudes which stultified all progress'.[34] In a parallel way, she admired the efforts of her grandfather's cousin, Sir Horace Curzon Plunkett (1854–1932), an agrarian reformer who preached a message of confidence in a new age.[35] Plunkett believed in the notion of '*noblesse oblige*' and that the resident gentry, of which he was a member, with their privileges of wealth, education and class, had a duty to foster moral courage, initiative, independence and self-reliance in the Irish people.[36] This family emphasis on confidence encouraged Eilís to promote similar ideals in her writing. Believing passionately in the possibilities for Ireland's future through an adherence to the best of Ireland's traditional values, Dillon made her own contribution by focusing on writing stories for young people that could make a difference to their outlook and allow them to become a dynamic force for the future.

Inspired by her early reading, she understood the potential of suitable books to influence, guide and to educate. She believed that 'fixing a sense of good taste is a great consideration in the choice of children's reading' since books that were true works of art were incapable of injuring a child's mind. But while quality books could be enjoyed, they were also, in Dillon's view, even more valuable for their capacity to improve and educate. She advocated that children could absorb, through the finest writings of their country, a reverence for their heritage and appreciate that they themselves are 'the descen-

the Irish Jacobite army in 1691, following the end of the Williamite war in Ireland. **33** Dillon, *Inside Ireland*, p. 11. **34** Dillon, *Inside Ireland*, p. 93. **35** Sir Horace Plunkett founded the innovative Irish Agricultural Co-Operative Movement in the 1890s. **36** Horace Plunkett, *Ireland in the new century* (1st ed., London, 1904; repr. London, 2006), p. x.

dants of an old aristocracy, which had a long tradition of scholarship and literature'. She commended Douglas Hyde for 'revealing to the English-speaking Irishman, that a long and honourable literary tradition existed in Ireland' that could be drawn upon as examples of excellence. Dillon echoed the Revivalist belief that to fail to introduce the finest Irish writing was to 'leave the child in the intolerable situation of not knowing the literature of his own country', and, by implication, the values that it imparts.

She wrote of 'the physical relief' that had descended on the population with the introduction from the early 1900s of books specifically written for Irish schools.[37] At last, Irish children could read stories from their own heritage instead of English school stories about the 'impropriety of going without one's hat and gloves' which, as Dillon pointed out, were 'quite ridiculous' to the children of rural Ireland, many of whom walked to school barefoot and wearing 'rags and tatters'. According to Dillon, these new books represented their own lives, with stories of Finn Mac Cool and Cúchulainn that they heard by the fireside at home. They also mirrored the Ireland familiar to the children, that of the 'family meal, the rosary and the cat'. For Dillon, these texts 'were the surest sign of a new Ireland' and an intimation of a developing country finding its identity. She noted that the coloured pictures they contained were the first ever seen in Connemara in a book of any kind – again, a sign of a new prosperity.[38]

At a summer course for librarians in 1963, Dillon articulated her strong views about the quality and content of appropriate reading for Irish young people. Her notes from that time exhibit an uncanny similarity to the writings of Charles Gavan Duffy (1816–1901) who, in an address to the Royal Society of Literature in London in 1892, had enthusiastically promoted the idea that literature could exert tremendous power on a new generation of Irish children. It is likely that Dillon was aware of Duffy's work, due to his close affiliation with her family through John Blake Dillon in founding the influential *Nation* newspaper.[39] Duffy had described books as a 'cabinet of ideas' that was capable of making young Irish people 'wiser, manlier, more honest' and could develop in them 'a practical and patriotic spirit'. Moreover, appalled that Irish children had been 'imperfectly acquainted' with their history, he was forceful in promoting the teaching of the subject, stating: 'Of all studies which a nation can least safely dispense with is a study of its own history', since through it, a people could recognize 'where weak places in national and individual character need to be fortified and strong ones developed'.[40]

37 Dillon, NLI, 33337, 'Irish books'. 38 Dillon, NLI, 33323, 'Forty years of freedom'. 39 Charles Gavan Duffy co-founded *The Nation* with Thomas Davis (1814–45) and Dillon's ancestor, John Blake Dillon (1814–66). 40 Charles G. Duffy et al., 'The revival of Irish literature' in *The revival of Irish literature and other addresses* [London, July 1892

Dillon, too, valued history as a means of understanding both the past and the present, as well as preparing young people for the future and, with this in mind, promoted material that was overtly nationalist in tone. She endorsed Frank O'Connor's *A book of Ireland* for its 'panoramic view of our literature and history' and suggested Alice Curtayne's *The Irish story* as being 'patriotic without being blind to our national feelings'. She believed that John Mitchel's *Jail journal* could 'make a child of 11 or 12 an Irishman for life' and saw *The Rising* by Desmond Ryan as essential reading since 'the Civil War has made us self-conscious in Ireland about instructing our children in patriotism'.[41] The use of the word 'instruct' is significant as it underlines her intended didacticism.

The list of over 200 titles that Dillon provided for her audience of librarians is comprehensive, prescriptive and extremely demanding in reading level and content by today's standards. Critic Declan Kiberd, when he was given this list in the 1980s for his own children, recalls his surprise at the very challenging nature of its contents.[42] It aimed to educate young people, not just in nationalist ideals and patriotic fervour but also in a wider well-rounded appreciation of international literature. Beginning with *The heroes* by Charles Kingsley for 7-year-olds, the list moves through Stevenson, Masefield and Ransome for 8-year-olds, on to Dickens and Shakespeare for children of 9 years and then through an eclectic range for the various age groups, ending with *Metamorphoses of Ovid* for those aged 17. Interspersed are books on the lives of the saints, works by Shaw, O'Casey, Synge and Stephens, as well as some of Dillon's own adventure stories. Dillon, undoubtedly influenced by the high standards of her own literary upbringing, which involved the reading of Dante, Chaucer, Milton and Swift, deliberately omits the popular and, in her view, less worthy British writing that Irish children were reading voraciously in the mid-twentieth century. For example, she overlooked works by Enid Blyton and Frank Richards, thereby ignoring the daily reality for the majority of children and that of the librarians she was addressing and the impossibility of the task she was setting them.[43] However, the greatest contradiction lies in Dillon's condemnation of didacticism in literature for young people. At a conference in 1981, she stated:

> The most obvious problem with children's literature is that so many writers are tempted to be didactic, to keep on and on pointing to a moral, dropping the philosophical principle that all art must stand on its own feet and be independent of lessons and morals.

& June 1893] www.gutenberg.org/files/32746/32746-h32746-h.htm, accessed 8 June 2010. 41 Dillon, NLI, 33337, 'Irish books'. 42 Declan Kiberd, personal interview with Anne Marie Herron, 1 Feb. 2011. 43 Dillon wrote a letter of complaint to the national broadcaster, RTÉ, regarding Richards' *Greyfriars School series* being read on radio.

Dillon regularly declared that it was always her intention to avoid any temptation 'to hammer the message home', preferring the freedom 'to attend to the artistic side' of her work.[44] Yet, despite her good intentions, the combination of an innate sense of duty to her country, the deep seated patriotism of her family and a genuine love of Irish language and tradition, all conspired to impede her imaginative flow at times. According to Kiberd, it resulted in her work being 'a little formulaic' and 'less instinctive and creative' than it might have been.[45] With a real sense of urgency and commitment, Dillon aimed to impart the best of Ireland to a new generation before it was lost forever. As someone who had experience of, and passion for, the more Irish Ireland, she took upon herself the responsibility of keeping that ancient flame alight in her writing.

Commentator Robert Dunbar summarizes Dillon's significant contribution to the canon of Irish children's literature, stating that 'she gave readers of the time, growing up in Ireland, who would not have had much access to other Irish material, something that definitely was recognizably their own', an achievement for which he believes she 'deserves much praise'.[46] Publisher Michael O'Brien also acknowledges Dillon as a catalyst in providing authentic Irish children's literature in what he describes as the 'scorched earth, barren, literary landscape' of mid-twentieth century Ireland. While admiring her 'emotional literary loyalty to her own culture', he believes that a 'lack of modernity' caused her to be overshadowed as the industry sought more contemporary voices and themes in the 1980s and 90s.[47] O'Brien describes how Dillon's work, with its 'good clean adventure stories' and honorable young male protagonists 'faded' in popularity as Irish children's publishing began to cater for a new generation of young readers who had little affinity with the Ireland of the hearth and heroics that Dillon portrayed.

However, Dillon's legacy as a successful author and champion of children's literature, at a time when few Irish authors devoted themselves to the genre, has been celebrated extensively by the children's literature community, not only through the annual Children's Books Ireland (CBI) Award for a first children's book but at successive conferences and talks held by the Irish Society for the Study of Children's Literature. Indeed, the ISSCL acknowledged Dillon's significant contribution as author, scholar and curator of identity by dedicating both its 2004 conference[48] and its subsequent publication, *Treasure islands*, to her memory.[49] Further analysis and consideration of

---

44 Dillon, 'Literature in a rural background', p. 10.   45 Kiberd interview, 1 Feb. 2011.
46 Robert Dunbar, personal interview with Anne Marie Herron, 20 Apr. 2010.   47 Michael O'Brien, personal interview with Anne Marie Herron, 28 Nov. 2009.   48 ISSCL 2nd annual conference, 'Treasure islands in children's literature', 20–22 Feb. 2004.   49 Mary Shine Thompson & Celia Keenan (eds), *Treasure islands: studies in children's literature* (Dublin, 2006).

Dillon's work and its place along the continuum of children's literature can, from a current, more mature political perspective, provide useful insights regarding the ways in which respect for indigenous culture and traditions have been transmitted to young people through fiction. It seems apposite now, as we enter an era of commemoration of Ireland's emergence as an independent state, to examine, from a historical viewpoint, Dillon's lessons on the preservation of Irish identity and her reverence for that symbolic flame of patriotism.

Recovery of origins: identity and ideology in the work of O.R. Melling

CIARA NÍ BHROIN

In a 2004 study of homecomings of diasporic peoples, the anthropologist Anders H. Stefansson argues that:

> [d]espite recent notions of postmodernism and anti-essentialism and the claim that the bond between people(s), culture, and territory has withered away, place and home, often in the shape of localized homelands or nation-states, continue to be of vital importance to individuals and communities as sources of identity, livelihood, legal rights and social relations.[1]

Migration research indicates that although there are many nuances of exilic conditions, 'exile is inexorably tied to homeland and to the possibility of return'.[2] Yet the actual return of emigrants, refugees and exiles received remarkably little attention from academics for much of the last century as homecoming tended to fall on the margins of the grand narratives in migration research, 'those of assimilation; multiculturalism / diaspora; and transnationalism / globalization'.[3] When return finally came to be recognized as a subject for academic analysis, it was generally treated in terms of a myth or as a source of symbolic belonging or, more recently, in the context of global mobility among 'transmigrants'. The recognition that many emigrants left their homelands with an intention to return that tended to become more aspirational than practical with the passage of time, led to the focus in research on 'the myth of return'[4] or the notion of the homeland as a symbolic resource. As Stefansson pointed out in 2004, 'the possibility that some displaced people may in fact return to the homeland, thereby 'demythologizing' the myth of return, remain[ed] strangely unexplored'.[5] Return to the place of

---

1 A.H. Stefansson, 'Homecomings to the future: from diasporic mythographies to social projects of return' in F. Markowitz & A.H. Stefansson (eds), *Homecomings: unsettling paths of return* (Maryland, 2004), pp 2–12. 2 H. Naficy, 'Introduction: framing exile: from homeland to homepage' in H. Naficy (ed.), *Home, exile, homeland: film, media and the politics of place* (London, 1999), p. 3. 3 Stefansson, 'Homecomings to the future', p. 5. 4 M. Anwar, *Myth of return: Pakistanis in Britain* (London, 1979); M. Al-Rasheed, 'The myth of return: Iraqi Arab and Assyrian refugees in London', *Journal of Refugee Studies*, 7:2–3 (1994), 199–219. 5 Stefansson, 'Homecomings to the future', p. 6.

origin can be a complicated process, involving issues of personal and national identity, since both the returnee and the homeland are likely to have undergone significant change. Indeed, return is often experienced as a new displacement whereby the returnee feels alienated from the home country.[6]

In light of the above, this essay aims to examine the interconnected themes of return, national identity and the tradition/modernity dialectic in the fantasy fiction of O.R. Melling, a writer of Irish birth and Canadian upbringing, whose extensive use of Irish mythology and romance is arguably impelled by her own desire as a returned emigrant to recover a lost past. It will be argued that Melling combines Canadian ideals with images of Irish national identity drawn from mythology to create a utopian vision of homecoming, of Irish unity and of unity between the Irish and the diaspora. Such unity is predicated upon reconnection with an ancient cultural heritage in danger of being lost in the drive to modernity. While return to Ireland is romanticized as a recovery of origins, recurring images of rupture and duality hint at a more fraught process than Melling's fiction overtly acknowledges.

As Morag Styles noted in her study of national identity in British poetry for children, '[n]ot only is the notion of national identity tricky and contested, but what it means to individuals is extremely variable'.[7] Melling (a pseudonym for Geraldine Whelan) was born in 1951 in Bray, Co. Wicklow, where she currently lives, but emigrated with her family to Canada when she was 4 years old. A strong sense of her Irish heritage was instilled in her from a young age by her mother's love of Celtic lore and by contact with relatives in Ireland.[8] Canada's multicultural policy, which was made official in 1971, encouraged retention of ethno-cultural heritage among its culturally diverse citizens and has resulted in a national children's literature with a strong international dimension. In their examination of local and global perspectives in Canadian, Australian and South African children's literature, Carpenter, Hillel and Van der Walt liken Canadian children's literature to a swing 'moving back and forward through time and place, through adult and child worlds but fastened on Canadian ideals that ground Canada as a nation and connect it internationally',[9] a metaphor that resonates in Melling's work. Whereas political turbulence and

---

6 C.D. Smith (ed.), *Strangers at home: essays on the effects of living overseas and coming 'home' to a strange land* (New York, 1996); H. Pilkington & M. Flynn, 'From "refugee" to "repatriate": Russian repatriation discourse in the making' in R. Black & K. Koser (eds), *The end of the refugee cycle: refugee repatriation and reconstruction* (New York, 1999), pp 171–96.   7 M. Styles, 'Voices of the world: national identity in British poetry for children' in M. Meek (ed.), *Children's literature and national identity* (Stoke on Trent, 2001), pp 61–9.   8 P. McGeever, 'Chronicling the land of faerie', *Inis: the Children's Books Ireland Magazine* 18 (Winter 2006), 15–17.   9 C. Carpenter, M. Hillel & T. Van der Walt (eds), 'The same but different: the dynamics of local and global in Australian, Canadian and South African children's literature' in E. O'Sullivan, K. Reynolds & R. Romøren (eds), *Children's literature global and local: social and aesthetic perspectives* (Oslo, 2005), pp 173–99.   10 Ibid., p. 176.

conflict characterized Ireland's history, 'settlement and the progress to nationhood in Canada were comparatively peaceful', requiring qualities of 'persistence, compromise, adaptability and consensual agreement',[10] qualities that Melling's Irish-Canadian protagonists tend to embody. There are, however, interesting parallels between both countries. Canada and Ireland share a British colonial past. Both countries have two official national languages with a literature in each, and each country has a publishing industry that exists in the shadow of a more powerful industry in a neighbouring country.

The druid's tune and *The singing stone* were first published in Canada in 1983 and 1986 respectively and subsequently revised and published for an Irish readership by the O'Brien Press in 1992 and 1993, while *The hunter's moon* was published both in Ireland and in Canada in 1993. All three have since been updated again with new editions brought out in Canada and the US within the last decade. This essay will focus primarily on the O'Brien editions of the 1990s, published at a time of major social, economic and political change in Ireland. This was the decade Ireland reinvented itself[11] to become an affluent, modern, metropolitan nation. Rapid modernization was accompanied by a major erosion of traditional values, particularly Catholicism and territorial nationalism, which were in the past central to Irish national identity. Closer integration with Europe and enhanced Anglo-Irish relations, due to the peace process of the 1990s, reflected an evolving national identity with a stronger international dimension. The international profile of Mary Robinson's presidency (1990–7), and in particular her emphasis on the Irish diaspora, redefined Irish national identity as outward, inclusive and modern. The economic boom caused a reverse in emigration trends and many emigrants returned to Ireland at this time. The Celtic Tiger Ireland of the 1990s was a very different place from the Ireland Melling had left as a young girl.

In a time of major social change myth can be a culturally stabilizing force, connecting the past and the present and contributing to a collective sense of identity. As an antidote to rapid modernization and increased globalization, fantasy novels that draw on tradition can provide 'images of an imaginary homeland that help sustain myths of national identity, community and common heritage'.[12] The link through myth with the imaginary homeland has particular significance for members of the diaspora; myth can help preserve an idealized place of origin as an emotional resource for those geographically distant from their land of birth or the land of their ancestors.[13] However, rec-

11 P. Kirby, L. Gibbons & M. Cronin (eds), *Reinventing Ireland: culture, society and the global economy* (London, 2002).   12 T. Watkins, 'Cultural studies, new historicism and children's literature' in P. Hunt (ed.), *Literature for children: contemporary criticism* (London, 2004), pp 173–5.   13 W. Safran, 'Diasporas in modern societies: myths of homeland and return' *Diaspora: a Journal of Transnational Studies* 1:1 (1991), 83–9. http://muse.jhu.edu/journals/diaspora-a-journal-of-transnational-studies/summaryv001/

onciling an imagined past with the modern present can involve complex tensions for returnees to the homeland.

The druid's tune, The singing stone and *The hunter's moon* feature Canadian or American teenage protagonists with Irish roots, who, while on holiday in Ireland, are transported back to a time of crisis in its mythical past. They befriend epic heroes from Irish mythology and their quest becomes a joint one in which the needs of the past and those of the present merge. The quest in each case involves journeying around Ireland, and the emphasis in the novels on topography and toponomy, characteristic of medieval Irish literature, along with the maps of Ireland in the paratext, render the geography of Ireland as central to these novels as is its mythical history. Landscape is part of the iconography of nationhood[14] and the primacy of the geographical in postcolonial literature has been interpreted in the context of repossession of the land, which is at first only imaginary.[15] In the case of the returned emigrant, imaginary repossession of the land may serve as compensation, not only for the initial loss of homeland on emigration, but also for the sense of displacement often felt on return. The map of the protagonist's journey has additional significance in graphically inscribing the returnee onto the land. At an even deeper level, the map of the journey, as Peter Hunt has pointed out, 'is not simply a map of places visited; the places link with the myths and traditions which lie deep behind the action'.[16] Following Joseph Campbell's model of separation, initiation and return,[17] all three novels end with some form of return as *Bildung*, involving a recovery of a lost shared past, an awakening of an inner source of power and, to varying degrees, a reintegration into their community and into modern life.

In *The druid's tune*, Rosemary and Jimmy Redding are sent to relatives in Ireland by their father, a Canadian judge, who disapproves of his children's wild friends, particularly of Rosemary's boyfriend who has appeared before him in court. While Canada is associated with the complexities of modern teenage life, Ireland is portrayed as a wholesome antidote. Judge Redding hopes that '[f]resh air, hard work and a good simple way of life' will keep his errant teenage offspring 'out of mischief for a while'.[18] The Ireland of *The druid's tune* is an Arcadian rural idyll far removed from the realities of Ireland at the end of the twentieth century. The regressive strain of much fantasy fiction for children has been noted by many critics[19] but in Melling's case it is

1.1.safran.html, accessed 10 Sept. 2012.   14 T. Watkins, 'Homeland: landscape and identity in children's literature' in W. Parsons & R. Goodwin (eds), *Landscape and identity: perspectives from Australia* (Adelaide, 1994), pp 3–20; Carpenter et al., 'The same but different: the dynamics of local and global in Australian, Canadian and South African children's literature', p. 174.   15 E. Said, 'Yeats and decolonization' in D. Walder (ed.), *Literature in the modern world* (Oxford, 1990), pp 34–41.   16 P. Hunt, 'Landscapes and journeys, metaphors and maps: the distinctive feature of English fantasy', *Children's Literature Association Quarterly*, 12:1 (1987), 11–14.   17 J. Campbell, *The hero with a thousand faces* (2nd ed. London, 1993).   18 O. Melling, *The druid's tune* (Dublin, 1992), p. 11.   19 P. Hunt & M. Lenz, *Alternative*

compounded by the nostalgia of the emigrant. The peace of Uncle Patsy's farm in the rolling Leitrim hills is unspoilt by traffic, machinery or technology of any kind. The hay is cut using a scythe and haystacks are made by pitchfork.

Melling does not specify the time in which her novels are set, although successive editions contain contemporary cultural allusions and there is a direct reference to the 1990s at the end of the O'Brien edition of *The singing stone*. Perhaps the novels capture nostalgic childhood memories of summer holidays in Ireland or perhaps they reflect her childhood reading. In a talk given in the Belfast Arts Club in August 1992 and subsequently published in *Children's Books in Ireland* in 1993,[20] Melling listed the Irish author, Patricia Lynch (1894–1972), among the writers whose work had a profound influence on her as a child, and, indeed, echoes of Lynch are evident in Rosemary's first impressions of her uncle and aunt's home:

> The old farmhouse was bright and cheerful with its fresh coat of whitewash. Geraniums blossomed in the window-boxes and wisps of smoke trailed from the stone chimney. Chickens chased each other noisily across the yard. An ageing sheep-dog dozed in the shade of the rust-coloured barn. All round were the hills of Leitrim, falling gently from the pillar posts at the end of the driveway, and rising up again behind the house and barn. She was in the heart of the hills, she realized, and she took a deep breath of the cool refreshing air.[21]

A ripple in the peace is caused by the erratic behaviour of the farmhand Peter, the druid of the title, whose agitation hints at unresolved tensions in the past. The siblings follow Peter on one of his nocturnal trips and are transported back to Ireland at the time of the *Táin*. Melling's choice of the *Táin*, the central epic of Irish heroic literature, is significant. As I have argued elsewhere,[22] the theme of dynastic conflict at the centre of the *Táin* is particularly relevant to Irish history. The civil strife depicted in the ancient saga was to become a reality in the Irish civil war, national partition and subsequent conflict in Northern Ireland, resonances exploited by Melling to highlight the futility of war. For the ancient Celts, the successful cattle raid had an important political

worlds in fantasy fiction (London, 2001); T. Watkins, 'Cultural studies, new historicism and children's literature'; S. Gilead, 'Magic abjured: closure in children's fantasy fiction' in P. Hunt (ed.), *Literature for children: contemporary criticism* (London, 2004), pp 80–109; C. Ní Bhroin, 'Mythologizing Ireland' in V. Coghlan & K. O'Sullivan (eds), *Irish children's literature and culture: new perspectives on contemporary writing* (London, 2011), pp 7–27. **20** O. Melling, 'Myth and history in fantasy literature' *Children's Books in Ireland* (November 1993). http://www.ormelling.com?Author% 20Pages/o.r.mellingmytha.html, accessed 15 Nov. 2012. **21** O. Melling, *The druid's tune*, p. 15. **22** C. Ní Bhroin, 'Recovering a heroic past: the *Táin* retold' in M. Shine Thompson (ed.), *Young Irelands: studies in children's literature* (Dublin, 2011), pp 67–80.

dimension in that it asserted the integrity of the community and the sovereignty of its leader,[23] issues that were particularly charged in Northern Ireland at the time of publication of the novel. Cúchulainn has been mythologically associated with Ireland's destiny but can be difficult to interpret as a character and the ideals for which he died are questionable. This poses a particular challenge for writers attempting to portray him as a hero with whom modern young readers can identify. Melling, with varying degrees of success, emphasizes his teenage status, something he has in common with the modern protagonists he befriends and with Melling's implied readers.

Melling adapts the *Táin* saga to allow her modern protagonists a proactive role. The siblings inadvertently find themselves in opposite camps in the epic conflict. Rosemary befriends Maine, a son of Maeve and Aillil, while Jimmy becomes Cúchulainn's charioteer. Crucially, in each case the modern protagonist plays a central role in saving the mythic hero's life, symbolic, perhaps, of the upcoming generation's role in keeping a culture's mythology alive but, even more significantly, of the importance of the diaspora to national regeneration. Melling's rendering of the epic saga is, of course, highly romanticized; the flowing silk dresses that Rosemary dons and the chivalrous, flirtatious Celtic warriors depicted are far removed from the Iron Age La Tène culture of the *Táin*. Melling is less concerned, however, with an authentic rendering of the myth than with a modern reimagining of it aimed at inspiring the younger generation. In this she is clearly influenced by idealized retellings of the Literary Revival. The epigraph prefacing the novel is a quote from Yeats' poem, 'To Ireland in the Coming Times', in which the poet claims his rightful place among the great poets of Ireland reaching back to the druids of ancient times. Similarly, in weaving her modern Canadian protagonists into the ancient Irish epic, Melling seeks to reclaim their Celtic identity, and perhaps by extension her own. In placing members of the diaspora, who were historically marginalized, into the very centre of Irish epic history, Melling endows them with heroic (national) significance. However, this is seriously undermined by the nostalgic, regressive strain running through the novel and by Melling's simplistic positioning of Canada and Ireland as binary opposites – the former signifying philistine modernity and the latter an ancient spirituality – in a rhetoric that echoes the Celticism of Matthew Arnold (1822–88) and of many writers of the Revival. When Rosemary and Maine partake in an ancient pagan lovers' rite of jumping over the campfire hand in hand, Rosemary casts off her modern Canadian exterior to uncover a supposedly authentic Celtic self:

> She was no longer Rosemary from modern Canada, but Rose, a Celtic girl, a warrior of the stone cairns, the timeless hills, the blood passions

23 P. MacCana, *The learned tales of medieval Ireland* (Dublin, 1980), p. 80.

of a warrior race. In that moment she understood an oath purged in fire, a bonding under the sight of the great moon goddess. She threw back her head as the spirit flooded through her and her face was exultant.[24]

A strong wish-fulfilment underlies this portrayal of belonging, of authenticity, in short, of return to source. In reality, casting off one identity to reveal a more authentic alternative is not possible, nor even desirable, for the returnee, whose hybrid identity has been formed by a myriad of factors, including life experience in the new home-country. The teenagers' final reluctance to return to 'shallow modern life',[25] and in particular to their home in Canada, outweighs the transcendence that Melling attempts to convey in the unifying vision that they experience at the end of the novel and ultimately portrays the modern world as deficient and unsatisfying. Thus, while the trajectory of children's books typically, and Melling's overt aim here, is to 'home the child subject, both the subject inside the book and the subject outside the book',[26] the ideological closure of home in this case is problematized by an underlying sense of dislocation.

A sense of estrangement and displacement, characteristic of literature of emigration and exile,[27] pervades the opening frame of *The singing stone*, in which the identity crisis at the heart of Melling's work is most overtly explored. Abandoned as a baby and raised in a series of unsatisfactory foster homes, Kay Warrick has always felt 'different', 'strange'[28] and friendless. A recurring vision of a red-haired maiden in distress and the arrival in the post of a mysterious parcel of old Irish books impel Kay to leave her home in an un-named city in North America and to travel to Ireland in search of her origins. Kay's arrival in Ireland is imbued with the romantic wish-fulfilment of the returned emigrant. A strong sense of place is created in stark contrast to the anonymity of the setting in the opening chapter. The landlady of the Bray boarding house in which Kay lodges shows a maternal concern for her welfare, and the Irish landscape is warm and welcoming:

> Green was the colour of the countryside, from the fields and hills that rolled along the horizon to the hedges that grew over the walls of every station stop. Having lived her life in a grey city, Kay was overcome by the bright beauty of the landscape. She felt it beckoning to her with warmth and promise.[29]

---

24 O. Melling, *The druid's tune*, p. 55. **25** Ibid., p. 184. **26** M. Reimer & C. Bradford, 'Home, homelessness, and liminal spaces: the uses of postcolonial theory for reading (national) children's literatures' in E. O'Sullivan et al. (eds), *Children's literature global and local: social and aesthetic perspectives* (Oslo, 2005), pp 200–17. **27** J. Whitlark & W.A. Aycock (eds), *The literature of emigration and exile* (Texas, 1992). **28** O. Melling, *The singing stone* (Dublin, 1993), p. 16. **29** Ibid., p. 18.

Kay's initial sense of security is short-lived as she is plunged into turmoil and uncertainty when she travels back in time to Ireland's distant past and finds herself in a 'vast and impenetrable forest'.[30] In a historical note prefacing the novel, Melling explains that *The singing stone* reaches even further back than *The druid's tune*, to the Gaedil ancestors of Cúchulainn's tribe and 'the Danaan gods of his people'. Melling's source here is the ancient *Leabhar gabhála Éireann* (Book of invasions), a pseudo history of Ireland, which culminates in the arrival of the Gaedil (Gael or Irish) and the naming of the land. It is, in effect, the book of origins of the Irish people. Kay's personal story, and by extension Melling's own, is thus written into the wider national story. Significantly, Kay's arrival in Ireland is aligned with that of Amergin, the first Gaedil to set foot on Irish soil. According to mythology, Amergin approached the three Tuatha Dé Danaan queens, Fódla, Banba and Éiriu (Éire), each of whom sanctioned his rule on condition that he name the island after her.

Kay befriends a Tuatha Dé Danaan girl suffering from memory loss due to trauma, only to discover as the novel unfolds that she is none other than Éiriu, the rising queen and the maiden of Kay's earlier visions. Both girls are symbolically linked; each is unsure of her identity, but, more overtly, in a scene in the first chapter, Kay sees Éiriu's face in her own reflection in a pool. Such narrative mirroring is a prominent feature of Melling's fiction. A literary device often used to portray the duality of the exilic/émigré experience,[31] narrative mirroring is generally employed by Melling to reconcile apparently opposing elements: Irish and Canadian; past and present; tradition and modernity; spiritual and temporal; as well as vying tribes and cultures. The two girls, bound by a strong affinity, undertake an arduous quest to retrieve the four treasures of the Tuatha Dé Danaan, the loss of which has led to their moral and cultural decline, as evidenced in their misrule and intolerance of other races on the island. The motifs of memory loss, confused identity, loss of heritage and tribal conflict bear relevance to the rapidly-changing Ireland of the late twentieth century and create a sense of impending doom. However, disaster is averted. As each treasure is recovered, Éiriu's memory and beauty are restored, as is the integrity of her race through reconnection with their past. The warring mythological races of the *Leabhar gabhála Éireann* are thus reconciled and as the Tuatha Dé Danaan return in glory to their celestial cities, the Gaedil peacefully take their place as leaders. The two other races of the Mythological Cycle are the Firbolg and the Formorians. In *The singing stone*, the Firbolg ally themselves with the Gaedil and although the Formorians secretly leave Ireland at the end of the novel, Amergin indicates that they would have been warmly welcomed by the Gaedil had they chosen to stay. Thus, the Canadian ideals referred to earlier,

30 Ibid., p. 26.   31 J. Pérez, 'The paradigms of exile in Danosso's Spanish fiction' in J. Whitlark & W.A. Aycock (eds), *The literature of emigration and exile*, pp 34–42.

of tolerance, adaptability and consensual agreement, embodied by Kay in her pivotal role as mediator, allow for a peaceful settlement.

In light of Ireland's turbulent progress to nationhood and continued partition, Melling's allegory of Irish unity and of unity with the wider diaspora is aspirational. Nevertheless, her portrayal of the reconciliation of vying traditions on the island bears direct relevance to the Northern Ireland peace process, which was in its initial stages at the time of publication[32] and was a process in which women's groups and the diaspora would indeed play a key role. However, the aesthetic symmetry evident throughout *The singing stone*, particularly in the familial romance of the closure, exposes Melling's ideological intent. John Stephens has drawn attention to the ideological power of narrative structure, especially closure. Intentionality, as Stephens points out, 'can only be fully attributed to a text from the perspective of the close'.[33] Ideological intent in a work of fiction is apparent when the plot resolution affirms an underlying ideology that otherwise might be unintentional. The contrived ending of *The singing stone* is a case in point. Following a peaceful resolution of conflict, the novel concludes with marriage between Amergin and Éiriu, Kay's discovery that she is their daughter from a different time and her happy return to North America fortified by an unbroken link to her Irish heritage. The very completeness of the novel's ending encourages readers to focus on its thematic significance: the importance of cultural heritage to personal and national identity, the need for tolerance and respect for diversity, and, most especially, the value of the diaspora to the Irish nation with whom it shares a heroic past and with whom it can build a peaceful present.

A greater orientation towards the present is evident in *The hunter's moon*, which, unlike the previous novels, was first published for an Irish readership. Although the narrative is largely focalized through the Canadian protagonist, Gwen, the reader is first introduced, via a prologue, to her Irish cousin, Findabhair. The prologue opens in the noise and grime of Dublin's city centre as Findabhair excitedly awaits Gwen's arrival on holiday. The cousins, both avid readers of fantasy fiction, have planned a trip around Ireland to discover if the Land of Faerie exists. Dressed in the black garb of urban youth of the 1990s, Findabhair initially appears the very antithesis of the Irish red-haired maiden of *The singing stone*. However, as the plot unfolds, she emerges as the maiden in distress in different guise. Her wild and passionate nature makes her more susceptible to the dangerous allure of the Land of Faerie

---

32 The Sinn Féin/SDLP peace initiative began in 1993, the year *The singing stone* was published in Ireland, but women's groups had been active in working towards peace and social justice through community work for many years before the novel was first published in Canada. The Women for Peace movement was founded in 1976 and its co-founders, Mairead Corrigan and Betty Williams, won the Nobel Peace Prize that year.   33 J. Stephens, *Language and ideology in children's fiction* (London, 1992), p. 42.

than her more rational Canadian cousin and when she is seduced by the enigmatic king of the fairies into remaining there, it is the practical Gwen who rescues her from ritual sacrifice and helps her return safely to the real world. While the Land of Faerie is a timeless place, the romantic medievalism with which Melling imbues it renders it evocative of the past. Once again, therefore, the Irish protagonist needs to be freed from a troubled past and the rescuer, as in the novels previously discussed, is a member of the diaspora who, by contrast, needs to be inscribed into the Irish past. A form of twinning occurs in each case, visibly manifest in the symmetry of the mirror images of the protagonists in the cover illustrations of the O'Brien editions. Ostensibly images of unity, these twinned images also signify the duality of the returnee. Gwenavere and Findabhair share a name from the same root and appear to be complementary opposites, more whole when united. Findabhair's impulsive nature is tempered by Gwen's common sense while, in turn, Findabhair awakens in Gwen a more courageous and adventurous spirit.

A particularly obvious image of unity in the novel is the idealized Inch Island in Donegal, which is featured in an enlarged inset of the map of Ireland in the paratext and serves as a metaphor for an ideal (united) Ireland. The map of Ireland in the paratext of the O'Brien edition of *The hunter's moon* is of the island as a whole with no demarcation of Northern Ireland. Following the Good Friday Agreement of 1998, citizens of the Republic agreed in a referendum on 23 May to remove from the constitution any territorial claim to the six counties of Northern Ireland. This is implicitly acknowledged in the map of Ireland in the paratext of the 2005 Amulet edition, which marks Northern Ireland as a distinct entity. However, aspirations of a United Ireland are still evident throughout the text, not only in the allegory of unity presented but also in overt references to the thirty-two counties of Ireland and to the island as a whole.

A strong unifying symbol in the novel is the figure of the island king. On some Donegal islands it is tradition to have an island king and Gwen is surprised to learn that the king of Inch Island is a teenage boy, Dara, who has befriended her. Although king of the island, Dara can no longer live there for economic reasons. Living on the mainland, he is in a sense an emigrant and an exemplar for Gwen herself. He remains firmly rooted and maintains very close ties with the islanders but is also forward and outward-looking. Like the islander protagonists in the novels of Eilís Dillon (1920–94), he embraces the benefits of modernity while retaining the best of tradition.[34] He is studying

---

34 Eilís Dillon's adventure stories feature boy protagonists who initiate change in their island communities, but always with due regard for their native traditions. For further discussion of the tradition/modernity dialectic in Dillon's adventure stories see C. Ní Bhroin, 'Forging national identity: the adventure stories of Éilís Dillon' in C. Keenan & M. Shine Thompson (eds), *Studies in children's literature, 1500–2000* (Dublin, 2004), pp 112–19.

business in college and is excited at the benefits that a United Europe could potentially bring Ireland.

Indeed, *The hunter's moon* features a number of idealized characters who serve as exemplars of what Melling regards as a successful blend of the traditional and the modern. The businessman, Mattie O' Shea, wears a smart suit and tie, carries a briefcase and drives a shiny Mercedes with leather interior but still has a healthy respect for the fairies and a genuine concern for the good of his workers. Having encouraged the workers to buy shares in a company that was formerly owned by a foreign multinational, he now runs it as a successful cooperative. There are definite echoes of Eilís Dillon in Melling's promotion of indigenous industry and in the character of Granny Harte whose kitchen, with its mixture of old and new, is a metaphor for herself. While demonization of urban modernity is still apparent – for example in the negative references to pollution, concrete towers and the blare of traffic in the novel's opening chapter – a more positive attitude towards modernity is evident in *The hunter's moon* than in the earlier novels in that the protagonists are happy and indeed relieved to return to the real world. Like *The druid's tune* and *The singing stone*, *The hunter's moon* contains images of rupture, conflict and violence but ends with a utopian image of unity in the form of a circle of friends and romantic unions.

In the three novels discussed here, return to Ireland is represented as a recovery of origins. However, it is also a process involving rupture and conflict for the returnee, who must negotiate her way through a crisis in Ireland's mythical past. A Canadian sensibility is brought to bear on a volatile Irish situation and proves to be a source of (national) salvation and regeneration. The returnee is thus written into the wider national story and endowed with heroic significance. Extensive narrative mirroring reflects the duality of the returnee but is ultimately aimed at balancing and reconciling apparently opposing elements to create a utopian image of homecoming, of Irish unity and of unity with the wider diaspora. However, the aesthetic symmetry of closure, in affirming the thematic significance, exposes Melling's ideological intent.

In 'The road from Damascus; children's authors and the crossing of national boundaries', Gillian Lathey commends those authors whose work springs from a sense of cultural duality, reflecting their own crossing of boundaries.[35] Like much Canadian children's literature, Melling's fiction is largely set outside of Canada, features female heroism and embodies Canadian national ideals such as tolerance, respect for diversity, negotiation and cooperation. Like much Irish children's literature, especially of the past, it is largely set in Ireland, draws on Irish mythology and folklore and tends to

35 G. Lathey, 'The road from Damascus: children's authors and the crossing of national boundaries' in M. Meek (ed.), *Children's literature and national identity* (Stoke on Trent, 2001), pp 3–9.

privilege the rural over the urban and the past over the present. In the O'Brien edition of *The hunter's moon*, both Gwen and Findabhair sport signifiers of their respective national identities on their knapsacks, in Gwen's case a red maple leaf and in Findabhair's a tricolour. In light of Gwen's repeated assertion of her Canadianness when she is taken for an American, it is highly ironic that she actually *is* American in the 2005 revised edition, published by Amulet in the US, from which all references to Canada have been removed. Pejorative references to American tourists and to foreign multinationals are also removed while added elements include a glossary of Irish language terms, a note on the Irish language and an updated map of Ireland, referred to earlier, acknowledging Northern Ireland as a distinct entity. It would appear that Irish distinctiveness is more palatable to the American public than Canadian distinctiveness, traces of which have been eradicated from American editions of these novels.

Notwithstanding this, in an interview with Susan Lawrence in 2001, Melling describes herself as a Canadian rather than an Irish writer: 'If you ask me what kind of writer I am, I'm Canadian. Maybe it's the greater opportunity in Canada – and the tolerance ... Thank God I'm not an Irish writer or I'd have given up before I started.'[36] Her work has certainly received less critical recognition in Ireland than in Canada, where she has received a number of prestigious awards. It is likely that the Ireland she portrays has more appeal for Canadian than for Irish readers. A note of disillusionment and a sense of rejection can be detected in her description of the Irish writing community as a 'boys' club' in which women writers are undervalued.[37] In the same interview Melling voices her intention to return to Canada to live and, indeed, her recent fiction shows a greater orientation towards Canada. At the end of *The light bearer's daughter* (2001) the protagonist leaves Ireland to live in Canada, while *The book of dreams* (2003), the final book of *The chronicles of faerie*, is set there. Migration research highlights the ambivalence and complexities of return to the homeland[38] and the likelihood that returnees will re-emigrate to the country of initial emigration or engage in circular transnational migration.[39] It would appear that the aesthetic completeness of Melling's fiction, in which loose ends are neatly tied up, belies the more open-ended complexity of life experience.

36 S. Lawrence, 'Between two worlds: O.R. Melling brings Irish myth to Canada' *Quill and Quire* (Feb. 2001). http://www.quillandquire.com/authors/profile.cfm?article-id=2002, accessed 7 Sept. 2012.   37 Ibid.   38 S. Jansen, 'Homelessness at home: narratives of post-Yugoslav identities' in N. Rapport & A. Dawson (eds), *Migrants of identity: perceptions of home in a world of movement* (Oxford, 1998), pp 85–109; G. Kibreab, 'When refugees come home: the relationship between stayees and returnees in post-conflict Eritrea', *Journal of Contemporary African Studies*, 20:1 (2002), 53–80.   39 H.L. Zarzosa, 'Internal exile, exile and return: a gendered view' *Journal of Refugee Studies*, 11:2 (1998), 189–98.

Distant districts and dark days: national identity in *The hunger games*

SUSAN SHAU MING TAN

> Was it like this then? Seventy-five years or so ago? Did a group of people sit around and cast their votes on initiating the Hunger Games? Was there dissent? Did someone make a case for mercy that was beaten down by the calls for the deaths of the districts' children? [...] Nothing has changed. Nothing will ever change now.[1]

Amid the countless fansites devoted to *The hunger games* trilogy, where followers are encouraged to share fan-fiction and art inspired by the series, the abundance of fan-created maps and their similarity across artists and sites is striking. In its initial description, the setting of *The hunger games* is characterized by geographic erasure. The nation of Panem, existing in the 'ruins of North America', has been eroded by 'encroaching seas' and ravaged by natural disasters.[2] In this devastated landscape, the districts that comprise Panem are represented only by numbers. Katniss' world is one where place is strictly controlled, where geography is unnamed, where contact with the natural world is denied and where the past is left in a similar state of inaccessibility – the only memory of national history narrated and controlled by the government as a tool of political propaganda. The focus, then, of fan-attention to maps is particularly revealing. Underlying the erasure of national memory and identity within the narrative is a geographic reality: that the thirteen districts of Panem exist in identifiable locations, specifically, within the United States. The world of *The hunger games* is meant to be a familiar one.

Parallels between Panem and the United States have been repeatedly noted in the budding field of critical work on *The hunger games* trilogy. In the recent *Of bread, blood and* The hunger games (2012),[3] an entire book-section has been devoted to issues of history, politics, economics and culture within the trilogy, pointing to the ways in which *The hunger games* exists in dialogue with contemporary America and tracing similarities between American government, media culture, war-time imagery and imaginings of space within Collins' work.[4] This recent scholarship supports the notion that *The hunger*

---

1 Suzanne Collins, *Mockingjay* (London, 2010), p. 432.   2 S. Collins, *The hunger games* (London, 2008), p. 18.   3 Mary F. Pharr & Leisa A. Clark (eds), *Of bread, blood and* The hunger games: *critical essays on the Suzanne Collins trilogy* (Jefferson, 2012).   4 My dis-

games trilogy fits the mould of the contemporary young adult dystopia, a narrative which acts as a cautionary tale and cultural critique, staging a vision of our own world gone wrong.[5]

In this essay, I will examine the interaction of space, history, and national identity in *The hunger games* trilogy. Drawing on this notion of dystopia as cultural and national critique, I intend to push these connections between American spaces and the spaces of the dystopian future further, considering how geographic representations are utilized in the creation and transmission of national memory within the world of Panem. It is my contention that an exploration of the politicized landscape reveals tensions that emerge between place and memory, as the future is envisioned as a site of dystopian destruction, yet firmly rooted in American geographic heritage and the foundational utopian ideals of the United States. I will demonstrate that *The hunger games* presents us with a world where the landscape itself is evocative of the monstrous potential of the future, and yet mired in the crimes of American history. As this narrative nightmare coagulates around a text for youth, I will examine this problematic intersection: a story of social 'nightmares' for the next generation that points towards the impossibility of escaping the sins of the past.[6]

Cultural geographer Tim Cresswell writes that 'place and memory are [...] inevitably intertwined' and 'one of the primary ways in which memories are constituted is through the production of places', a physical manifestation of memory, legacy, and identity that we see in museums, heritage sites, and monuments.[7] For Cresswell, 'the very materiality of a place means that memory is not abandoned to the vagaries of mental processes and is instead inscribed in the landscape – as public memory'.[8] Similarly, Leo Marx discusses 'mental maps', a people's vision of nation that corresponds to cultural self-image, rather than the actual physical landscape. Marx writes that:

> [a] nation's mental map [...] is a shared expressive, highly distorted representation of a people's actual geographic situation. It is a mental map, in other words, because the literal, objective geographic image has been reshaped by shared assumptions, beliefs, or ideology.[9]

cussion in this essay is limited to a focus on the United States of America and assumes that most, if not all, of Collins' Panem is located within the borders of the US. Thus, I will use the terms 'United States' and 'America' both to refer to the US.   5 Carrie Hintz & Elaine Ostry, 'Introduction' in C. Hintz & E. Ostry (eds), *Utopian and dystopian writing for children and young adults* (New York, 2003).   6 J. Sargent, 'Afterword' in C. Hintz & E. Ostry (eds), *Utopian and dystopian writing*, p. 234.   7 T. Cresswell, *Place: a short introduction* (Malden, 2004), p. 85.   8 Ibid.   9 L. Marx, 'The American ideology of space' in S. Wrede & W. Adams (eds), *Dematured visions: landscape and culture in the twentieth century* (New York, 1991), p. 63.

Both Cresswell and Marx point to the centrality of landscape in the fashioning of identity, as notions of place – inscribed through the physical presence of memorials and landmarks and in their imagined existence in cultural narratives – shape and root a collective sense of self.

This notion of collective memory through the meaningful establishment of place, or the mental construction of place, however, is denied within the world of *The hunger games*. As the landscapes of the districts are illustrated in vivid detail, Panem resembles the frozen, immobile spaces of the panoptic prison.[10] No movement is allowed between the districts, and within them, space is violently marked, with fences that trap their citizens and cut them off from any areas not under constant government surveillance. The establishment of meaning around places is actively denied, and Katniss observes that the District square, 'one of the few places in District 12 that can be pleasant', is calculatingly used to host the lottery of the Hunger Games, infusing a potential locus of community identity with a perpetual 'air of grimness'.[11]

Denial of ownership over place and landscape within Panem corresponds to a similar denial of historical knowledge. The period of time which saw the formation of the Capitol and its districts, as well as a failed rebellion against the Capitol, is known only as 'The Dark Days'.[12] These nebulous Dark Days are the only narrative of history that Panem possesses. It was this period of cultural void that gave birth to the institution of the Hunger Games: paradoxically, the only source of a shared physical, cultural, and national community available to the citizens of Panem.

The eponymous Games emerge at the intersection between these tensions of place and fragmented notions of cultural memory. The Games are a 'yearly reminder that the Dark Days must never be repeated', a punishment for the failed rebellion and an annual reminder of the Capitol's power over its people. At the same time however, the history that the Games are meant to commemorate is quickly eclipsed by the Games themselves. I have argued elsewhere that, like Baudrillard's system of signs and simulations, the simulation of the Hunger Games has become far more 'real' than the cloudy memory of 'Dark Days'.[13] While the Games are meant to 'make fresh the memory' of the Dark Days, we see that this historical event, shrouded in the darkness that its name suggests, is unknown and inaccessible;[14] its memory cannot be resuscitated. For the citizens of Panem, then, the only real knowledge of the past, in fact, comes from the Hunger Games themselves. The Hunger Games have surpassed their commem-

10 M. Foucault, *Discipline and punish: the birth of the prison*, trans. A. Sheridan (London, 1979). 11 Collins, *Hunger*, p. 16. 12 Ibid., p. 18. 13 J. Baudrillard, *Simulacra and simulation*, trans. S.F. Glaser (Ann Arbor, 2004); S. Tan, '"Burn with us": sacrificing childhood in *The hunger games*', *The Lion and the Unicorn*, 37:1 (Jan. 2013), 54–73. 14 S. Collins, *Catching fire* (London, 2009), p. 207.

orative function: the televised images of Games offer the only source of any sense of 'history'.

As the Games emerge as Panem's sole source of collective history and identity, essentially the 'cultural heritage' of Panem, the spaces of the arenas reflect this significance. The arenas themselves are the only landscapes endowed with any sense of Cresswell's notion of memory: ascribed with the national and communal meaning that all other spaces are denied. This is taken to its extreme by Capitol audiences, for whom the arenas are:

> [h]istoric sites, preserved after the Games. Popular destinations for Capitol residents to visit, to vacation. Go for a month, re-watch the Games, tour the catacombs, visit the sites where the deaths took place. You can even take part in re-enactments.[15]

This macabre invocation of the landmarks that Cresswell sees as so crucial to community identity has another valence: that of the theme park. I have argued previously for a connection between Disneyland and the spaces of the arenas, following Baudrillard's model of Disney as the true 'real' of the United States.[16] I want to turn here, however, to place-theorist Edward Relph, who focuses on the power implicit in what he terms 'disneyfication'.[17] For Relph, the sanitization of Disney acts as 'a popular [...] expression of belief in the objective mastery of nature and of change: monsters and history and wild animals are brought safely under control'.[18] This idea of mastery through the land, and, specifically, through a simulation of the land, is telling. As the Games become an ultimate act of power over a population, we see this power reflected in control over the very land itself. The notion of taming 'monsters' and 'history' is evoked through control of the spaces of the districts and within the painstakingly constructed arenas of the games. Power is demonstrated through the literal creation of 'monsters' to torment the tributes, but alongside this, the arenas demonstrate power over memory. The arenas preserve landscapes long-forgotten, and, as Katniss stares on the unfamiliar landscape of an arena, she realizes that it is a jungle, a 'foreign, almost obsolete word [...] Something [she] heard from another Hunger Games'.[19] At the same time, however, this jungle is inherently unnatural, 'nature' laced with traps and mutations as 'everything in this pretty place – the luscious fruit dangling from the bushes, the water in the crystalline streams, even the scent of the flowers when inhaled too directly – is deadly poisonous'.[20]

If arenas represent the only physical markers of legacy and heritage, then we see that this national identity of Hunger Games is bound up in simula-

---

15 Collins, *Hunger*, p. 175.   16 Tan, '"Burn with us"' (Jan. 2013), 65–9.   17 E. Relph, *Place and placelessness* (London, 1976), p. 99.   18 Ibid.   19 Collins, *Catching fire*, p. 330. 20 Ibid., p. 239.

tion, erasure and similar distortion. The historical void at Panem's centre is made manifest, as a nation defines itself through these false landscapes, warped spaces and manipulated histories. And, for the citizens of the districts, while these spaces are remote and completely inaccessible, they are simultaneously horrifically intimate, as the people of Panem must watch their children face these spaces and die. Memory and space are indeed intertwined. But power over each is articulated in opposition: while space is painfully delineated – in the restriction of the districts, in the geographic specificity of the districts, in the detailed construction of the arenas – memory is comprised of absence, of the void of the past and the literal destruction of the future. Thus, it is in the very tensions and paradoxes they embody that the arenas truly adhere to Cresswell's notion of 'placing of memory':[21] the spaces of the arenas endowed with fraught significance within what little cultural memory Panem possesses.

And yet, even as *The hunger games* trilogy envisions a world that has lost any sense of heritage, there are two districts, District 12 and District 11, Katniss' district and Rue's district, that emerge as telling exceptions. These are the most vividly described districts within Panem, and each evokes a specific moment in American cultural history. District 12, located in the remains of Appalachia, is a mining center. The conditions of the coal mines and the poverty-stricken lives they offer is drawn in lurid detail, from 'the stomach-churning elevator ride into the depths of the earth' where miners spend their days 'pounding away at a coal seam' to the 'claustrophobic tunnels, foul air, [and] suffocating darkness on all sides'.[22] These descriptions become reminiscent of the coal pits that indeed existed in Appalachia, whose poor and dangerous conditions were the epicentre of early American labour disputes and often violently put-down attempts at unionization.[23] Similarly, District 11 evokes the spectre that haunts all American foundational history: slavery. While race is rarely mentioned in *The hunger games* trilogy, citizens of District 11 are noted for their 'satiny brown skin'.[24] And, as District 11 presents visions of 'crops [...] stretch[ing] out as far as the eye can see' with scores of 'men, women and children' laboring in the fields, living in 'small communities of shacks', the image of the plantation or sharecropping community is inescapable.[25]

With District 11 and District 12, historical moments of violence within the American cultural make-up are evoked and projected into the future. The place-identities that remain of the current United States are those that carry valences of historical discomfort, of national shame and failure. The 'cultural baggage' of slavery and forced labour is imagined to engulf the entire nation in a vision of heritage which allows only for an inheritance of cultural vio-

21 Cresswell, *Place*, p. 85.   22 Collins, *Catching fire*, p. 5.   23 Ibid., p. 159.   24 Collins, *Hunger*, p. 98.   25 Collins, *Catching fire*, p. 68.

lence; the injustices that have dwelt in the United States' past are imagined to consume its future. *The hunger games* trilogy then, as it stages these cycles of historical remembering, forgetting, and revisiting, seems as much a caution against the cultural ills that plague us now as it is a warning against forgetting the history – in all its positives and evils – which comprises heritage and memory. When public memory is allowed to fade, when the 'placing' of memory is uprooted, nation becomes vulnerable to cultures of arenas and simulation.

Indeed, the distortion of the natural world within the arenas reflects this greater distortion: a distortion of American history and contemporary American traditions implicit within the Games. Despite assertions of national amnesia, the Games themselves are based on traditional American rhetoric. Represented as 'a time for thanks',[26] the Games evoke the foundational holiday of Thanksgiving and imagery associated with Thanksgiving, including the central cornucopia of the arenas, reinforces this connection. Similarly, every District contains a justice building, a site of political power, which in Districts 12 and 11 reside in the ruins of contemporary spaces that evoke old governmental spaces: the justice building in District 11 is a 'huge marble structure',[27] with tall columns, and 'a big flight of marble stairs' beneath a domed roof.[28] Selection for the Hunger Games, as well as the ensuing Victory Tour, takes place before this building, a space that '[o]nce [...] must have been a thing of beauty', but time has taken its toll. Even on television you can see ivy overtaking the crumbling façade, the sag of the roof.[29] Just as the evocation of Thanksgiving distorts the holiday's commemoration of foundation and unity, so too do the bones of the American system stand in decay, the monuments and political buildings of the contemporary American world used to further the agenda of a government that actively wages war on its children. The spaces and rhetoric of 'traditional' America are once again used in a foundational event: appropriated to explain and justify the project of Hunger Games. But this resuscitation of history is warped and bloody: the Games themselves a tool of disunion, a weapon employed *against* the future.

On a larger scale, history within Panem is envisioned as operating within similar overarching cycles of cultural disconnect. The Capitol is based on, and named after, the Roman model of *Panem et circenses* [bread and circuses]. In this model, as is explained to Katniss, 'in return for full bellies and entertainment' the people of a nation '[give] up their political responsibilities and therefore their power'.[30] The idealized notions of individualism and responsibility of founding-America have been relinquished, sacrificed for a life of pure pleasure. Similarly, the notion of a 'United' states has fallen away, the infrastructures of the districts organized to provide the Capitol with their luxuries,

---

26 Collins, *Hunger*, p. 19.   27 Collins, *Catching fire*, p. 56.   28 Ibid., p. 58.   29 Ibid., p. 56.   30 Ibid., p. 261.

and then, of course, with tributes for their 'circus'. Each district is responsible for the provision of one type of product, and this stratification facilitates the view of children-as-objects. Indeed, on their initial reception to the Capitol, tributes are dressed in costumes that '[suggest] [their] district's principal industry', reduced to the commodity they provide.[31] The nation that has risen from 'the ashes of a place [...] once called North America' has turned to its ancient foundations for structure, and from the worst of those foundations created a dystopian future that is entirely of our own making – based on the previous historical wrongs and abuses that form American cultural history.

Much dystopian literature deals with cultural critique.[32] Dystopian narratives are seen to reflect the logical conclusions of present-day excesses and *The hunger games* trilogy is no exception. However, as *The hunger games* evokes American traditions and rhetoric, the evils of the past come to the fore. Sifting through the silt of American history, the horrors that *The hunger games* unearth are those that muddy the American self-image: its greatest evils, complications and stains. Thus, *The hunger games* does indeed emerge with a critical function, but its overall caution seems to be that the evils of history are inescapable. Just as the Games stage a visitation of the sins of the father upon each succeeding generation, the narrative whole suggests that nation is doomed to repeat historical ills, to be punished for its crimes in perpetuity.

In the growing bulk of academic writing on dystopian literature, technology within dystopias, and as an agent of dystopia, has received great attention.[33] In *The hunger games* however, while technology is central in the facilitation of dystopia, the true evils of the narrative are not technologically based. The world has not been overtaken by computers, television or machinery, though, admittedly, the world is not better off for them. Rather, the evils that target the children of Panem are all too human: a decadence that has plagued civilization since the Romans – slavery, labour exploitation and political oppression. The desire to watch the suffering that television communicates, it is made clear, is as old as Western civilization itself. The evils of television only transmit the horrors of the Games, broadcasting these primal human impulses and desires and the death that the Games bring is not dealt by the screen but by the prisons of the arenas: those spaces of warped preservation and primal stagnancy, the technologically manipulated fossils of the past.

In a narrative that seems to empower youth, endowing them with the responsibility, but also – centrally – the *ability* to change their worlds, this

31 Collins, *Hunger*, p. 80.   32 Raffaella Baccolini & Tom Moylan, 'Introduction: dystopia and histories' in R. Baccolini & T. Moylan (eds), *Dark horizons: science fiction and the dystopian imagination* (New York, 2003), pp 1–11.   33 See, for example, K. Reynolds, *Radical children's literature* (New York, 2007); Hintz & Ostry (eds), *Utopian and dystopian writing* (New York, 2003).

message of historical entrapment is problematic. As audiences look to the future to imagine youth empowerment and change, they are told that even the most innocent of children will suffer the responsibilities of past sins. At the same time, there is an undeniable honesty to this portrayal. The imagining of a warped Thanksgiving within the space of the arena captures the historical events more accurately than the American myth of the holiday: the historical narrative does not end with a peaceful meal between two reconciled groups, brought together by need, but rather with the slaughter of the Native Americans. War over territory, mass relocation of Native American tribes and systematic violence – often centering around issues of resources and food – signal the true ending of this foundational American story. And the resulting reservations, the only spaces allowed to the surviving Native Americans, which are today plagued with violence, alcoholism and poverty, are perhaps the closest US society comes in modern America to Collins' imagined districts. These competing visions of national self-image – the clash between visions of ideal-America and the realities of America – perhaps point towards the necessity of violent confrontation in the 'reclamation' of nation for youth. As imagery of America's idealized-myths is woven back into a narrative of violence, the mantle of 'national identity' is left to the young to be claimed. Through their sacrifices and disillusionment, the children of Katniss' generation win the ability to perpetuate or, conversely, to cast off these national illusions.

By the end of the trilogy, the political narratives of Panem have been prised open: national history unearthed, national heroes cut down and complicated, national past-times denounced and destroyed. At the same time, as the myths and hierarchies of Panem are disassembled, so too is narrative conclusion exposed as myth. The end of *The hunger games* trilogy is couched in the trappings of positive resolution. A just president has been appointed, with a reimagining of thirteen colonies coming together to form a new nation, a chance to go back in time and stage a rebirth of American democracy. But stability is uncertain, and one of the leaders of the rebellion sums it up well as he tells Katniss:

> [w]e're in the sweet period where everyone agrees that our recent horrors should never be repeated ... But collective thinking is usually short-lived. We're fickle, stupid beings with poor memories and a great gift for self-destruction.[34]

The historically cogent reader knows what is to come: recognizing that the cultural ills of slavery, labour disputes and war historically follow this idyllic establishment of a land of liberty. And the historically unaware reader has been granted initiation into these realities through the overarching narrative of the

34 Collins, *Mockinjay*, p. 442.

trilogy itself. The resolution, and its hope for peace, is yet another myth, yet another dream in the larger scope of political and national evolution.

The hunger games taps into a recent trend in young adult literature; staging a dystopian vision of the future, and placing hope, but simultaneously, the burden of the future, upon the young. Successfully trolling this vein, the trilogy's popularity encompasses adult and child audiences alike, pointing to the profound cultural power contained within this vision of a future world gone wrong. But an exploration of national identity within *The hunger games* demonstrates that there is more to this vision, as the evils of the American past are evoked and resuscitated. The nightmare of dystopia is revealed to be less a fantastic imagining of the future and more a re-visitation of what has come before. This notion clearly resonates with audiences, as they look to the future and see themselves.

In a world where justice buildings lie in decay and the preserved landscape rises up to kill, *The hunger games* trilogy points to the need to interrogate contemporary visions of ourselves – contemporary narratives of nation, history, and space. The importance of historical transmission becomes paramount. Indeed, as bleak as the trilogy has been argued to be, the ending, perhaps, points a way forward: not the political ending, of tenuous peace, but Katniss' own conclusions. As she looks on her children, emblematic of everything she has fought for, and both won and lost, she wonders how she will tell them about the past. Katniss worries '[h]ow [she] can [...] tell them about that world without frightening them to death'.[35] In her fears for her children, Katniss recognizes that the past can be dangerous: that the horror that must accompany revelations of past atrocity can be actively damaging. But Katniss resolves that she will tell her children. She will find a way to explain it, in all its ugliness, 'in a way that will make them braver'.[36] *The hunger games* trilogy has attempted to do the same: presenting readers with a vision of past and future selves, refusing to forget or gloss over the evils that dwell in American history, and cautioning against forgetting them. In its imagining of the future, *The hunger games* trilogy acts as a reminder that the United States was built on the backs of slave labourers, bought with the bodies of indigenous peoples and industrialized through the exploitation of workers. Katniss' children play in a graveyard. In contemporary America, *The hunger games* reminds us, it cannot be forgotten that we do the same.

35 Ibid., p. 389.   36 Ibid., p. 390.

'You are the hope of the world!': the figure of the child in First World War children's literature

ELIZABETH A. GALWAY

As anyone working in the field of child studies knows, childhood is an ever-shifting notion, varying between cultures, classes, genders and historical periods. The difficulty in defining childhood also affects how we perceive and define children's literature.[1] The recent popularity of such works as the *Harry Potter* and *The hunger games* series, among both adult and child readers, further highlights the blurred boundaries between children's, young adult and adult literature, raising new questions about how we conceive of childhood, adolescence and adulthood. The flexibility of these concepts is especially evident during wartime and, as Karin Westman observes, 'the boundaries of children's literature are particularly fluid when read within the context of war: during times of war [...] the ideological work of "children's literature" carries greater weight and has a wider reach'.[2] Evidence of this can be found in English-language children's literature from the First World War which, in promoting certain ideologies, presents child figures in myriad ways, demonstrating the fluidity of both children's literature and the very concept of childhood itself.

Much English-language children's literature from the First World War reflects pro-war sentiment, but writers, in fact, had many outlooks on the conflict, and the complexities of these have not yet been fully explored by scholars. Different attitudes are often manifested in the figure of the child, which appears in various guises that include victim, soldier and the embodiment of hope. These figures serve several ideological functions and reveal a variety of perspectives on the war, on the role of children in the conflict and on the nature of childhood. Together, they help illuminate how First World War children's literature may have helped to shape attitudes towards militarism, pacifism, gender and politics in a generation of young readers who would witness not one, but two global wars. What is more, they reveal the

The author gratefully acknowledges that this work was supported by a SSHRC Standard Research Grant, received in 2008.

1 The difficulties of defining children's literature and the fact that it often serves adult needs and desires are topics first explored in depth by Jacqueline Rose and taken up more recently by critics such as Perry Nodelman. 2 K.E. Westman, '"Forsaken spots": at the intersection of children's literature and modern war', *Children's Literature Association Quarterly*, 34:3 (Fall 2009), 213–17 at 216.

mutability of the concept of 'the child', raising questions about how children's literature may have influenced the ways in which young readers conceived of their identity as children. During the war years, this construct of 'the child' was packaged in a variety of ways by adult authors and sold to children, shaping not just adult understandings of childhood, but the ways in which wartime children saw themselves. This essay is structured therefore around a discussion of the child in these different guises – as victim, soldier and peacemaker. The literature chosen for this discourse includes a select range of widely-read English-language periodicals and annuals aimed at school-going children, in addition to a key publication for young American readers by Hermann Hagedorn, which is referenced in the essay title. Contemporary popular visual imagery, whether propaganda posters or commercial advertisements, are introduced throughout, to reflect on the diversity of the child figure in publications for children during the period spanning from 1914 to the immediate post-war era.

THE CHILD VICTIM

A common figure in literature from the First World War is the child victim, embodied in characters such as orphans and refugees, and acknowledged in accounts of children injured or killed in the conflict. These literary representations simultaneously replicate, and complicate, a Romantic conception of childhood innocence. For example, the figure of the child victim perpetuates the notion that children are vulnerable, innocent, and disempowered and, according to this view, war is an aberration, filled with horrors that are at odds with a so-called natural state of childhood. In such depictions, the figure of the innocent victim is utilized to highlight the absurdity of war and to argue for its end. Yet this image of innocence and potential slaughter, made manifest in the figure of the suffering child, can also be employed to garner support for the war effort.

One example of this complicated representation is found in the long-running British juvenile periodical, *Work and Play: the Scholars' Own Magazine.*[3] The front page of the November 1916 issue contains an illustration of a soldier in the midst of a fray, carrying a young girl in his arms. The caption draws attention to the child's vulnerability:

---

3 Published in London as *Scholars' Own* from 1893–1914 and then as *Work and Play* from 1914–17, this periodical for school-aged children demonstrates some of the ways in which child figures were presented to young readers. A. Tropp, 'Some sources for the history of educational periodicals in England', *British Journal of Educational Studies*, 6:2 (May 1958), 151–63 at 161.

> In the villages captured by the British desperate hand-to-hand fighting
> often takes place [...] and the lives of [...] civilians [...] are [...] in
> great danger. Our picture shows a Highland soldier carrying a terrified
> little French girl to a place of safety.[4]

A casualty of the war, the child is depicted as passive and vulnerable, but in
this instance the image of the suffering child is not used as part of a pacifist
argument. Rather, it serves to celebrate the contributions of Allied soldiers,
who are presented as protective, masculine figures. This image both contrasts
and echoes the well-known Ellsworth Young's 1918 propaganda poster
'Remember Belgium' that pictured the silhouette of a young Belgian girl
being dragged away in the night by a German soldier as a town burns in the
background. In Young's illustration, the masculine soldier is clearly presented
as a threat to the innocent girl.[5]

The depiction of the little girl being rescued by a Highland soldier justi-
fies Allied involvement in the war, supporting the argument that continued
fighting is necessary in order to protect vulnerable children. This is a clear
example of how the figure of the innocent child can be exploited to serve as
pro-war propaganda, but in other literature from the period the responsibility of saving victimized children is not presented as belonging to adults alone.
Often, writers encourage young readers to contribute to the war effort, paradoxically creating an image of the child as both a victim, and an empowered
citizen. Indeed, while there are many examples of innocent victims in literature from the period, they were by no means the only type of child figure in
wartime writing. Much juvenile literature depicts children not as victims, but
as soldiers, both literally and figuratively. Kimberley Reynolds questions just
how large a role children's literature played in 'making so many young people
[...] desperate to take part in the action' during the First World War,[6] rightly
pointing out that many other factors contributed to one's decision to become
a soldier. While it is difficult to measure the success individual writers may
have had in persuading readers to enlist, it is nevertheless evident that this
was the intent of many wartime authors.

THE CHILD SOLDIER

One means in particular by which writers sought to foster a desire to take
part in the action was through the portrayal of child figures fighting for the

---

4 *Work and Play*, 11:123 (Nov. 1916), 33.   5 Ellsworth Young, *Remember Belgium: buy
bonds, Fourth Liberty Loan* (New York, [1918]). Young (1866–1952) was an American magazine and book illustrator.   6 K. Reynolds, 'Words about war for boys: representations of
soldiers and conflict in writing for children before World War I', *Children's Literature
Association Quarterly*, 34:3 (Fall 2009), 255–71 at 255.

cause.[7] Such titles as 'Boy Heroes of the Present War'[8] help to illustrate Reynolds' argument that 'children's writers [...] began very explicitly to groom readers to accept the need for boys to head for the battlefields by showing children [...] as resourceful, responsible, and valued members of society who could start contributing at an early age'.[9] Several examples of underage soldiers can be found in the popular British periodical, the *Boys' Own Paper*. One writer notes that the war 'has seen several youthful heroes come to the front – a number of these were referred to in our February issue',[10] suggesting that young fighters were a frequent topic in this widely-read boys' periodical. Indeed, the same volume contains several tales about underage fighters, including accounts of French teenagers, Gustave Chatain and Charles Trottemont. In each case the young age of the boy is a cause for celebration rather than concern, with the author noting that 15-year-old Chatain 'has been nominated for the French Military Medal, and, despite his youth, it is confidently expected that this decoration will be awarded him for his repeated bravery'.[11] Chatain demonstrates to young readers that boys can act bravely, can serve their nation, and can expect to be rewarded for their efforts. Similarly, the figure of 13-year-old Trottemont establishes the importance of young men serving their nation: '"It is necessary," said Charles immediately mobilization began, "that at least one member of every family shall defend France." So when, in August last, the 146th Regiment passed through [...] his native town, he followed it, full of martial ardour'.[12]

These examples of young French boys fighting to defend their nation seem intended to inspire a young male, British readership to do the same, in part by presenting war as a liberating activity for young men who, as children, might otherwise lack autonomy. As Joseph Kestner argues in his study of masculinity in British adventure fiction, some 'of the attraction of the adventure genre is that it provides males with a way out of and beyond the domestic and legal constraints of shore life or the home country'.[13] The image of boys casting off the constraints of home life is present in the stories of both Trottemont and Chatain who, without any hesitation, run off and join a passing regiment. The notion of war as an appealing alternative to domestic restraint is particularly apparent in the account of Chatain who:

7 For a detailed discussion of the figure of the boy soldier, see Elizabeth A. Galway's 'Competing representations of boy soldiers in First World War children's literature', *Children in Armed Conflicts*. Spec. issue of *Peace Review: A Journal of Social Justice*, 24:3 (Sept. 2012), 298–304.   8 A. Tegnier, 'Boy heroes of the present war' in *Young Canada: An Illustrated Magazine for Boys* (London, 1916).   9 Reynolds, 'Words about war', 266. 10 A.L. Haydon, 'A young French hero', *Boy's Own Paper*, 37 (1914–15), 483–4.   11 Ibid., p. 484.   12 Ibid.   13 J.A. Kestner, *Masculinities in British adventure fiction, 1880–1915* (Farnham, 2010), p. 27.

[w]as working in the fields [...] one day [...] when the 92nd Regiment
of the line came marching by. At the sight the boy threw down his
hoe, ran out into the road and joined the line. He refused to be
rebuffed; it was his ambition to be a soldier, and now that the chance
had come he meant to take it. In the end the regiment adopted him.[14]

Here, the regiment is presented as offering freedom and opportunity while,
simultaneously, the image of Chatain being 'adopted' suggests that joining up
provides him with a new family, making the realm of war appear to be a natural and appropriate place for the boy. Rather than expressing concern over
the involvement of underage fighters, such stories hold up the figure of the
child soldier as an example for readers to follow.

Boys were not the only children depicted as fighters. Edward Shirley's
The jolly book for boys and girls, published by the highly successful English
publishing company, Thomas Nelson, includes a story entitled 'The heroine
of Loos', about Émilienne Moreau. The author describes this young French
girl as playing 'a noble part in the fighting at Loos' and recounts how she
'bandaged the British wounded and ministered to them tenderly'.[15] Moreau
does not remain in this caretaking role, however, and is instead transformed
into a fierce fighter:

When [...] she saw Germans attacking wounded Highlanders who
were no longer able to defend themselves, she was roused to fury.
Seizing a revolver, she shot down several of the inhuman Germans,
and afterwards flung grenades at them. Right well does she deserve to
be called the Heroine of Loos [...] this gallant girl was summoned to
Versailles, and there [...] [had] pinned on her breast the Military
Cross, as a tribute to her great courage [...] She stood [...] amidst the
bravest soldiers of France, all of whom were eager to acclaim her as
the bravest of them all.[16]

As this account demonstrates, girls too were sometimes cast in the role of
child soldier in literature from the period. Moreau encourages bravery in
young female readers and suggests that in a time of great need, a young girl
can stand on equal footing with 'the bravest soldiers' and can serve her nation
in ways that go beyond traditional female duties.

Though she demonstrates strength and valour by stepping into a role that
is unconventional for both a child and a woman when she takes up arms
against German aggressors, Moreau simultaneously serves as a representation
of ideal femininity. This is suggested in her tender nursing of the wounded,

---

14 Haydon, 'A young French hero', 483.   15 E. Shirley (ed.), 'The heroine of Loos', *The
jolly book for boys and girls* (London, *c*.1916), pp 31–3.   16 Ibid., p. 32.

and in her humility while being honoured by the General. In recounting the moment when she was awarded the Military Cross, the author notes that she 'was very modest, and cast down her eyes when the General addressed her'. As both a soldier figure springing to the rescue of those being attacked, and a model of traditional feminine modesty, Moreau 'will ever remain an inspiring example, not only to the women of France, but to the women and girls of Britain as well'.[17] The figure of the adolescent girl soldier serves to foster pro-war sentiment, inspiring the girls of Britain to be brave and to contribute to the defeat of the Germans, while also upholding traditional notions of gender during a time when these were in flux. Moreau's dual role as both tender nurse and capable soldier reflects anxieties over the changing role of women on the home front during the First World War. Women were needed to help with traditional male occupations, including farm labour and munitions work. Through the figure of Moreau, girl readers are encouraged to do their bit for their nation, to be brave, and even to fight if necessary, while at the same time the need to exhibit traditional feminine propriety is reiterated.

Such accounts of children joining the fighting serve as inspiring examples for young British readers, but the figure of the child soldier appeared in a number of guises and served a range of purposes, even being co-opted as part of a marketing ploy. A 1916 issue of *Work and Play* features an image of a small boy smiling broadly while holding a rifle. The advertisement reads: 'One of Britain's future hopes lies in a virile, dominant manhood. *"We are what we assimilate"* and growing boys and girls [...] will find that a Pure Cocoa (like Fry's) is All Goodness, unrivalled for family use'.[18] The idea that the child represents the future is made manifest here.[19] In particular, the advertisement emphasizes the importance of masculinity to the nation. Just as the figure of Moreau reinforces popular notions of femininity in the face of changing social realities, so too does Fry's advertisement reaffirm a traditional code of masculinity based on military prowess and physical strength, privileging it as key to Britain's future success. The picture of an armed child in an advertisement for cocoa might strike some as being out of place, but it reveals just how pervasive and acceptable the image of the child soldier was during the period of the First World War.

In addition to tales of underage fighters engaged in combat, children were also pictured as soldiers metaphorically. Literature from the period is filled with examples of patriotic children contributing to the war effort in a number of ways, such as practising thrift, growing food, knitting and raising funds for

17 Ibid., p. 33. 18 'One of Britain's future hopes', *Work and Play: The Scholars' Own Magazine*, 10:114 (1916), 112. 19 The advertisement's citing of Hippocrates' claim that 'we are what we assimilate' provides further food for thought regarding children's literature: to what extent do children 'assimilate' what they read, and to what degree does this shape the people they become?

various causes. One work published in 1915, entitled *French toys*, even suggests that American children can help the 'widows [and] orphans' of the war in Europe by buying the right kinds of toys; in other words, those made in France, rather than in Germany.[20] *French toys* is one example of how the image of the child victim – in this case the orphan figure – was used to encourage young readers to contribute to the Allied cause and to come to the aid of other young people. This work, which was published before the United States entered the war, implies that American children have the power and the duty to help their European peers, suggesting that children's literature may have been a means of persuading that nation to join the Allied cause. In this case, however, the American child is not encouraged to be a soldier on the battlefield, but to help in other small, but important ways behind the front line.

THE CHILD PEACEMAKER

The above examples of young victims and soldiers shed light on some of the ways in which child figures were part of a widespread attempt to garner support for the war effort, but some served a slightly different function. A third dominant image of the child draws on revived Romantic notions of the child as an incarnation of mankind's potential, picturing the child as the embodiment of hope for the future. These figures suggest that the child has the potential to rejuvenate society by producing significant political and social change. The post-war British publication the *Children's Newspaper*,[21] subtitled *The story of the world today for the men and women of tomorrow*, suggests that the success of organizations like the League of Nations lies in the hands of children, claiming 'nothing on earth can save the League of Nations unless the children are on its side'.[22] According to this work, children represent the world's hope for future peace: 'To make peace you must begin at fifteen or sixteen, at twelve or thirteen, at nine or ten. You must grow up loving peace and hating war. You must fill your heart and head with the great idea of a united world. You must understand that justice means as much to other people as to you'.[23] This publication explicitly figures the child as key to the world's ability to rebuild itself in the post-war period.

---

20 A. Hellé (ill.), *French toys* (Paris, 1915), p. 3.   21 The debut issue of the *Children's Newspaper* was published 22 March 1919. This periodical was hugely successful, running for 46 years and publishing more than 2,000 issues. *The History of the Children's Newspaper. Look and Learn History Picture Library*. n.d. http://www.lookandlearn.com/childrens-newspaper/history.php., accessed 10 Oct. 2012.   22 'The children's League of Nations: what the conference has forgotten' in *The Children's Newspaper: the story of the world today for the men and women of tomorrow* (22 March 1919), 1.   23 'The one

This image of the child is also evident in works that were published while war was still being waged. One example, addressed specifically to American readers, is Hermann Hagedorn's propaganda title, *You are the hope of the world! An appeal to the girls and boys of America* published in 1917. Hagedorn is probably best known for his biographies of Theodore Roosevelt, but he was also a poet, and a founder of the Vigilantes,[24] a group of writers and artists who sought to inspire patriotism and support for the war effort in America, particularly among the nation's youth.[25] Hagedorn's work places a marked emphasis on the importance of children themselves to the events unfolding in 1917, but he encourages a particular type of participation in the war. Rather than exhorting young readers to contribute directly to the war effort as soldiers, or even by being thrifty or growing food, he suggests that the possibility for global peace rests with American children. He begins by impressing on his young American readers that the greatest tragedy of war has been the deaths of young people, describing the victimization of European children:

> In Europe, boys of your age are dying daily [...] Boys who might have been leaders of men [...] boys who might have been great scientists, great poets, great tellers of tales, great inventors, great merchants, great physicians, great preachers. Europe does not know yet what she has lost.[26]

For Hagedorn, the negative effects of the war on Europe's young people will continue to be felt long after the battles cease, and he suggests that what 'remains of the youth of Europe after the War will be crippled and scarred in body or spirit'.[27]

The way in which Hagedorn presents the European child is very much in keeping with some of the images of victims discussed earlier, but in this instance this figure serves as a foil for American youth. Hagedorn quickly turns his attention from the suffering of European children to explain what this means for American children themselves: 'Before the War', Hagedorn claims, 'the civilized world looked to Europe for leadership and inspiration. After the War, the world will look [...] to America. We shall have the wealth, we shall have the youth, we shall have the energy'.[28] Historian David M. Kennedy sums up this attitude as follows:

hope for the world: unless the children support the league they labour in vain who build it. Has the Peace Conference forgotten boys and girls?' *Children's Newspaper* (22 March 1919), 5. **24** 'Hagedorn, Hermann', *Marquis Who Was Who in America, 1607–1984* (New Providence, 2009), http://osearch.credoreference.com.darius.uleth.ca/content/entry/marqwas/hagedorn_hermann/0?searchId=192047680722388000&result=0, accessed 7 Sept. 2012. **25** D.M. Kennedy, *Over here: the First World War and American society* (25th anniversary ed. New York, 2004), p. 41. **26** H. Hagedorn, *You are the hope of the world! An appeal to the girls and boys of America* (New York, 1917), pp 1–3. **27** Ibid., p. 14. **28** Ibid., p. 18.

There was much confidence to be found in the image of a young United States rescuing decadent Europe from the burden of her feudal past, and many Americans cheerfully accepted that view of the war, with its implications of a new world order in which their country could at last take its rightfully premier place.[29]

In Hagedorn's work, this feeling emerges in his imagery of the child; in contrast to the European victim the American child is full of life, energy and inspiration.

The primary duty of American youth, according to Hagedorn, will be to 'live for the service of democracy' and thus to 'build, out of the agony and the ashes, a better world than the sun has yet shone upon'.[30] Unlike many other wartime works, this piece does not suggest that the child's ability to serve his or her country resides in the ability to serve as a soldier. In fact, the author directly challenges the popular image of the child sacrificing himself on the battlefield, saying at one point: 'To you, girls and boys [...] is given a work every bit as grand as dying for your country; and that is, living for the highest interests of your country!'. Rather than envision the child as either victim or soldier, Hagedorn presents the American child as a thinker, a leader and an ambassador for democracy: 'Young America, ten to seventeen [...] The world [...] doesn't ask you to [...] enlist. The world asks you to sit down and think about [...] what America stands for, what America is, and what America might be'. Youth are pictured as holding the key to future peace and success and Hagedorn refers to what he calls the 'cramping conservatism of the elder generation', encouraging his young readers to utilize their power, arguing that democracy needs the 'impassioned enthusiasm for freedom [...] which only youth has, which only you, girls and boys, can give!'.[31]

Repeatedly emphasizing that children have the future in their hands, Hagedorn commands, 'If your elders [...] will not volunteer to lead you, lead yourselves, and demand their support! Speak gently to Teacher, but if words don't wake him [...] girls and boys of America! [...] Fight! Not with guns, but with your brains!'.[32] This image of the child as a fighter differs significantly from those discussed earlier; in this case, it is not Germany that needs to be defeated, but the older generation itself. Tropes of generational hierarchy and devotion, evident in the familiar metaphor of the nation as a 'motherland' to which the child must be dutiful, are overturned and in their place is an image of the child holding the power.[33] This reflects what Kennedy

29 Kennedy, *Over here*, p. 43.   30 Hagedorn, *You are the hope*, pp 48–9.   31 Ibid., pp 99, 49–51, 96–7.   32 Ibid., pp 96–9.   33 Hagedorn's rallying cry against the older generation may also speak to his own family history. Born in New York City to German immigrants, he 'grew up speaking German at home. The fact that some of his family members returned to Germany from the United States influenced his interest in "divided loyalties"

refs to as the American view of themselves as 'a new, youthful force in the planet's affairs', that 'going to war was not simply against Germany but against [...] all that Europe historically represented in the American mind: coercive government, irrationality, barbarism, feudalism [...] America, in other words, was going to war against the past'.[34] In Hagedorn's view, it is not simply winning the war that is important; the true cause is to promote the 'interests of the world. In that struggle, the goal is [...] democracy. It is a lasting peace among nations; and, as far as it is humanly possible, amity among men. Go to it! Go to it, girls and boys of America! You are the hope of the world!'.[35]

CONCLUSION

The image of the child challenging the older generation, evident in both the *Children's Newspaper* and Hagedorn's work, brings to mind the poetry of Wilfred Owen, who famously refers to Horace's well-known verse, 'It is sweet and proper to die for one's country/and death pursues even the man who flees/nor spares the hamstrings or cowardly/backs of battle-shy youths'.[36] Owen revolts against this, writing, 'My friend, you would not tell with such high zest/ To children ardent for some desperate glory,/The old lie; Dulce et decorum est/Pro patria mori'.[37] Such works are part of a broader expression of desire for a world characterized by peace, not war, and some writers for children encouraged the younger generation to take active steps to secure this brighter future. Be they soldiers, contributors on the home front, or participants in a new political landscape, the children envisioned in much juvenile literature from the First World War are not cowardly, battle-shy youth, nor are they simply hapless victims in need of adult protection. Although such child figures appear in children's literature from the period, they are found alongside images of brave and selfless children who fight for their countries, who embody hope for the future, and who have the capacity to create a better society. The figures discussed here demonstrate how complex

of "hyphenated-Americans"'. 'Hagedorn, Hermann' *Theodore Roosevelt Center*. Theodore Roosevelt Center at Dickinson State University. n.d. http://www.theodorerooseveltcenter.org/Learn-About-TR/Themes/Family-and-Friends/Hermann-Hagedorn.aspx., accessed 10 Oct. 2012. Hagedorn's call to reject the old in favour of the new can be read in light of his own identity as a loyal American. Among his written works is *Where do you stand? An appeal to Americans of German origin* (New York, 1918), in which he calls for Americans of German ancestry to stand against Germany in the war. **34** Kennedy, *Over here*, p. 42. **35** Hagedorn, *You are the hope*, pp 99–100. **36** Horace, 'Ode 2, Book III: Angustam Amice' in W.G. Shepherd (trans.), *Horace: the complete odes and epodes* (London, 1986), pp 130–1. **37** W. Owen, 'Dulce et decorum est' in Brian Busby (ed.), *In Flanders fields and other poems of the First World War* (London, 2008), pp 175–6.

the notion of 'the child' was during this tumultuous period. Young readers were presented with representations of the child figure that extended far beyond simple notions of childhood innocence or obedience to embrace the idea that children have the power to change the political landscape, and that they are 'the hope of the world'.

'A noi!': the emergence of the gallant Fascist in Italian children's literature of the inter-war period

JESSICA D'EATH

> *Cibanti era un ragazzo come tutti gli altri ragazzi del mondo; non aveva il naso lungo, il vestituccio di carta e la testa di legno; era proprio un figliuolo vero come voi che leggete questa storia.*[1]

> [Cibanti was a boy just like any other boy in the world; he didn't have a long nose, paper clothes or a wooden head; he was a real little boy, like those of you reading this story.][2]

The opening passage of Eros Belloni's 1933 novel *Guerra! Romanzo fascista per i giovani* [War! Fascist novel for young people] makes obvious allusion to Carlo Collodi's canonical work *Le avventure di Pinocchio*. The inter-textual reference that permeates the story serves as a device to align the tale with traditional Italian children's literature and provides an interpretative key for the stark tone of passages such as the following:

> *In questa storia non sentirete mai parlare di Fate che scendono dalla cappa del camino, di cani che parlano, di lumicini lontani lontani che insegnano la strada a un bambino sperduto nella notte. No. Lasciamo le Fate dormire il loro sonno interminabile nel buio delle foreste favolose. State pure tranquilli ch'esse non si svegliano più, neppure se i bambini battono i piedi e si strappano i capelli uno per uno.*[3]

> [You won't hear tell, in this story, of Fairies who fly down from the chimney-top, of talking dogs and little lights far far away that guide the little lost child in the night. No. We'll leave the fairies to their never-ending sleep in the dark forests of fairy-tales. And you can be sure that they won't awaken ever again, even if children stamp their feet and pull out their hair, strand by strand.]

Collodi's own story opens with a similar (though admittedly less foreboding) caveat – that what follows is not the story of a king, but of a piece of wood that one might use to kindle the fire – and, just as Collodi's cautionary words

---

1 Eros Belloni, *Guerra! Romanzo fascista per i giovani* (Lanciano, 1933), p. 7.   2 All translations provided in this article are by Jessica D'Eath.   3 Belloni, *Guerra!*, p. 8.

pave the way for a tale which explores many of the darker sides of nine-teenth-century life – albeit in the guise of an innovative fantasy – Belloni's forewarning is intended to prepare his reader for an unsettling snapshot of early twentieth-century society.[4]

Belloni's *Guerra!* is but one of a body of texts which emerged in Italy in the 1930s, featuring the exploits of the 'gallant Fascist' – the heroic guardian of the Italian people who metes out 'justice' through recourse to acts of brutal and often humiliating violence. These depictions are glorified representations of Fascist *squadristi* [squad members], historical figures of the 1920s, who used public beatings and castor oil 'purges' amongst other methods to silence and punish their declared enemies. Though one may not be unduly surprised to discover that Fascist prepotency was depicted and celebrated in literature during the years of the dictatorial regime, in actuality, the figure of the *squadrista* is conspicuously absent from Italian popular and literary culture prior to the 1930s. The Fascist squads' controversial methods resulted in them being consciously marginalized in the late 1920s by their political counterparts through a process of calculated revisionism, only to be retrospectively reintegrated into official Fascist history upon consolidation of the dictatorial regime.[5]

The cultic image of Benito Mussolini as omnipotent *Duce* and exclusive orchestrator of the Fascist revolution was carefully cultivated in the 1920s but began to concede space to the commemoration of grassroots fascism in the 1930s. Public manifestations of this shifting perspective included the alloca-tion of a proportion of government positions to ex-*squadristi* and the acknowl-

---

4 *Le avventure di Pinocchio* opens as follows: '*C'era una volta ... – Un re! – diranno subito i miei piccolo lettori. No, ragazzi, avete sbagliato. C'era una volta un pezzo di legno. Non era un legno di lusso, ma un semplice pezzo da castata, di quelli che d'inverno si mettono nelle stufe e nei caminetti per accendere il fuoco e per riscaldare le stanze.*' [Once upon a time there was ... – A king! – my young readers will cry immediately. No, children, you are mistaken. Once upon a time there was a piece of wood. It was not an expensive piece of wood. It was a simple block of firewood, of the kind used to fuel stoves and fireplaces and warm up rooms in the winter-time.] Carlo Collodi, *Le avventure di Pinocchio: storia di un burat-tino* (Florence, 1883).   5 The term Fascism in the context of early 1920s Italy refers simultaneously to an emergent political power – of which Benito Mussolini would become the revered leader – and to a grassroots movement known as *squadrismo*. While a signifi-cant degree of overlap existed between the two groups, and while they shared many common interests and objectives, they cannot be considered to represent a homogenous Fascist movement with a coherent agenda. The actions of the squads facilitated Fascism's rise to political power, but the political leaders were quick to dissociate themselves from *squadrista* violence in the early years of Mussolini's reign. For a discussion on the position of the *squadristi* within the context of the Fascist regime see Emilio Gentile, 'The problem of the party in Italian Fascism', *Journal of Contemporary History*, 19:2 (1984), 251–84; Paul Corner, *The Fascist Party and popular opinion in Mussolini's Italy* (Oxford, 2012) and Roberta Suzzi Valli, 'The myth of *squadrismo* in the Fascist regime', *Journal of Contemporary History*, 35:2 (2000), 131–50.

edgment and celebration of the action of the squads in the *Mostra della Rivoluzione Fascista* [Exhibition of the Fascist Revolution] in 1932. Such initiatives by the authoritarian government demanded public acquiescence and resulted in the previously taboo topic of *squadrismo* being revived within Italian collective memory.

While the cultural rehabilitation of *squadrismo* is tentatively evident in adult literature and film, it is within the field of children's literature that the fluctuations in attitude towards the *squadristi* are particularly manifest. Little research has taken place to date on the literary representations of the squads, though recent articles by Italian scholars have provided interesting insights into the trends common to literary and cinematic depictions.[6] This essay will consider the emergence of the figure of the *squadrista* in Italian children's fiction of the 1930s. Following a consideration of the socio-cultural context, it will evaluate a range of devices employed by authors to court the child reader's fullest engagement with the revised ideological construction of *squadrismo*.

CHILDREN'S LITERATURE AS A FORUM FOR THE VALORIZATION OF *SQUADRISMO*

The Fascist regime put much faith in the power of children's literature as a tool to inculcate hegemonic values and proactively retained tight control over its production. As Pino Boero and Carmine De Luca note:

> *La letteratura giovanile è il terreno sul quale, forse meglio che su altri, è possibile misurare la capacità del fascismo a acquisire consensi incidendo sui comportamenti mentali degli italiani. Nel campo della produzione editoriale, l'ambito specifico dei libri e dei periodici destinati ai ragazzi e alle ragazze [...] trova, infatti, a essere più immediatamente soggetto a processi di strumentalizzazione da parte del potere costituito e ad essere privilegiato come canale di propaganda.[7]*

> [it is within the field of children's literature – perhaps more so than any other – that it is possible to measure Fascism's capacity to acquire consensus, inscribing itself upon the mental behaviour of Italians. Editorial production of books and periodicals destined for consumption by boys and girls was, in fact [...] most immediately subject to processes of instrumentalization by the authorities, and privileged as a vehicle for propaganda.]

6 For a discussion on the cultural representation of *squadrismo* see Cristina Baldassini, 'Fascismo e memoria. L'autorappresentazione dello squadrismo', *Rivista di Storia dell'800 e del '900*, 3 (2002), 485–506 and M. Millan, 'L'essenza del fascismo: la parabola dello squadrismo tra terrorismo e normalizzazione (1919–32)' (PhD, University of Padua, 2011).
7 P. Boero & C. De Luca, *La letteratura per l'infanzia* (Rome, 1995), p. 168.

This observation is certainly apposite to the sudden prevalence of the figure of the *squadrista* in children's fiction in the 1930s, despite the continued scarcity of representations in adult literary and cinematic culture. The regime's own contentious relationship with the actions of the squads indicated that its members were acutely aware of the general negative perception of *squadrismo* in the 1920s and were thus conscious of the challenge inherent in seeking to re-evaluate their role in the nation's recent history. Subverting the attitudes of adults who had personal experience of the period posed particular difficulties; dictating the version of events offered to the youngest generation was far less problematic.

In order to fully rehabilitate the figure of the *squadrista* then, it was important to take control of the narrative offered to children and to direct their responses. Equally crucial was the incorporation into the official narrative of all aspects of *squadrismo* that might filter into children's consciousness by way of anecdote or folklore. Despite the unpalatabilty of the methods of the squads, and the seeming irreconcilability of these with the principles of the regime, a deliberate decision appears to have been taken not to censor the violence and aggression central to the movement. An omission of these elements would create dissonance between official and anecdotal history. By embracing these aspects, however, and presenting them as legitimate, noble and necessary, authors shifted the lens through which *squadrismo* was perceived and provided children with a comprehensive and persuasive interpretation of the movement and its motivations.

Throughout the 1920s, Fascist children's literature had served to perpetuate the myth of Mussolini as a Christic saviour who had delivered Italy from the threat of socialism, and to promote the values central to the regime such as hard work, family integrity and national pride.[8] Violence was integral to Fascist culture – the Balilla youth groups trained their members to handle weapons – and acceptable in children's literature, but was governed by an implicit ethical code: militarization of society's youth was necessary to ensure the safeguarding of the nation, but gratuitous, spontaneous acts of aggression were strongly condemned.

Representations of violence had been integral to Italian children's literature since its inception. Edmondo De Amicis' *Cuore* – the novel which, together with *Pinocchio*, best epitomizes nineteenth-century Italian children's fiction – is saturated with reference to Risorgimento battle, child soldiers and mutilated veterans, while Emilio Salgari's colonial tales centre on conflict and battle overseas. Italian children's authors writing during and after the Great War, meanwhile, regularly sent protagonists – both adult and child – to the battlefield to experience the realities of war and death first-hand.[9]

8 See Antonio Gibelli, *Il popolo bambino. Infanzia e nazione dalla Grande Guerra a Salò* (Turin, 2005), pp 219–49 for a discussion on these texts.   9 For a detailed discussion on

A tradition of violence was thus firmly established in Italian children's fiction prior to the emergence of the *squadrista* as a literary figure. What sets the *squadrista* novels apart, however, are the identities of the perpetrator and victim of the violence, the context within which the episodes occur and the peculiarly gratuitous nature of the acts committed. De Amicis' *Cuore*, Salgari's colonial tales and the novels of the Great War all relied on the 'otherness' of the enemy to justify the unflinching violence inherent in the works. Where acts of aggression by Italians are depicted, they are invariably portrayed as a reaction to the barbaric nature of the 'other' which demands a firm and definitive response. The physical setting of these novels is also 'other', reference to conflict in De Amicis' work is retrospective and therefore at a remove from the readers' world, while Salgari's works and the novels of the Great War are situated abroad and on distant battlefields respectively. The *squadrista* novels, however, depict squad attacks occurring in Italian towns, village streets and countrysides, thus situating the scenes described firmly within a space familiar to the reader. Furthermore, both the aggressor and victim of the violence in these novels were generally depicted as being Italian. In light of this, mitigating devices were necessary to ensure that readers could accept rather than reject the hegemonic ideology inherent in the *squadrista* novels and imbibe the concept of *squadrismo* as legitimate, noble and necessary.

COMIC RELIEF: USING HUMOUR TO MITIGATE SQUAD VIOLENCE

In *Guerra!* Belloni combines surreal comic illustrations, a child focalizer and simple, playful language in a narrative that explores Italy's experience of the First World War and subsequent journey into Fascism. Despite the carefully constructed surface levity, the story is punctuated with episodes of violence characteristic of the context in which it was set. A consummate example is provided by the scene in which Cibanti and his father bear witness to a *spedizione punitive* [punitive expedition] by a group of *squadristi* [members of the Fascist attack squads]:

> [...] Ora – *proseguì il ragazzo della camicia uni aperta sul petto* – ora, non scomoderò più il mio fedelissimo manganello che, come vedete, porto appeso alla cintura, ma ho qualche cosa di meglio per voi, rispettabilissimo signore: credo, che le emozioni di questi giorni [...] devono avervi prodotto un certo disordine nelle viscere: per regolare il loro funzionamento, sarà bene che voi beviate il magico liquore contenuto in questa uniti, che vi offro.

the novels see J. D'Eath, 'Approaching war: representations of the Great War in Italian children's novels, 1915 to the present' (PhD, NUIG, 2012).

[...] E' veramente salutare ed è raccomandabilissimo per il vostro caso – proseguì fra le risa dei compagni – in Italia, questo liquore si chiama: olio di ricino.

[...] Lo straniero provò a svincolarsi dalla stretta dei due fascisti, che lo tenevano, e di fuggire.

Il giovine scherzoso, allora, trasse il pugnale dalla cintura e, puntandolo al petto dello straniero, disse, facendosi scuro in volto:

– Ora basta con le chiacchiere, o bere, o [...] affogare.

Con le unit tremanti dalla paura, l'uomo avvicinò la bocca all'apertura della uniti e, d'un fiato, trangugiò il contenuto....

Quando ebbe bevuto, i due fascisti lo lasciarono e, uno di essi, dandogli una pedata nella parte più carnosa del corpo, gli disse:

– Ora vai all'inferno, a raccontare al diavolo l'effetto che produce una unit di mezzo litro d'olio di ricino!

Lo straniero s'allontanò di corsa, gesticolando, e disparve nella uni, come se quella pedata l'avesse veramente mandato nel regno di Belzebù.[10]

[Now – continued the boy with the black shirt open at his chest – now, I won't inconvenience my trusty cudgel (which, as you see, I wear on my belt) any further. I have something even better for you, Illustrious Sir: I imagine that the excitement of the last few days [...] must surely have taken its toll on your bowels: you must drink the magic liquor from this flask to regulate them.

[...] It's very good for you, and comes highly recommended for your condition – he continued, amidst the laughter of his companions – in Italy, this liquor is called: castor oil.

[...] The foreigner tried to disentangle himself from the grip of the two Fascists who held him, and to escape. And so the playful youth pulled the dagger from his belt and, as his face became dark, pressed it against the foreigner's chest and said:

– Now enough chatting, either drink, or ... drown.

The man's lips trembled with fear as he brought his mouth close to the mouth of the bottle and, in one go, gulped down the contents...

Having watched him drink, the two Fascists left him and one, kicking him in the fleshiest part of his body, told him:

– Now, go to hell, and tell the devil of the effects that half a litre of castor oil produce!

The foreigner ran away, gesticulating, and disappeared into the night, as though that kick truly had sent him to the land of Beelzebub.]

Reading this passage out of context, one might reasonably assume that the *squadristi* are intended to be perceived as the villains of the scene, as vigilante

10 E. Belloni, *Guerra!*, p. 157.

thugs who delight in torturing their adversaries. The true ideological persuasion of the novel is apparent however, if one considers the above episode in light of Cibanti's father's reaction to the arrival of the *squadristi*. Intimidated by the presence of socialists in his local tavern, he rejoices at the sight of the Fascists, exclaiming '*Siamo salvi! I fascisti, giungono i fascisti!*'[11] [We're safe! The Fascists, the Fascists are coming!]

Writing on the subject of Roald Dahl's novels, Felicity O'Dell observes that '[n]arrative suspense, cathartic pleasure and surreal comic effects are all part of the delicate weave that constitutes the appeal of violence for children'.[12] Belloni's *Guerra!* relies masterfully on comic imagery and blithe use of language to counter the aggression of the narrated acts. The dialogue is quick and simple, the novel is illustrated in a caricatural and surreal style, the protagonist is depicted as being a *monello* – a mischievously roguish character-type of which Pinocchio is the forebear – and it is these details, together with an intimate narrative style, which establish in the work a sense of complicity, merriment and wicked fun.

The above-quoted passage is brimming with mirth despite the grotesque nature of the episode described. The staccato rhythm of the dialogue, the explicit reference to the cudgel, and the implicit threat contained therein, result – within the context of the overall tone of the work – in a slapstick sort of humour. Indeed the potentially slapstick quality of *squadrismo* as a movement was acknowledged by Margherita Sarfatti – Mussolini's mistress and Fascist party member – who, according to David Forgacs, in her writings on the topic 'slots the punitive expedition into the tradition of the *beffa*, a sometimes vicious practical joke, and puts the cudgel in a line of descent from Punch's stick.'[13] Belloni's novel courts the acquiescence of the child by implicitly aligning the *spedizione punitive* with playground pranks.

The humorous potential of the scene is reinforced by the scatological nature of the punishment meted out. Castor oil purges were but one of a repertoire of 'punishments' inflicted by *squadristi* on their victims; the decision to foreground this particular technique suggests a calculated desire by the author to appeal to what O'Dell describes as the 'child's appetite for the grotesque and the macabre'.[14] Children of the period would have been familiar with the intended effects of the 'magic liquor' – which was administered in small doses to alleviate stomach problems – and the suspense created in this scene is clearly designed to elicit a sense of anticipation and subversive delight in the reader. Further contributing to establishing a sense of wicked glee is the cowardice demonstrated by the victim of the purge; his 'trembling

11 Ibid.   12 Felicity O'Dell, *Socialisation through children's literature: the Soviet example* (Cambridge, 1978), p. 81.   13 David Forgacs, 'Fascism, violence and modernity' in P.W. Hutchings (ed.), *The violent muse: violence and the artistic imagination, 1910–1939* (Manchester, 1993), p. 8.   14 O'Dell, *Socialisation through children's literature*, p. 78.

lips' and his readiness to flee 'as though that kick really had sent him to the land of Beelzebub' indicate a pusillanimity which serves as a marked counterpoint to the virility and power of the perpetrator.

JUSTIFYING SQUAD VIOLENCE BY RECOURSE TO TRADITION

Though Belloni's novel constitutes a perfect example of the use of humour to normalize *squadrista* violence in 1930s novels for children, it should be noted that the majority of depictions of *squadrismo* in this period occur in more sombre, realist children's fiction. Indeed it is likely that most authors chose to shun more comical styles – fantasy and frivolity were considered incompatible with the disciplined nature of Fascism – in favour of more unequivocally 'noble' representations of *squadrismo*. Communicating a sense of the sobriety of the squad campaigns was certainly a priority for children's author Armando Michieli; the narrator of his 1938 novel *Piede sull'orma* [In his footsteps] observes that '[g]li squadristi, ormai noti per le loro azioni audaci e vittoriose contro quelli che gettavano la Patria in rovina, ispiravano ai due ragazzi ear timore che nasce a chi si trova improvvisamente in una casa ignota, e con gente che non earzo'.[15] [The *squadristi* – by now famous for their daring and triumphant actions against those who threatened to destroy the Fatherland – inspired reverential awe in the two boys, the sort of awe you feel upon finding yourself in an unknown house, with people who do not mess around.]

   Unwilling to rely on humour to palliate the violence inherent to *squadrismo*, authors turned to other devices to facilitate the acceptance of the movement by the child reader. Recourse is thus made to symbols and archetypes familiar to the child and integral to Fascist culture. Rumino, the protagonist of Ugo Scotti Berni's 1930 novel *Fiamma nel cuore* [Flame in heart] is constructed in accordance with the tropes of *romanità* [Roman-ness] and is thus portrayed as embodying the Fascist claim to classical Roman lineage. He is depicted as a 'legionario romano ... soldato garibaldino'[16] [Roman legionnaire ... Garibaldinian soldier] long before he joins the ranks of the *squadristi*, thus conditioning the readers' response to his actions. As Romke Visser asserts, during the Fascist regime 'Roman symbols and rhetoric [...] were part of a very efficient semiotic language intended to arouse popular enthusiasm'.[17] Likewise, the cult of the Risorgimento – the nineteenth-century process of unification – formed part of a distinct but correlate semiotic language. Literary and cultural references to Giuseppe Garibaldi – the iconic

15 Armando Michieli, *Piede sull'orma: romanzo per la gioventù* (Turin, 1938), p. 155.   16 Ugo Scotti Berni, *Fiamma nel cuore* (Florence, 1930), p. 189.   17 Romke Visser, 'Fascist doctrine and the cult of Romanità', *Journal of Contemporary History*, 27:1 (1992), 5–22 at 6.

soldier figure of Italy's wars of independence – invariably cast him as handsome, blonde and kindly, and it is clearly this familiar paradigm upon which Belloni draws when he describes the *squadrista* leader in his novel as 'un bel giovane alto e biondo; portava le maniche della camicia ear rimboccate fino al gomito e il fez calcato sulle ventitrè; aveva un aspetto allegro e franco'.[18] [a handsome youth, tall and blonde; he wore the cuffs of his black shirt rolled up around his elbows and his fez at an angle; he had a cheerful and open countenance.] By reproposing such familiar and reassuring archetypes of benevolent heroism so omnipresent in Fascist culture, the authors succeed in normalizing acts of aggression by associating the perpetrators with traditional, noble, irreproachable warriors.

SQUADRISMO: DEFENDING THE MEMORY OF THE GREAT WAR

The most common and effective device applied by authors in their pursuit to ameliorate the image of the squads, however, consists of presenting the birth and development of *squadrismo* within the framing narrative of a Great War story. Representations of the First World War had abounded in Italian children's literature during the conflict and into the 1920s, and the formulaic tales of this category were invariably preoccupied with glory, heroism and ultimate victory. This interpretation of Italy's experience of the war was consonant with that espoused by the Fascist regime; the expression of sentiments of pacifism or disillusionment was regarded as a betrayal of the memory of those who had fought the war and was expressly prohibited. Ex-officers proliferated in the ranks of the *squadristi*, and the protection of the sanctity and solemnity of Italy's victory was a declared purpose of the movement. Clashes regularly occurred between the attack squads and those members of society who refused to acknowledge the necessity and positive legacy of the war.

The decision to foreground a link between *squadrismo* and the Great War was, therefore, an obvious one, yet the *squadristi* were notably absent from the Great War novels of the earlier period. Children's fiction published as late as 1928 – years after the nation's experience of *squadrismo* – present the aftermath of the conflict in utopian terms: inter-war society is portrayed as being civilized, harmonious and reconciliatory. Beginning with Scotti Berni's *Fiamma nel cuore* in 1930, however, a formulaic plot structure begins to emerge that depicts a period of inter-war turmoil from which the *squadristi* emerge to champion and safeguard the memory of the war and its veterans. Scotti Berni's hero, Rumino, volunteers as a soldier in the Great War and fights valiantly for Italy, driven by the conviction of the greatness of the nation. He is horrified, in the wake of the war, to discover that a wave of

18 E. Belloni, *Guerra!*, p. 152.

socialism has poisoned people's hearts and numbed their sense of patriotism, thus desecrating the memory of the dead. It is to combat this abhorrence that Rumino proudly joins the *squadristi* and partakes in a civil war against socialists and pacifists. The genesis of the movement is depicted as being both aggressive and noble; Great War veterans are called to arms as 'Bisogna preparare nuovamente armi di ferro, armati di ferro, e picchiare senza pietà!'[19] [[t]he time has come once again to establish iron armies, armed with iron, and to dole out beatings without mercy!] He describes the resultant conflict as:

> *Triste guerra, deprecabile guerra, perché avevamo di fronte, o spesso alle spalle, gente dello stesso sangue. Ma chi rinnega la patria non è forse peggiore e più spregevole nemico di chi ci assale come straniero [...]? Guerra dolorosa, sì, ma necessaria come l'altra: perché l'altra diede all'Italia i suoi naturali confine terrestri [...] questa dava all'Italia la dignità di se stessa.*[20]

> [a sad war, a deplorable war, because before us, or often at our backs, were people of the same blood. But is he who renounces his fatherland not, perhaps, a worse and more despicable enemy than he who assaults us as a foreigner? [...] A sad war certainly, but as necessary as the last: because, while the last re-established Italy's natural territorial borders [...] this one restored Italy's dignity.]

The inter-war climate in Renzo Pezzani's *Corcontento* [Happyheart] is depicted as being so infested with malice that, prior to the intervention of the Fascist squads, '[u]n mutilato che aveva tentato di difendere in un pubblico locale le ragioni della Guerra, l'orgoglio della vittoria, la santità delle proprie ferite, era stato percosso a sangue.'[21] [a disabled veteran who had tried to defend the motivations of the war, the pride of Victory, the sacredness of his injuries, was beaten in a public house until he bled.] In Belloni's *Guerra!*, the castor-oil purge scene is a reaction to the perceived persecution of war veterans by socialist representatives, while in Michieli's *Piede sull'orma* the *squadristi* are called upon to ensure the correct and honourable burial of a war veteran in the context of socialist disapproval.

CONCLUSION

It is the memory of the war, then – a fundamental point of reference in Fascist culture and an established theme in children's fiction – that retro-

---

19 U. Scotti Berni, *Fiamma nel cuore*, p. 343.   20 Ibid., p. 344.   21 Renzo Pezzani, *Corcontento* (Turin, 1931), p. 152.

spectively legitimizes the brutality of the attack squads and guarantees them a place amongst children's literary heroes of the 1930s. That this appropriation is specific to the 30s and represents a deliberate and concerted effort to revise the previous historical perception of the *squadristi* is further demonstrated by some final observations. Salvator Gotta's *Piccolo alpino* [The little alpine soldier] is the single most successful Italian Great War novel for children. Published in 1926, it was written in the wake of the *squadrista* movement, yet Gotta, a committed Fascist cardholder, concluded his initial story by depicting inter-war society as peaceful and untroubled by the rumblings of civil conflict. It was not until 1935 that he published the sequel to his highly successful novel entitled *L'altra guerra del piccolo alpino* [The other war of the little alpine soldier], which concludes the story of the child hero, Giacomino, depicting his experience as a precocious member of the Fascist attack squads.

The link between the Great War and the legitimization of *squadrismo* in children's literature is definitively confirmed at the *Convegno nazionale per la letteratura infantile e giovanile* [National conference on children's and youth literature] in Bologna in 1938. In his introduction to the conference proceedings, F.T. Marinetti – leader of the Futurist movement, which shared common elements with *squadrismo* – includes among the criteria that good Fascist children's literature must satisfy:

> *L'orgoglio italiano solidamente costruito sulla Grande Guerra i cui sette-centomila morti produssero la massima vittoria della storia italiana e [...] sulla Rivoluzione Fascista che dallo squadrismo sanguinoso di piazza è giunta alle più liete organizzazioni agricole commerciali industriali portu-arie ferroviarie aviatorie.*[22]

> [Italian pride, solidly constructed during the Great War whose seven-hundred thousand dead produced the greatest victory in Italian history [...] and during the Fascist revolution which built upon the bloody grass-roots *squadrismo* movement to establish the most impressive agricultural, commercial, industrial, naval, rail and aviational organizations.]

Marinetti's speech encourages authors to foreground the Great War, the birth of the Fascist regime and *squadrismo* as key episodes in recent history that contribute towards the creation of the great nation. The degree of accuracy that these narratives should strive to achieve is also prescribed, Marinetti demands 'La verità storica rispettata ma sottomessa all'orgoglio italiano per

---

22 *Convegno nazionale per la letteratura infantile e giovanile. Bologna 1938–17: relazioni con prefazione manifesto di F.T. Marinetti* (Rome, 1939), p. 7.

modo che in tutte le narrazioni i nostri infortuni siano trattati con laconismo e le nostre numerose vittorie con lirismo'[23] [respect for historical fact though [this should be] subordinate to Italian pride so that in all narratives our misfortunes are glossed over and our numerous victories exalted].

It is impossible to assess the commercial success of the *squadrista* novels – though those referred to in this article enjoyed critical success under the regime – and equally difficult to evaluate the impact that such works had on the collective memory of *squadrismo*. What is certain, however, is that such novels were written with the deliberate intention of celebrating and retrospectively endorsing the actions of a group that had, until recently, been regarded as radical and unworthy of a place in the official narrative of Fascism. The shifting ideological perspective is most clearly notable in literature for children, and it is through this medium that we can best perceive the interpretation of the movement that the regime wished to establish and perpetuate.

23 Ibid.

Out of the Hitler time: growing up in exile

ÁINE McGILLICUDDY

In 'The road from Damascus; children's authors and the crossing of national boundaries', Gillian Lathey points out that '[w]hatever their origins, cultural transitions in children's books are as infinitely varied as the lives of those who write about them'.[1] For Judith Kerr, British children's author and illustrator, who was born in Berlin in 1923, the cultural transitions described in her autobiographical trilogy, *Out of the Hitler time* (1994),[2] are very much informed by her personal experiences. As a 9-year-old German refugee, she was forced to leave her native land and cross linguistic, cultural and national boundaries during her childhood and adolescence. The forthright, public criticism of Nazism by her father, Alfred Kerr, a renowned writer, journalist and theatre critic,[3] coupled with the family's Jewish origins, meant that the family had to flee Berlin just before Hitler came to power in 1933. So began a new and often unpredictable existence for young Kerr and her family, as political refugees moving first to German-speaking Switzerland, then to France before finally settling in England, where Kerr has remained ever since. As author and illustrator of the much-loved children's picturebooks, *The tiger who came to tea* (1968) and the *Mog* series, written between 1970 and 2002, Kerr's work continues to delight young readers.

Scholars debate as to whether or not her picturebooks should be read in light of the upheaval she experienced in her childhood. Louise Sylvester, for example, argues that 'traces of Kerr's traumatic childhood experiences may be found throughout her writing' in contrast to Lathey's suggestion that 'the picturebooks and autobiographical fiction [...] be viewed entirely separately'.[4]

---

1 Gillian Lathey, 'The road from Damascus: children's authors and the crossing of national boundaries' in M. Meek (ed.), *Children's literature and national identity* (Stoke on Trent, 2001), p. 5. 2 Judith Kerr, *Out of the Hitler time* (London, 1994). All citations from the trilogy will be from this edition, rather than from the three individually published volumes: *When Hitler stole Pink Rabbit* (London, 1971); *The other way round* (London, 1975); *A small person far away* (London, 1978). However, for the sake of clarity, all quotations will refer to the relevant novel title. 3 Alfred Kerr, originally Kempner, (1867–1948) was nicknamed the 'cultural pope' (Kulturpapst) in interwar Germany, due to the enormous influence he wielded in matters of culture and literature, particularly as drama critic for a leading German newspaper, *Berliner Tageblatt* (September 1919–January 1933). He often used the opportunity in these articles to criticize the growing power of the Nazi party and repudiate their Fascist ideology. 4 Louise Sylvester, 'A knock at the door:

Other scholars discuss Kerr's trilogy within the genre of Holocaust and war fiction and see in it valuable lessons about the past and a warning that '[i]gnorance of history is an invitation to tragedy'.[5] The first volume of *Out of the Hitler time*, entitled *When Hitler stole Pink Rabbit* (1971), has garnered widespread praise both in its original English and translated German versions, for its poignant and compassionate portrayal of the experiences of a Jewish child refugee.[6]

In this essay, I will discuss Kerr's trilogy from another angle, one that examines issues of identity around growing up in exile, loss of homeland and eventual homecoming (however short-lived the duration of return). This encompasses treatment of differing images of German identity and perceptions of diverse cultural identities, encountered and described by the protagonist Anna, as she and her family move from one country to another. Physical and psychological shifts, in migrating from one cultural and linguistic space to another, as described in *Out of the Hitler time*, can therefore be analysed in terms of self and the other. Questions of identity are notoriously complex, contested and multi-layered. Individuals, for example, can simultaneously identify with quite different groupings, be they ethnic or national or along age or gender lines. Furthermore, individual identification with particular groups is subject to permutation: at the beginning of *Out of the Hitler time*, Anna possesses both a German and Jewish identity; she is a child and a girl. However, over time, her identity and self-image changes, as will be discussed in more detail later. Group identity is described by Joep Leerssen as a balancing act, where cohesion within a particular group is more important than how each member of the group distinguishes themselves from one another. Rather, differences from the other are emphasized to reinforce group identity.[7] Thus, as Anna and her family find themselves

---

reading Judith Kerr's picture books in the context of her Holocaust fiction', *The Lion and the Unicorn*, 26:1 (2002), 16–30 at 17. Sylvester here refers to Gillian Lathey, *The impossible legacy. Identity and purpose in autobiographical children's literature set in the Third Reich and the Second World War* (London, 1995), p. 33. Sylvester argues that the eponymous tiger in *The tiger who came to tea* does not observe the rules of civilized society and reveals Kerr's underlying fears that, 'a knock at the door offers real menace' (Sylvester, 'A knock at the door', 23). In the same article, she points to the significance of the title of another of Kerr's picture books, *Mog and bunny* (1988), and how the illustrations throughout depict a pink toy rabbit (24). The same pink rabbit re-appears in another *Mog* tale, *Mog on fox night* (1993), underlining how 'Kerr cannot help but return again and again to the trauma of being severed from the toy that she represents as the chief companion of [...] childhood' (Sylvester, 'A knock at the door', 25).   5 Judy Mitchell, 'Children of the Holocaust', *The English Journal*, 69:7 (1980), 14–18 at 18. See also Lydia Kokkola, 'Holocaust narratives and the ethics of truthfulness', *Bookbird. A Journal of International Children's Literature*, 45:4 (2007), 5–12.   6 *When Hitler stole Pink Rabbit* won the prestigious German Youth Literature Prize (*Deutscher Jugendliteraturpreis*) in 1974 and has often featured on school curricula both in Britain and (in German translation) in Germany.   7 Manfred Beller & Joep Leerssen (ed.),

identified as outsiders in a variety of contexts, the bond between them strengthens, despite differences in their individual identities, characterized by gender or age. They distance themselves from those Germans who support Nazi Germany and increasingly identify themselves as Jewish refugees rather than as German citizens. For Anna and her brother Max, assimilation into their host cultures, through the acquisition of foreign languages and cultural practices, becomes a crucial part of their changing identity formation as they are disconnected from their identity of origin.

In examining issues of identity it is also important to take into consideration that *Out of the Hitler time* is neither a work of pure fiction nor wholly autobiographical but rather a fictionalized autobiography, where Kerr draws upon her own experiences without necessarily having to relate exact political and historical details as they happened. As Lathey argues in her study of autobiographical children's literature set in Nazi Germany and the Second World War, 'it is not [...] carefully documented historical facts which [...] writers wish to emphasize, but rather the *emotional* truth of childhood experience in a time of extreme stress and disorientation'. There is 'a need on the part of some writers to fictionalize in order to [...] express feelings about the past without the impediment of having to achieve historical accuracy'.[8] Kerr's work certainly supports such an argument, demonstrating, as it does, a greater concern with personal, everyday experiences of life in exile and family relations rather than political events of the time.[9] It is important to note too that Kerr chooses not to tell the story from the perspective of an adult/first person narrator, recalling events and emotions from the past but rather in the third person beginning with the voice of her alter ego Anna, a 9-year-old child. Such a narrative choice, which focalizes the story through a child protagonist, renders the experiences of growing up in exile more immediate. However, it also suggests a certain disconnection on the part of Kerr from her childhood self, 'a distancing of childhood which only appears to be resolved in the final volume'.[10]

Imagology: the cultural construction and literary representation of national characters. (Amsterdam, 2007), p. 337. Imagology is a domain of study within the discipline of comparative literature studies which examines literary representations of ethnic groups and nationalities.   8 Lathey, *The impossible legacy*, p. 44.   9 Kerr's trilogy has been criticized in some quarters for failing to address the history of Germany under Nazi rule in a more thorough and critical manner. See, for example, Zohar Shavit, *A past without shadow* (New York, 2005). Yet, such criticism seems unjustified when one considers that Kerr left Germany as a child in March 1933 before the Nazi party came to power and her story draws on her life experiences. The first novel is told from the perspective of a child who has an incomplete understanding of the events of the time. The content is adapted to suit a child readership being gently introduced to this historical period and its legacy.   10 Lathey, *The impossible legacy*, p. 73. Lathey also refers here to Kerr's description of her childhood during a lecture in Berlin on 7 October 1990 as 'frozen in time, inaccessible and

Before proceeding with an analysis of *Out of the Hitler time*, the significance of each title of the trilogy will first be outlined. These highlight the different temporal stages in the protagonist's life and the shift from a child's to an adult's view of the experience of exile against the backdrop of Nazism, war and its aftermath. The first book of the trilogy, *When Hitler stole Pink Rabbit*, is told from the perspective of Anna, the young heroine who, soon after her departure from Berlin, learns that the Nazis have confiscated her family home and all its contents. She imagines Hitler playing with her favourite toy, Pink Rabbit, which she had left behind and is now irretrievable. 'For a moment she was terribly sad about Pink Rabbit' and although she laughed at the thought of Hitler cuddling her cherished toy, 'some tears had come into her eyes and were running down her cheeks all at the same time'.[11] This irrevocable loss of Pink Rabbit symbolizes the loss of her carefree childhood but also, it later transpires, the loss of her German citizenship/identity. In the second book, *The other way round* (1975), we follow the fortunes of Anna's family in war-time London, after their experiences in Switzerland and France as described in the first book. In the second volume, it is not their parents, but rather an adolescent Anna and her older and much admired brother Max (modelled closely on Kerr's older brother Michael), who increasingly gain independence in this new, if at times precarious, environment. The children are now capable of providing their parents with a much-needed sense of security. This reflects both Anna's and Max's growing maturity and independence, moving from childhood into young adulthood, '[n]ow I suppose it's the other way round [...] the only times *they* don't feel like refugees is when they're with us'.[12] It implies, for their parents at least, that 'home' has been reduced to their family circle since their move to England and, with it, their increased reliance on their children. In the final book, entitled *A small person far away* (1978), Anna, now a young married woman living in post-war London, returns rather reluctantly to Berlin to nurse her widowed mother. In Berlin, she is confronted by her suppressed past identity and lingering memories of her childhood re-surface. The small person, speaking in German, seems so far removed from whom she has become, 'Somewhere very far away, a small person in boots was running up some steps, shouting, "Ist Mami da?"'.[13]

Questions of identity are central to this work from a variety of perspectives: how the four main characters change; the permutations of their familial roles; and the changes to their social and financial status as they move from one linguistic and cultural space to another. With each crossing and re-crossing of a national boundary, Anna's sense of self-identity evolves.

without connection to her present self'.   11 Kerr, *When Hitler stole Pink Rabbit*, p. 65.
12 Kerr, *The other way round*, p. 577.   13 Kerr, *A small person far away*, p. 810.

So too do her images of the other, which initially tend to be influenced by stereotypical impressions, before she becomes better acquainted with the new country and culture to which she moves. Language acquisition also plays a crucial role in the process of successful integration into and understanding of another culture. Since Kerr experienced the challenges and frustrations of learning more than one new language in her childhood, her descriptions of Anna's attempts to grapple with French, and her ultimate success, in tandem with her adaptation to French culture, are very realistic and, at times, humorous. Lathey reflects on Kerr's 'insights into the functional, everyday inconveniences of learning a new language', reminding us that 'learning a language is an adaptation of mind and linguistic sensibility, and not just the acquisition of vocabulary and functional phrases'.[14] This adaptation of a cultural and linguistic sensibility by Anna's family will form the main focus of this essay, drawing chiefly on the first volume of the trilogy. It provides the richest source for analysis of questions of identity and diverse cultural encounters. Commentary on the subsequent volumes will be included to a lesser extent.

At the beginning of *When Hitler stole Pink Rabbit*, Anna is leading a happy untroubled childhood in an affluent suburb of Berlin where her main preoccupations concern schoolwork and friends. Although it is soon evident that the novel opens in 1933, on the eve of Hitler's accession to power, Anna, as a typical 9-year-old, is not much concerned about politics and the rise of the Nazi party. Her parents are wealthy and respected members of the Berlin intelligentsia, leading a cultivated and seemingly carefree existence. We learn that Anna's father is a famous writer, her mother an accomplished musician and they live in a big house attended upon by servants, unencumbered by financial worries or domestic duties. As Anna later recalls, '[e]very day while Papa wrote in his study, Mama had played and even composed'.[15]

Anna's identity as a child growing up and going to school in Berlin is at first unambiguously German. However, on the way home from school one afternoon, she casually mentions to her friend Elsbeth that she is also Jewish. It is evident from her friend's surprised reaction that this Jewish aspect of Anna's identity was until then unknown to Elsbeth. Quite innocently they agree that she doesn't 'look Jewish', drawing on a familiar negative stereotype of the Jewish hooked nose as grounds for believing that Anna may not be correct in claiming her Jewish identity after all. Their familiarity, as children, with this image of the Jew, promoted extensively through Nazi propaganda, indicates not just the prevalence but also the unquestioning acceptance of such a stereotype.[16] Anna hardly seems to know what being a Jew signifies,

14 Gillian Lathey, 'Where Britain meets "the Continent": language and cultural exchange in fiction', *Children's Literature in Education*, 32:4 (2001), 295–303 at 300.   15 Kerr, *A small person far away*, p. 662.   16 The stereotype of the Jewish hooked nose has been doc-

due to her family's lack of religious observations or practices. She surmises that it has to do with family background, '[I]t's because my mother and father are Jews',[17] and concedes that until her father had mentioned it only the previous week, she had never given it much thought. It would appear that in the face of growing anti-Semitic sentiment, Anna's father, as a staunch opponent of Nazism, now wishes his family to become aware of and affirm this aspect of their identity so that they no longer regard themselves simply as German but as German Jews. 'My father said [...] we were Jews and no matter what happened my brother and I must never forget it'.[18] The 'imagined community'[19] of Germans as a unified *Volk* is thus fractured. Anna and her family, like many other excluded groups, are repudiated by the Nazi regime because they no longer conform to the prevailing discourse and image of what constituted wholesome German identity. Anna's sense of identity already begins to be shaped by an awareness of being somehow perceived as a stranger within, in line with the Kristevan formulation: 'Who is the stranger? He, who is not part of the group, he who "*is not*", the *Other*'.[20]

This 'otherness' or Jewish aspect of the family's identity becomes increasingly fore-grounded once they leave their home in Germany and move to Switzerland. On the eve of their departure to what is to be their first destination of exile, Anna is excited rather than anxious about the prospect of what she perceives to be the start of a thrilling adventure. Similar to her mother and their close family friend, affectionately known as Onkel Julius, she believes that it will be a short stay of no more than six months, a holiday rather than a flight from imminent danger. From her imaginings of life in Switzerland, it is apparent that she has but a sketchy knowledge of this country and its inhabitants, apart from some vague, stereotypical notions about mountains and a rural way of life ('a house in the mountains [...] goats [...] or was it cows?').[21] Emer O'Sullivan identifies such topographical cultural stereotypes as an important feature of imagology, citing the Alps as one of the

umented as far back as the thirteenth century in Europe. Klaus Hoedl, 'Physical characteristics of the Jews', *Jewish Studies at the Central European University: Public Lectures, 1996–1999* (Budapest, 2000), 59–70. Although appearing five years after 1933 (the opening date in *When Hitler stole Pink Rabbit*), a widely-read, children's picturebook *Der Giftpilz* (literal translation: The poisonous mushroom), published by Julius Streicher in Nuremberg in 1938, is a good example of such anti-Semitic propaganda. Its illustrated description of a school child being taught to draw the Jewish hooked nose like the number 6 on a black board, highlights the systematic way in which children were indoctrinated with negative stereotypical images of the Jews in Nazi Germany.   17 Kerr, *When Hitler stole Pink Rabbit*, p. 9.   18 Ibid., p. 8.   19 Benedict Anderson, *Imagined communities: reflections on the origins and spread of nationalism* (London, 1983, 2nd ed. London, 1991), p. 4.   20 Julia Kristeva, *Étrangers à nous-mêmes* (Paris, 1988), p. 139. Emphasis is in original. Translation is by Áine McGillicuddy.   21 Kerr, *When Hitler stole Pink Rabbit*, p. 23.

most common associations with Switzerland in children's literature.[22] Although Anna and her family have crossed a national border from Germany into neutral Switzerland, they are still living in a German-speaking land. This, to an important extent, facilitates initial adaptation to their life as political refugees. At the outset, Anna seems to view her new identity as a refugee in a positive light, rather than being troubled by it: 'It seemed rather fine and adventurous to be a refugee, to have no home and not to know where one was going to live.'[23] Life in exile and departure from Germany does appear at first to be more akin to a holiday, as the family stays in a luxurious hotel in Zurich and enjoys idyllic lake outings. Anna's father is also, at this point, still optimistic that he can continue to earn a lucrative living as a writer and critic. A few weeks later, when these hopes are dashed, due to a ban in Nazi Germany on printing anything he writes, the family's finances become a source of concern. Eventually, Anna's parents deem it wiser to move from cosmopolitan Zurich and their expensive hotel to a more modest guesthouse run by the friendly Zwirn family, located further down the lake in the heart of the Swiss countryside.

It is only at this stage, once the 'holiday' period is over, that Anna appears to encounter in earnest, the otherness of Switzerland and its inhabitants, most notably through her initial difficulty in understanding the local Swiss German dialect, which nonetheless she soon masters. Everyday life must continue, even in exile and Anna begins to attend the village school. There she observes that, unlike her teachers in Berlin, the Swiss schoolmaster Herr Graupe 'was not a very good teacher of the more conventional subjects ... [but] was a remarkable yodeller',[24] an allusion to the stereotypical image of the yodelling Swiss. She finds the behaviour of her new schoolmates alienating, notably their preference to go barefoot to school and their inscrutable and unspoken rules regarding interactions between boys and girls. When Anna both inadvertently and intentionally breaks these rules she is snubbed by the girls in the class while the boys chase her and throw stones at her. Such behaviour suggests that she is rejected for being different, a misunderstood outsider. However, when she is given to understand that Swiss country boys demonstrate their admiration by throwing things at the object of their affections, she feels more reassured. Thus, even if Anna's otherness as an outsider, an exile in a foreign land, is underlined here by her failure to understand and decipher these Swiss codes of behaviour, nevertheless, she, along with her family, appear to be accepted locally and they generally enjoy living in this 'pleasant atmosphere'.[25]

22 Emer O'Sullivan, 'Imagology meets children's literature', *International Research in Children's Literature*, 4:1 (2011), 1–14 at 8. In this article O'Sullivan advocates analysis of children's literature (both text and image) through an imagological lens. See also footnote 7. 23 Kerr, *When Hitler stole Pink Rabbit* , p. 93. 24 Ibid., p. 76. 25 Ibid., p. 68.

This convivial atmosphere is soured by the arrival of another German family from Munich, with two children of a similar age to Max and Anna, who book in as holidaymakers to the same guesthouse. At first Gudrun and Siegfried happily play with Max and Anna, as well as with the guesthouse owners' the Zwirns' own children, Vreneli and Franz. It is not long, however, before the new arrivals are forbidden by their parents to play or even speak with Max and Anna because of their Jewish identity. Subsequently Vreneli's and Franz's hesitation in choosing which group of German children they would prefer to play with, prompts Anna's father to exclaim: "'I think Vreneli and Franz will have to decide who their friends are [...] Swiss neutrality is all very well but it can be taken too far".'[26] With the parents' involvement, either by forbidding the children to play together or by commenting on their allegiances, it is evident that even play and choice of playmates can be politicized and polarized in this particular historical context. Although Anna's father refers to Gudrun and Siegfried as Nazis, Anna instead refers to them as the Germans, suggesting that they are of a different nationality to her and indicating a distancing from her original identity. This growing disconnection from Germany and her German identity is further reinforced by a conversation Anna overhears, in horror, between her mother and grandmother concerning the tragic fate of a Jewish professor in a concentration camp. Her instinctive response is to suppress the memory of this conversation and she consciously decides that '[i]n future she would try never to think about Germany at all'.[27] This reference to the treatment of Jews in Germany and Anna's horrified reaction are a reminder that, however agreeable life in exile may appear to be on the surface, disturbing news of the political situation in Germany and Nazi atrocities, although not directly experienced, hover in the background.

As time progresses there is a growing realization that a return to Germany is an impossibility for Anna and her family. Six months later, as Anna celebrates her tenth birthday on a steamer boat on Lake Zurich, her father informs her they will soon leave Switzerland for France where he hopes to find more opportunities for journalistic work. From the moment that they alight on the platform in a train station in Paris, Anna finds her first encounter with France and the French overwhelmingly alien:

> All around her there were people shouting, greeting each other, talking, laughing. Their lips moved quickly, their mobile faces kept pace with them. They shrugged, embraced each other and waved their hands to emphasize what they were saying – and she could not understand a word. For a moment [...] she felt quite lost.[28]

26 Ibid., p. 101. 27 Ibid., p. 114. 28 Ibid., p. 133.

Here again, Anna's initial impressions allude to stereotypical images, this time of French volubility and excitable Latin temperaments.[29] Her sense of alienation, of being an exile in a foreign land is accentuated by the fact that Anna has not just crossed a national boundary but a linguistic one, where not only the culture but also the language is unfamiliar to her. With the passage of time, Anna soon views the unfamiliarity of her new surroundings in a more positive light. Many of these favourable observations of Parisian life are derived from her sensory impressions of this new culture. She comments for example on the 'peculiar smell' in the metro, which was 'a mixture of garlic and French cigarettes', adding that she 'rather liked it'. If the sights, smells and bustling energy appeal to her senses, she is a little more circumspect about the 'prospect of going to a school where no one spoke anything but French' and she finds the idea 'rather daunting'.[30] Her brother Max finds the language barrier even more of a trial, possibly because he is older than Anna and is more self-conscious. Anna notices that he tries to fit in by changing his dress and hairstyle to look more like his French schoolmates. Once they master the French language, which they find frustrating and difficult at first, they both excel in school and feel less like outsiders. The moment of Anna's linguistic and psychological shift, when she no longer speaks French like a foreigner but quite effortlessly, is an important milestone: '[O]ne day her whole world changed [...] The words just seemed to arrive from nowhere in perfect French, without her having to think at all [...] It was as though she had suddenly found out she could fly'.[31] This underscores Lathey's point that, 'awareness that language is the key to the adoption of a new identity in the country of exile is a central theme'[32] in Kerr's trilogy.

Once they attain fluency in French, Max and Anna adapt so well to their new life in Paris that on their return to France after summer holidays spent at the invitation of the Zwirn family in Switzerland, they feel like they are coming home. This further emphasizes their continuing estrangement from their homeland and German identity. Nevertheless, sporadic news from an increasingly despondent Onkel Julius, back in Berlin, who eventually kills himself due to his unbearable existence in Nazi Germany, coupled with the ever-growing number of exiles arriving from Germany to Paris with tales of Nazi atrocities, ensure that the sinister development of political events in Germany continues to cast a long shadow. Anna's father, in particular, is affected by this and in their new, more cramped living arrangements, Anna is only too aware of the frequency of his nightmares. Life for Anna's parents is more taxing in different ways, despite the fact that they both speak French

---

29 Leerssen, for example, documents how the word 'garrulous' was used to describe the French from the early Enlightenment period in Germany. Beller & Leerssen (eds), *Imagology*, p. 156. 30 Kerr, *When Hitler stole Pink Rabbit*, p. 142, p. 152. 31 Ibid., pp 218–19. 32 Lathey, *The impossible legacy*, pp 96–7.

and make new friends. Apart from the enormous changes in their physical surroundings – a new country, a new city and a tiny apartment rather than the large house with servants that they were used to in Berlin, or the comfortable guesthouse by Lake Zurich – they must also adapt to severely straitened financial circumstances. For the first time, Anna's mother must cook for her family and mend their clothes. Her father finds it difficult to get work, despite his prestigious reputation and he seems at a loss to know what to do to earn a living, apart from writing. Anna notes how her mother worries constantly about money. Her parents simply cannot adjust as well as their children to their new life, perhaps partly due to their older age but also to the fact that they are regarded as 'the two most impractical people in the world'.[33] The change in social and financial status, added to their increased identification as part of an ever-growing community of Jewish refugees, stripped of German nationality, underlines the extent to which their identity has changed: from wealthy and respected German intellectuals to impoverished Jewish refugees. That they are also perceived as the latter by others in their immediate circle is highlighted in an unpleasant confrontation with their landlady about non-payment of rent, when she exclaims that Hitler was right to get rid of 'people like them'.[34]

After two years in exile in Paris, Anna's family is given the opportunity to improve their financial situation by moving to London to begin afresh. Feelings of upheaval and alienation are experienced once again by Anna, who remarks how '[i]t seemed strange to be leaving for yet another country'.[35] Like Max, she is saddened at the prospect of having to leave their adopted home in France. On her arrival in England (described at the very end of *When Hitler stole Pink Rabbit*), her first impressions of her future home and its inhabitants are not particularly positive, reflecting her reluctance to move and start a new life in a foreign country all over again. Anna finds the English to be a 'very quiet people' and 'the landscape is anonymous and dark', 'it was cold' and their cousin Otto who meets them off the train in London solemnly advises them to 'always wear woollen underclothes'. Anna notes that it is damp and 'her nostrils are filled with the smell of rubber from the mackintoshes which nearly all the English people were wearing'.[36] She remarks too on the polite behaviour of the English at the train station, who do not push or shove like the Germans and the French. As the volume concludes, and as Anna and her family are being whisked off in a taxi to begin a new life as political refugees in England, she reflects on her childhood – moving from Germany to Switzerland and then to France – and surmises that '[s]ome things had been difficult, but it had always been interesting and often funny [...]. As long as they were together she could never have a

33 Kerr, *When Hitler stole Pink Rabbit*, p. 232.   34 Ibid., p. 252.   35 Ibid., p. 264.   36 Ibid., p. 267, p. 269, p. 270.

difficult childhood'.[37] This brief summary of two-and-a-half years spent in exile would seem to minimize the very real trauma of losing her home and language, in addition to the disruption of her hitherto secure childhood. Perhaps it stems from the sense of guilt, commonly experienced by Holocaust survivors, that Kerr underplays this aspect so as to counter the few descriptions of self-pity to be found in this volume, such as Anna's dismay at losing Pink Rabbit.[38]

The next novel in the trilogy, *The other way round*, brings the story of Anna and her family forward by almost five years. Our protagonist is no longer a child but an adolescent growing up in war-time London. Max, and to a lesser extent, Anna, again find it easier than their parents to integrate into life in a new country. This can in part be attributed to their successful acquisition of the English language. We learn that the brother and sister converse in English rather than in German when alone. Anna is described as speaking like a native English speaker and '[a]fter four years of public school and nearly two terms at Cambridge, Max looked, sounded and felt English. It was maddening for him not to be legally English as well.'[39] The fact that Max is not legally English, although culturally and linguistically he appears to have wholeheartedly adopted this identity, has serious implications when he is interned for four months as an enemy alien while waiting to become a naturalized British citizen.[40] Thus, on an official level at least, he remains an outsider due to his German background and in the given political climate is treated with suspicion. Anna, despite sounding English, finds it more difficult to adapt to life in England than in France. She nostalgically recalls that in Paris '[s]he felt as though she belonged [...] not like a refugee'.[41] This sense of alienation is compounded by the challenges of adolescence and all the problems and dilemmas that can accompany this phase, such as crippling shyness and a burning desire to conform, so that at times Anna is no longer sure where she belongs. When she develops a crush on her art teacher, she fervently wishes that she were English in order to understand the subtleties of his questions and not appear foolish. Thus, once again, issues of language and identity are shown in this volume, to be inextricably linked.

External factors linked to the political times also play a role in hindering Anna's smoother adaptation to English life. The Second World War has broken out and 'France, like Germany had become a black hole on the map, a place you could no longer think about'.[42] One of the consequences of the Nazi occupation of France was that many more refugees now flocked to

37 Ibid., p. 272.   38 Lathey, *The impossible legacy*, p. 146.   39 Kerr, *The other way round*, p. 292.   40 For more information on British internment of aliens and political dissenters on the Isle of Man, known as the British army defence regulation 18b, see Connery Chappell, *Island of barbed wire: the remarkable story of World War Two internment on the Isle of Man* (London, 2005).   41 Kerr, *The other way round*, p. 301.   42 Ibid., p. 351.

England, one of the few remaining countries not under Hitler's sway, and it was difficult to be regarded as anything other than a stateless refugee. For Anna, this signifies further disconnection from her German identity. Her parents, along with the many other refugees fleeing war-torn Europe, live in relentless poverty in the run-down Hotel Continental in central London, in constant fear of German air raids. As Anna's father speaks little English and is no longer able to publish in either German or French, he is now 'a writer without a language'[43] and her mother bitterly resents having to constantly worry about family finances. Although assimilation is most difficult for the family in England, it is English citizenship they all adopt in the end. For Max and Anna, this new identity will be easier to accept as they are younger, more open to change and less isolated than their parents. As Max remarks to Anna, '[y]ou and I will be all right, but they'll never belong. Not here. Not anywhere I suppose'.[44] However, against the backdrop of the horrors of the Holocaust they so narrowly missed, Anna's father is philosophical rather than bitter about their changed identity and social situation; 'The four of us are together. After seven years of emigration, perhaps one shouldn't ask for more luck than that.'[45]

In *A small person far away*, the last book in the trilogy, Anna and Max have married into English families in the post-war period and to all intents and purposes appear to be thoroughly English themselves. Yet, when Anna is obliged to return to her native Berlin for an extended stay to look after her widowed mother who has ended up in hospital after a suicide attempt, she is catapulted back to her earliest memories and identity as a German child. This re-crossing of a cultural and linguistic border is the catalyst for deeply embedded and forgotten childhood experiences and memories to resurface: 'She did not remember the streets, only the feel of them';[46] '[t]he conversation slid from English into German and back again in a way that she found curiously soothing'.[47] Time and again, in the descriptions of Anna's stay in Berlin, we witness how visceral these memories are, despite her initial feelings of reluctance and unease with re-engaging with German language and culture. Since her childhood in exile, Anna had attempted to suppress this aspect of her identity along with the stories of horror from Nazi Germany. Now, as an adult, she finally comes to terms with her buried past on a last symbolic visit to her old family home as a 'young Englishwoman in a thin tweed coat'[48] before her return to her adopted home in England to start a new family of her own. This may appear a neat and satisfactory ending to a story of a life full of change and upheaval, of disconnection and alienation and to some extent it is. Nevertheless, even if the trilogy is in some regards 'too neatly Freudian in its resolution [with] the recovery of the childhood self

---

43 Ibid., p. 300.   44 Ibid., p. 576.   45 Ibid., p. 290.   46 Kerr, *A small person far away*, p. 637.   47 Ibid., p. 639.   48 Ibid., p. 772.

during a visit to the childhood home',[49] Anna remains resolutely English and has no regrets about returning to her adopted homeland. Likewise, she determines not to teach her unborn child her own mother tongue, as 'it wouldn't be the same'.[50]

As a migration narrative in both directions: Germany to England and back again via Switzerland and France, *Out of the Hitler time* describes encounters with different nations and their inhabitants against the backdrop of Nazi Germany, the Holocaust, the Second World War and the plight of Jewish exiles. Political exile affects Anna, her brother Max and her parents in different ways and they are challenged, not just by upheaval and poverty, but also in their negotiation of cultural and linguistic boundaries. The prime importance of the family as a safe haven from these challenges is reiterated throughout the trilogy. As Anna reminds her family at one point, '[i]f you haven't got a home, you've got to be with your people'.[51] This is a fate reminiscent of that of the Wandering Jew, a figure to which Anna compares herself at one point in *The other way round*.[52] The family bond is indeed strengthened by their shared trials, adventures and experiences. Ultimately, the message in *Out of the Hitler time* is a positive one. Kerr's trilogy not only sheds light on a Jewish child's experiences of exile in a particular historical epoch for readers who grew up after the Second World War but also encourages empathy in contemporary readers for the plight of refugees in other contexts.[53]

Drawing so closely on her own experiences infuses Kerr's trilogy with authenticity so that she genuinely achieves what she describes as her aim in writing this story based on her memories, 'I wanted to describe what it was like – what it was really like to flee from the Nazis, go to schools where they don't speak your language, live through air raids and [...] grow up.'[54] In *Out of the Hitler time*, she re-establishes a connection with the past experiences of a childhood in exile. Her writings portray how the crossing of linguistic and physical boundaries, encounters with other cultures and disconnection from one's country, language and culture of origin can have a lasting and profound

49 Lathey, *The impossible legacy*, p. 87.   50 Kerr, *A small person far away*, p. 808.   51 Kerr, *When Hitler stole Pink Rabbit*, p. 255.   52 Kerr, *The other way round*, p. 317. The Wandering Jew, according to medieval legend, was a Jew who mocked Jesus on the way to his Crucifixion and, as a result, was cursed to wander the earth until the Day of Judgment. 53 As part of an exhibition on Kerr's life and work, entitled, 'Tiger, Mog and Pink Rabbit: a Judith Kerr retrospective', organized by Seven Stories National Centre for Children's Books in Newcastle upon Tyne, England (2010), a group of children from nearby Christchurch primary school were filmed as they discussed issues of war and displacement with Kerr and their continuing relevance today. Some of the children filmed also came to England as refugees. The two-part film, entitled *When Judith found Pink Rabbit*, can be viewed at: http://exhibitions.sevenstories.org.uk/18/film.   54 Kerr, *Out of the Hitler time*, author's note.

effect.[55] In light of Kerr's experiences, Sylvester's assertion in her article, referred to at the beginning of this essay, that 'Kerr's picturebooks for young children cannot be separated from her other writing'[56] is convincing. We are challenged to reconsider Kerr's life's work as a way, both consciously and subconsciously, of dealing with the trauma of exile, an experience re-echoed in seemingly innocuous images of tea-drinking tigers and cuddly pink rabbits.

---

55 Kerr's continuing preoccupation with her past is highlighted in her latest autobiographical book, *Judith Kerr's creatures* (London, 2013), published to celebrate her 90th birthday in June 2013. It is a beautifully illustrated retrospective of her life, with a particular focus on her adult life and work as a children's author and illustrator. 56 Sylvester, 'A knock at the door', 28.

Paratexts and gender politics: a study of selected works by Anna Maria Fielding Hall

MARIAN THÉRÈSE KEYES

INTRODUCTION TO THE PARATEXT

Paratexts play an important role in literary and bibliographic history and interpretation. The theorist most closely identified with the notion of the paratext is the French literary scholar Gérard Genette for his work *Seuils* published in 1987.[1] He describes the paratext as a kind of vestibule or threshold, arguing that texts are rarely presented in an unadorned state without such elements as book covers, endpapers, prefaces, forwards, footnotes, illustrations, typography and advertisements.[2] Sometimes, these paratextual elements are fully approved by the author or editor but in other cases, the publisher makes the final decision for a variety of reasons, both commercial and ideological. Genette defines the paratext as:

> [a] zone between text and off-text, a zone not only of transition but also of *transaction*: a privileged place of pragmatics and a strategy, of an influence on the public, [...][facilitating] a better reception for the text and a more pertinent reading of it.[3]

Paratexts prepare the reader, guiding them subliminally over the vestibule or threshold and expectations can be manipulated in a variety of subtle or indeed explicit ways.

This essay examines a number of publications by Anna Maria Fielding Hall (1800–81),[4] exploring first how a selection of frontispiece portraits of the author prepared the reader for what lay ahead and second how, as an editor, she was able to utilize the many paratextual elements of *The Juvenile Forget-Me-Not* which she edited from 1829 to 1837. Hall was an intensely self-aware writer and she makes for a rewarding study in narratology. Quoting Genette again, he defines three basic types of narrators: the heterodiegetic where the

---

1 Gérard Genette, *Seuils* (Paris, 1987). It was translated into English as *Paratexts, thresholds of interpretation* (Cambridge, 1997). *Seuils* translates literally as 'thresholds'. 2 Ibid., p. 2. 3 Ibid. 4 Anna Maria Fielding Hall will be referred to as Hall or Mrs Hall throughout the essay to differentiate between her and her husband who will be referred to as S.C. Hall (1800–89) (an abbreviation for Samuel Carter Hall).

narrator is absent from their narrative; the homodiegetic where the narrator is inside the narrative, as in a story recounted in the first person; and autodiegetic where the narrator is inside the narrative and also the main character.[5] Hall was most at home with the latter two or a combination of both. At all times she endeavoured to keep the reader within sight of the narrator, vital for her didactic aims which were to encourage and promote good behaviour and hard work.[6] Retaining the viewpoint of an omniscient narrator gave her the flexibility to shift perspectives and to comment freely to her readers on education, morality, family duties and values. The paratextual elements provided Hall with a range of devices that could reinforce her didactic thrust, providing today's readers with many insights into children's literature and gender politics during the period from 1829 to 1850.

By focusing on a select number of works by Hall, this essay is divided into two parts: the first part examines three portraits of Hall, highlighting the power of the frontispiece authorial portrait;[7] and the second part explores a variety of paratextual elements in *The Juvenile Forget-Me-Not*. These elements include bindings, dedication plates, frontispieces, prefaces and publishers' advertisements.

PART 1

HALL: THE AUTHOR PORTRAIT AS PARATEXT

Hall was born in Dublin, spent her childhood in Bannow, Co. Wexford, and at the age of 15, she moved to London with her mother, where, in 1824, she married the Irish journalist and editor, Samuel Carter Hall. Encouraged initially by her husband to write her Irish sketches, Hall gained widespread success with her two series of *Sketches of Irish character* when they appeared in 1829 and 1831.[8] The following three decades were immensely prolific as she produced further sketches, plays, novels and children's books.

Numerous portraits exist of Mrs Hall, which comes as no surprise due to her personal friendship with many of the leading artists of the era. Her hus-

5 G. Genette, *Narrative discourse revisited* (Ithaca, 1980), pp 244–5.   6 In the story 'A great trial', the scene opens with a child requesting a true life story from the author. He says 'Mrs Hall knows very well what I mean – I want facts'. There is no pretence as to her identity – she positions herself in the room with her audience of children. Mrs S.C. Hall, 'A great trial', *St. James's Magazine*, 2 (1861), 251.   7 In his conclusion, Genette acknowledges that he did not go into detail in his book on three major areas that would require a separate book on each aspect. These areas included translation, serial publication and illustration – the latter he described as constituting an 'immense continent'. Genette, *Paratexts*, pp 405–6.   8 Mrs S.C. Hall, *Sketches of Irish character*, 2 vols (London, 1829) and *Sketches of Irish character* (London, 1831).

band's high profile position as editor of *The Art Journal* may also have been a factor, eliciting a ready response from eager artists. As the authors of *A guide to Victorian & Edwardian portraits* point out, commissions remained the principal reason for portraits during this period but there were other reasons, chief among them as a gift of friendship to a sitter.[9] Portraits, many by notable Irish artists such as Henry MacManus (1810–78) and Daniel Maclise (1806–70), depict Hall variously as a modest wife, a vivacious young woman of accomplishments, a hard-working author and a role model to her fellow countrywomen.

Like many of her contemporaries, Hall participated enthusiastically in the making of her public persona, not only through portraits but through autobiographical sketches, letters and memoirs. Annette Federico summarizes it aptly:

> Images of popular authors in photographs, frontispieces, postcards, and portraits sold books for publishers and authors were expected to cooperate in the commodification of their faces, bodies, pets, houses, and favourite haunts, all in the name of art, if not profit.[10]

The following section examines three portraits of Hall at different stages of her life – as a child, as a writer in the first flush of literary success and finally in her library, as a well established and admired author. The portraits chronicle the development of the writer towards greater autonomy. Functioning as frontispieces, they prepared the reader at the threshold of each title, providing important initial impressions. The portraits are taken from *Grandmamma's pockets* (1849), *Sketches of Irish character* (1844 edition) and *Midsummer Eve* (1848). While Hall may have selected these images as frontispieces, it is worth noting that the artists also brought their own ideological perspectives to bear on how the author was portrayed.

PORTRAIT OF THE AUTHOR AS A YOUNG CHILD

Between 1848 and 1851, Hall wrote four books for a new series entitled Chambers's Library for Young People, described by the publisher as consisting 'principally of moral and religious tales likely to influence the conduct and feelings of youth'.[11] The frontispiece to the first edition of *Grandmamma's*

9 Peter Funnell & Jan Marsh, *A guide to Victorian & Edwardian portraits* (London, 2011), pp 4–5. 10 Annette Federico, *Idol of suburbia: Maria Corelli and late Victorian literary culture* (Charlottesville, 2000), p. 21. 11 Review of *Orlandino* by Maria Edgeworth, *The Art-Union* (Jan. 1848), 35. *Orlandino* was the first in the series. Hall's works included *Uncle Sam's money-box* (Edinburgh, 1848), *Grandmamma's pockets* (Edinburgh, 1849), *The whisperer* (Edinburgh, 1850) and *The swan's egg* (Edinburgh, 1851).

pockets, dated 1849, portrays the young Annie Fielder (a thinly disguised
Anna Maria Fielding) on the top step outside an impressive doorway. Annie
lives at Dove Hall, and the author describes her life here with great affec-
tion.[12] The doorway includes some intricate stonework around the entrance
portico. A stone lion grasping an armorial plate stands on an elevated plinth
to the side of the entrance, and another can be seen behind the central figures. These elements add to the sense of aristocracy and privilege. This is no
humble country cabin but a home that exudes taste and heralds wealthy
inhabitants within. On the ornate steps, the young girl, dressed in veiled
bonnet and long dress and apron feeds pigeons from a wicker basket. The
pigeons fly around and peck seeds from the steps and basket, apparently
oblivious to any possible threat from the large dog and woolly ram on either
side of Annie. It is a peaceful scene and the only illustration in the publication. It captures the spirit of the book, which outlines in a lengthy first chapter what life was like for the lonely young girl who had no playmates other
than her pets.

> Annie had neither brother, sister, cousin, nor companions – that is to
> say, as she once said herself, 'human-being companions'; but a little
> cottage in the plantations was sacred to her favourites, and there she
> had a great number of birds and animals of many kinds.[13]

Set wholly in Ireland, there is little doubt that it is autobiographical, not
only because of the name of the heroine but in S.C. Hall's *Retrospect of a long
life*, he included a paragraph from *Grandmamma's pockets* where he referred
to his wife's great love of animals and the sea nearby.[14] Many women writers,
and it is particularly true of Hall, placed a major emphasis on their childhood,
returning to it frequently throughout their writing career. Patricia Meyer
Spacks has referred to this phenomenon, noting that for women 'adulthood –
marriage or spinsterhood implied loss of self. Unlike men, therefore, they
looked back fondly to the relative freedom and power of childhood and
youth'.[15] Richard Coe also suggests that this may explain why women were
drawn to writing *Jugenderinnerungen* (recounting the experiences and sensa-
tions of childhood) in preference to the *Bildungsroman* (an account of one's
whole life story).[16]

The first chapter refers to one of Annie's tasks being to take care of the
dovecot and the poultry yard but she also had an Angora ram called Mallow,

---

12 Dove Hall was no doubt inspired by memories of Graige House in Bannow where Hall
spent her childhood. 13 Hall, *Grandmamma's pockets*, p. 13. 14 S.C. Hall, *Retrospect of
a long life: from 1815 to 1883*, vol. 2 (London, 1883), p. 424. 15 Patricia Meyer Spacks,
'Stages of self: notes on autobiography and the life cycle' in Albert F. Stone (ed.), *The
American autobiography* (Englewood, NJ, 1981), p. 48. 16 Richard Coe, *When the grass
was taller: autobiography and the experience of childhood* (New Haven, 1984), pp 1–40.

and any number of dogs including 'Emp' or 'Emperor' the great mastiff.[17] The frontispiece portrays Annie with Emp and Mallow by her side. It could not, however, have been a direct portrait of Hall, as she was in her late forties when she wrote the book. Unlike the plates used in her annual, *The Juvenile Forget-Me-Not*, where stories and poems were penned in response to the expensive plates, the frontispiece in this publication followed the text very closely. It is signed by 'G. Millar, Edinr' but little is known about the artist/engraver, unlike the well-established artists and engravers who worked on the annuals for the Halls and who could command high prices.[18]

The tranquil scene of the 1849 frontispiece is worlds apart from that chosen for the later edition *c.*1899. Here the illustration highlights an incident that occupies a minor role in the book, where Annie's relative saves a toddler from being mauled by a grizzly bear. The illustration shows bear and man locked in fierce combat at the side of a steep mountain pathway. The publisher's ploy is to focus on high drama in order to stimulate reader interest during an era when more sensational tales sold well. In this case, the paratext misleads the reader into a false sense of the overall thrust of the gentle memoir, perhaps with a view to marketing the book to male readers.

PORTRAIT OF THE AUTHOR AS A YOUNG WOMAN

The second portrait of Hall is a steel engraved plate by Henry Thomas Ryall (1811–67) from a drawing by Henry MacManus, dating from the mid-1830s.[19] It is the frontispiece for the illustrated version of her *Sketches of Irish character* in 1844. Ryall was held in high regard for the rich tonal effects of his engravings and was appointed royal engraver by Queen Victoria. This was an early-career work for MacManus, an Irish artist who lived in London from the mid-1830s to 1844, and thus important for his status in London artistic circles. He depicts the seated Hall as a beautiful young woman, with her gaze directed to the viewer's left. Her eyes are not cast down and she has a gentle smile, exuding an air both of modesty and quiet confidence. She is dressed in a dark silk dress, wears a posy and chained crucifix on her bosom, a velvet hair band with a central cameo and a rose clipped over her left ear. She wears a number

---

17 Hall, *Grandmamma's pockets*, pp [11]–21.   18 G. Millar received £9 12s. 6d. for the frontispiece to *Grandmamma's pockets* (Chambers'Archive Dep 341/275. Publication Ledger No. 2, with title index 1845–67, National Library of Scotland, Edinburgh). With prints for the annuals, large sums of money were exchanged with artists for the loan of pictures and engravers for the plates. S.C. Hall refers to one image alone (*The Crucifixion* by John Martin, engraved by Henry Le Keux) which cost 210 guineas for the drawing and 180 guineas for the engraving. S.C. Hall, *The spirit and manners of the age* (London, 1829), p. 802.   19 Exact date unknown – based on the period that the artist was known to be working in London (1830s) and the date of the book she holds in her hand (1836–8).

of rings on her fingers and ornate bracelets on her wrists. Moreover, the book she clutches in both hands is not one of her own popular publications but her husband's most successful publication. It is tilted towards the reader, leaving the title easily read: *The book of gems: the poets and artists of Great Britain* which was published in three volumes between 1836 and 1838.

The convention of the author portrait, used as a frontispiece in many eighteenth- and nineteenth-century publications was widespread. In many cases it was the only visual in the entire publication, an image for the reader to ponder every time the book was opened. Frontispiece author portraits can play a distinctive and strategic role. According to Lynn A. Casmier-Paz, such portraits 'introduce, identify, or signal the presence of a narrator in the text' but 'such identification has always been potentially misleading and even ironic'.[20] Casmier-Paz' discussion related to slave narratives but it has useful parallels in a discussion of the woman author and her position in society in the first half of the nineteenth century.

Hall was a professional woman and that in itself was deemed transgressive by Victorian norms. The ideal woman was passive, docile and submissive so she had to negotiate her way in the marketplace very carefully. How her work was received in reviews was a matter of great importance as her reputation as a woman, a professional writer and a wife were always under scrutiny in a very public way. Evidence, both visual and textual, make up the raw material for a kind of battleground according to Colleen Denney, who referred to Victorian portraiture of women as follows:

> Such fixation speaks to their desire to hold themselves accountable and above reproach, cognisant of their place in history and time and their impact on the world and their responsibility to future generations.[21]

Hall had a complex relationship with her husband. Certainly he helped and encouraged her throughout her writing career but he was jealous of her success. She consistently strove not to alienate or humiliate him and a strategy such as the inclusion of this portrait of her holding her husband's book in the frontispiece of her own best-selling volume, publicly acknowledged her endorsement of her husband's professional superiority. For women writers it was often a delicate balancing act juggling self-promotion on the one hand yet self-effacement on the other.

20 Lynn A. Casmier-Paz, 'Slave narratives and the rhetoric of author portraiture', *New Literary History*, 34:1 (2003): 91–116. http://muse.jhu.edu.remote.library.dcu.ie/journals/new_literary_history/v034/34.1casmier-paz.html, accessed 10 Oct. 2012.   21 Colleen Denney, *Women, portraiture and the crisis of identity in Victorian England* (Aldershot, 2009), p. 2.

PORTRAIT OF THE AUTHOR AS A WORKING WOMAN

The final portrait shows Mrs Hall working at her desk in her library in The Rosery, Old Brompton, Kensington, the Halls' address from 1839 to 1850. The engraving, entitled 'The Library', was used as the overall frontispiece to *Midsummer Eve: a fairy tale of love* (1848), set in Killarney. It was drawn by the antiquarian artist and family friend, Frederick W. Fairholt (1814–66), most likely dating from the early 1840s, and it was engraved by J. Bastin who worked on many projects for the Halls.

In this portrait, Hall is shown in a magnificent baronial style library. As an antiquarian artist, Fairholt was keen to portray the interior in a painstaking fashion. The baronial style, popularized by Walter Scott's home at Abbotsford and completed in 1824, conveyed a romantic image of national identity, harking back to the castles and turrets of medieval architecture and reflecting the revival of interest in antiquarian concerns. For Hall, her library was the perfect room for a busy writer, replete with bookshelves, paintings and period furniture. Hall, wearing the same hair band and cameo as in the last portrait, sits at a highly decorative desk, immersed in her writing. To her left the large stained glass window, framed with elaborate curtain drapes, gives her ample light, adjacent to a tall column with floral foliage. Behind the author, there is a well-stocked library underneath a number of sculptural busts – one of whom appears to be of Shakespeare, one of her literary heroes. The fireplace, cabinet dresser, chandelier, ceiling and arched doorway are carefully depicted and the paintings and sculptural pieces could no doubt be matched with a household inventory if one existed. Hall is a small figure in her library – the artist wishes to convey how well she fits into her tasteful environment and also perhaps alludes to her modesty. As it is a fairy tale, one senses that the roaring fire and empty chair close to her desk represent a warm welcome to the reader to come closer and enjoy the tale that is about to unfold.

Keeping up with the hectic social round of invitations for a busy literary figure was a challenge for someone of Hall's stature and she was highly disciplined in her routines, working daily in her library until after lunch.[22] As her husband noted, referring to his wife:

> A well organized mind cannot fail if being orderly in all things and a mind that is not well organized can rarely inform or even amuse, except by its absurdities. Neatness of attire is the outward and visible sign of a well-regulated mind and a comfortable home.[23]

22 They entertained such notables as Charles Dickens (1812–70), Mary Howitt (1799–1888), Jenny Lind (1820–87), Thomas Moore (1779–1852) and William Wordsworth (1770–1850) at this address. 23 S.C. Hall, *Retrospect of a long life* (London, 1883), vol. 2, p. 428.

This portrait, therefore, of Hall in her library, confirms in every way the impression she wished to convey – she was a model Victorian woman exuding class, taste, modesty, hard work and erudition. These traits were deeply ingrained in her writings as it was vital that she set an exemplary model for her readers.

PART 2

The next section explores the first three volumes of *The Juvenile Forget-Me-Not*, an annual edited by Hall from its inception in 1829 until the final issue in 1837. It examines how the paratextual elements of these annuals contributed to the exposure of numerous ideologies but also informed the reader of the subtle ways in which gender politics were crystallized. These paratextual elements include the bindings, the dedication or presentation plates and the title page vignettes, the frontispiece plates, the prefaces and the publishers' advertisements.

INTRODUCTION TO THE JUVENILE FORGET-ME-NOT

Hall's growing reputation as a writer led to a variety of editorial appointments which in turn helped to market her own work. She had worked with her husband on the annual he founded three years earlier, *The Amulet* (1826–36),[24] providing short essays and editorial assistance, so was well equipped to take on new responsibilities. Her first major position was as editor of *The Juvenile Forget-Me-Not*. It was one of the earliest of these popular children's annuals, boasting a mixture of prose and poetry, interspersed with carefully chosen engravings.[25] While popular demand existed, writing for these annuals proved highly lucrative. Hall formed solid professional relationships with many women in particular, who provided stories and poems for this publication.[26] Recurrent themes in the annual included childhood mortality, poverty, Christian values and virtues (including prayers, poems and homilies) and the importance of avoiding cruelty to others and to animals. The didactic nature of the annuals harks back to the legacy of Mary Sherwood (1775–1851) and

---

24 http://www.britannuals.com/mes/mesp4.php?userID=britannuals&pageref=7, accessed 12 May 2013. 25 H. Carpenter & M. Prichard (eds), *The Oxford companion to children's literature* (Oxford, 1984), p. 26. The entry for 'Annual' quotes Thomas Crofton Croker who claimed that *The Christmas Box*, published in 1828, was the first annual for children, followed by Hall's *The Juvenile Forget-Me-Not*. 26 http://www.britannuals.com/mes/mesp4.php?userID=britannuals&pageref=7, accessed 12 May 2013. The chief contributors to *The Juvenile Forget-Me-Not* during its run included Hall herself (19 items), Maria Jane Jewsbury (1800–33) (14), Mary Howitt (1799–1888) (13) and Letitia E. Landon (1802–38) (12).

Maria Edgeworth (1768–1849), the latter a close friend and inspiration to the young Hall.

BINDINGS

Hall saw the importance of well-designed children's books, and urged that children should not be short-changed in terms of quality with all aspects of production. Her preface to *The Juvenile Forget-Me-Not* for 1829 states this at the outset:

> It will be evident that no expense has been spared to combine taste and elegance with qualities of greater importance [...] the production of a volume beneficial to those whose future character must in a great measure depend on their early impressions.[27]

As her writing for children spans the best part of fifty years, a study of the bindings used for her many juvenile publications proves both rewarding and informative.[28] The bindings for *The Juvenile Forget-Me-Not* appear to be of two kinds, initially a plain affair of brown half morocco over waxed yellow boards, with the title embossed in gilt on the spine and the second, a beautiful production of dark green morocco elaborately embossed in a classical design by De La Rue of London. According to Sara Hilton, after 1830 the annual was published with two trade bindings: a plain version reflecting its utilitarian purpose and the fact that it would be handled by children; and a later, presumably more expensive version, so designed that it would appear 'not misplaced in a well-appointed library'.[29] However, Hall alludes to the binding in the preface to the 1831 annual, pleased that the new design would, in fact, be even better suited to juvenile usage:

> I do not hesitate to submit the present volume as a considerable improvement on those by which it has been preceded. It will be at once obvious that such is the case with reference to the embellishments and the binding; the former being of a class by no means unworthy of the advanced state to which the arts of our country have arrived, and the latter being both more elegant and more durable than the delicate paper hitherto used, which faded at the touch of the gentlest and most careful reader.[30]

27 Mrs S.C. Hall, preface, *The Juvenile Forget-Me-Not* (London, 1829), p. iv.   28 Further discussion in chapters 4 and 6 in M.T. Keyes, '"Taken from the Life". Mimetic truth and ekphrastic eloquence in the writings of Anna Maria Fielding Hall (1800–81)', (PhD, DCU – St Patrick's College, 2010).   29 http://library.sc.edu/digital/collections/juvenileforgetmenotabout.html, accessed 4 Oct. 2013.   30 Mrs S.C. Hall, preface, *The*

Matthew Grenby notes that books were prized as luxury possessions by children in the first half of the nineteenth century, thus the physical appearance of the book was important.[31] To Hall, children deserved the greatest respect and their publications given due regard. In the April issue of *The Art-Union* (1846), her article entitled 'Thoughts on Juvenile Illustrated Literature' provides further evidence of her views on the importance of good quality publications. Adamant that children needed sufficient time away from their studies and an equal quantity of amusement to a 'given quantity of mental labour', she rejoiced in the modern improvements:

> The coarse covers, inappropriate and ill-drawn illustrations, are succeeded by beautiful bindings that encourage a child to be careful; and the illustrations are of such a nature, as I have already said, as to create a feeling and love of the beautiful which cannot be taught at too early an age.[32]

As a child grows up, so too their taste matures as their well-educated eye appreciates harmony and beauty in every sphere in their lives. Hall went to great lengths to point out that she was not advocating expensive habits for those who may not have the means to indulge them but saw the long-term benefit of familiarity with the principles of well wrought art and appropriate design: 'Habitual good order will prevent wasteful expenditure; and its soothing influence, felt rather than proclaimed, will extend like a halo around an habitation'.[33] These didactic sentiments were entirely consistent with her overall oeuvre, where she encouraged her readers to learn and imitate that which emanated from sound principles of the best art and design.

DEDICATION OR PRESENTATION PLATES AND TITLE PAGE
VIGNETTES

The dedication page (frequently referred to as the presentation plate) for *The Juvenile Forget-Me-Not* remained the same throughout the run of the annual. It features a bright-eyed greyhound seated on a low cushioned pedestal with the word 'Fidelity' underneath. He is depicted on his side and he gazes straight in front of him towards the left side. He is situated between two decorative plant containers out of which fuchsia plants grow, reaching up and

Juvenile Forget-Me-Not (London, 1831) [iii].   31 M.O. Grenby, 'Adults only? Children and children's books in British circulating libraries 1748–1848', *Book History*, 5 (2002), 27. 32 Mrs S.C. Hall, 'Thoughts on juvenile illustrated literature', *The Art-Union* (Apr. 1846), 111.   33 Ibid.

around a blank area, suitable for dedications. The dog in the dedication portrait may have been a portrait of one of the many that Hall owned.[34] Dogs
appear in practically every story written by Hall and she readily employed
them in her stories for children. They served numerous purposes: to educate
about animals and their behaviour; to elucidate a moral; to comment on
human nature and to teach respect towards the animal kingdom.

The title page vignette used in the 1829–32 annuals was designed by
William Harvey and shows two children reaching for forget-me-nots at a pool
surrounded by a wreath of such flowers. The girl leans around the tree, holding onto the wrist of her young friend while he reaches precariously over the
water to grasp some forget-me-nots. This wood-engraving is used as a tail-
piece for the annuals dated 1833–7 and a different design by William Harvey
is used for the title page for those years. This one features a central cameo of
three putti smiling and looking at a shared book placed between them. The
central cameo is surrounded by garlands of flowers and the publisher's details
are adorned with swags. The title and editor are on top of the page, the
former printed on a large shell and the latter on a decorative panel.

As with all of Hall's work, these plates were not random but careful
thought went into any selection process. The significance of flowers and their
symbolic meaning, for example, was widely understood in the nineteenth century. Lady Mary Wortley Montagu was credited with popularizing the secret
language of flowers to England in 1716 with Charlotte de la Tour's *Le lan-
gage des fleurs* published in 1818, followed by many others on this topic.
According to these accounts, fuchsia represented humble love, confiding love
and good taste. The forget-me-not represented true love, memories and a plea
to remember forever. Hall herself provided an introduction in 1877 to
Gertrude P. Dyer's *Stories of the flowers* and she commented that it was 'a
happy if not an entirely original idea to make flowers tell their stories'.[35]

Danielle Price has described how gender politics saturated nineteenth-century theories and that the use of floral codes in both literature and bouquets
was ubiquitous:

> Among myriad ideological associations between women and gardens, a
> clear program emerges, one familiar to readers of Foucault. To pro-
> duce perfection in women and nature requires enclosure, imprison-
> ment, and instruction, so that ultimately they will provide beauty and
> comfort.[36]

---

34 'Wherever Mrs Hall went there were sure to be birds and flowers, and a group of little
white Maltese dogs was a perennial feature in the establishment'. Isabella Fyvie Mayo, 'A
recollection of two old friends: Mr and Mrs S.C. Hall, *The Leisure Hour*, May 1889 [303]–
7.   35 Mrs S.C. Hall, Introduction, in Gertrude P. Dyer, *Stories of the flowers* (London,
1877), p. iii.   36 Danielle E. Price, 'Cultivating Mary: the Victorian secret garden',

The garden became an extension of the domestic and the symbolism of flowers readily understood.[37] Numerous literary outpourings addressed the ideological overtones of floral symbolism and horticultural activities, succinctly summarized in an excerpt from a poem entitled *The ministry of flowers* by Hall's good friend Lydia Sigourney:

> The matron fills her crystal vase
> With gems that summer lends
> [...]
> Her husband's eye is on the skill
> With which she decks his bower,
> And dearer is his praise to her
> Than earth's most precious flower.[38]

Dedication plates and title pages served to prepare the reader for what lay ahead in a variety of subtle ways that would have been picked up subliminally by any attentive child reader of the period.

FRONTISPIECES

The greatest care was taken with the 'embellishments' because the Halls championed contemporary British artists and Hall went to great pains to ensure that the engravings she selected were wholly appropriate for her young readers and reflected acceptable gender politics of the period. The frontispiece plates for the first three years of *The Juvenile Forget-Me-Not* were all engraved by the well-known portraitist James Thomson (1788–1850), ensuring the highest production values. In general, however, the market for children during this period was not always given equal weight as that for adults and, frequently, poor quality engravings were sometimes reissued and recycled rather than commissioned especially for their audience.

Whalley and Chester have addressed the fact that the art in the children's annuals reflected an earlier era with a fondness for sober neoclassical depictions rather than the art styles of the current time.[39] This is in evidence in the frontispiece for the 1829 annual that depicts a portrait bust entitled *The Princess Victoria*, drawn by H. Corbould (1787–1864) from a sculptural work 'in the

Children's Literature Association Quarterly, 26:1 (2001), 4–14 at 5.   **37** See Nicolette Scourse, *The Victorians and their flowers* (Portland, 1983); Michael Waters, *The garden in Victorian literature* (Aldershot, 1988); Beverly Seaton, *The language of flowers* (Charlottesville, 1995). **38** Lydia H. Sigourney, *The ministry of flowers*, quoted in Seaton, *The language of flowers*. **39** J.I. Whalley & T.R. Chester, *A history of children's book illustration* (London, 1986), pp 52–8.

possession of His Most Gracious Majesty by Behnes'.[40] It is neoclassical to the core – Victoria is dressed in classical attire, it is an idealized portrait giving no sense of her personality or individuality and the bust is displayed on a plinth with curtains draped back on either side. It exudes gravity and dignity and is a deliberate homage to the young princess, entirely fitting for the first frontispiece of the series. As the century progressed, a conscious effort was gradually made in the actual depiction of children. No longer shown as young adults, there was a heightened awareness of their difference in dress, behaviour and needs. A greater sense of fun and enjoyment replaced the restraint and sobriety more typical of the early decades of the century.

The frontispiece of the 1830 annual is entitled *My Brother* by the portrait miniaturist William Charles Ross (1794–1860) and it depicts a little girl who looks out towards the reader, with a gentle smile while hugging her younger brother. He is slightly higher up than his sister and looks rather regal as he gazes into the far distance, perhaps towards a noble future. Rose petals are strewn on his lap and he clutches a rose in his left hand. Lest the reader be in any doubt as to the gender dynamics, the poem, inspired by the plate and penned by Revd Thomas Greenwood, spells it out for the reader:

> Boy, love thy sister: how she loveth thee,
> Well that embrace, and well that look expresses;
> When added years reverse the tender duty,
> Guard thou, as fondly, her defenceless beauty.
> [...] When danger threats – and with that look of boldness,
> Stand forth her champion. Of her tenderness
> In childhood think, and shield her from distress.[41]

Hall's readers would identify with the superiority of the male infant and the sense of duty and responsibility that rests on his shoulders once he attains maturity. His little sister, is charming, loving and caring – essential prerequisites as she too grows into expected social norms.

It was no accident that an image such as the heavily gendered *Docility* was chosen by Hall as frontispiece for the 1831 annual. This engraving, after a painting by Andrew Robertson (1777–1845), could be a mirror image of the dutiful Hall in the MacManus engraving discussed earlier. The pose is similar with the young adolescent gazing into the left distance in an obedient non-threatening and non-confrontational manner. Like Hall, she holds a book and wears a crucifix and exudes an air of earnest contemplation and scholarly endeavour. It is not possible to see the titles of the book she reads, nor the one

---

40 Caption on the engraving. William Behnes (1795–1864) studied in Dublin, was appointed to the court of Queen Victoria and was noted for his portrait busts of children.
41 Hall, *Forget-Me-Not* (1830), pp 228–9.

on the table by the pen and ink.[42] As was the case in many annuals and gift books of this kind, the plates were selected first and the stories and poems built around the image. The accompanying poem in the annual was written by the editor's husband and its ideological slant leaves the reader in no doubt as to the edifying nature of the volume as evidenced by the following excerpt:

> From books, with information fraught –
> At once the nurse and child of thought [...]
> But oh! There may be found in books
> Lessons that tempt the heart to roam;
> And the good girl, before she looks,
> Consults the elders of her home.[43]

There are strong marketing reasons therefore why a frontispiece such as this is selected for the juvenile annual. Hall's mission was to educate as well as entertain so a plate of this kind highlights the didactic nature of the publication. Just as Hall looked to her husband for guidance and affirmation as portrayed in the MacManus frontispiece, so too is the young reader in *Docility* expected to consult her elders for guidance. Alexander Monro's advice to his daughter in the 1730s was that a girl ought to learn to read well so that she may 'entertain her companions', 'amuse and instruct her husband', and, most importantly, 'to convey her instructions to her children in a persuasive way'.[44] Kate Flint details how supervision was commonly exercised over the reading material of childhood and adolescence right through until the late Victorian and Edwardian periods. She also notes the 'prevalent assumption that different types of books were considered desirable and suitable for girls and for boys'[45] and that '[n]umerous narratives of prohibitions, warnings, and censorship are told [...] particularly concerning the ideas and emotions which were considered suitable for girls to encounter'.[46]

PREFACES

Hall's objective is unambiguously stated in the preface to the first volume in 1829: '[t]o produce a volume for youth [...] as to make the heart cheerful

---

42 Harriet Martineau had lamented that in her youth, it was not thought proper for young ladies to study conspicuously, and certainly not with pen in hand. Harriet Martineau, *Harriet Martineau's autobiography*, ed. Maria Weston Chapman, 2 vols (Boston, 1877), I, p. 77, qtd in Kate Flint, *The woman reader, 1837–1914* (Oxford, 1993), p. 192.   43 S.C. Hall, 'Docility', *The Juvenile Forget-Me-Not* (1831), 211–12.   44 Alexander Monro, *The professor's daughter* [...] (1739, Cambridge, 1995), p. 2, qted in M.O. Grenby, *The child reader, 1700–1840* (Cambridge, 2011), p. 259.   45 Flint, *The woman reader, 1837–1914*, p. 192.   46 Ibid., p. 209.

while the mind was improved'. In her preface for 1830, she reiterates 'that amusement is, at least, useless, if it [does] not contribute to information – and that the mind and heart may be improved even during the gayest moments'. Likewise in 1831, 'amusement is not much better than idleness [...] that knowledge and pleasure may go hand in hand'.

Influenced by the writings of educationalists such as John Locke (1632–1704), Jean-Jacques Rousseau (1712–78) and Maria Edgeworth, Hall believed that the right kind of education was vital to bring about a child's potential – a balanced combination of fresh air, healthy exercise and plenty of sleep. By extolling the importance of acquiring knowledge and instruction through well-written, carefully designed books, she could bring her readers on board and achieve her aim to guide in the formation of their characters from their early years.

PUBLISHERS' ADVERTISEMENTS

The inclusion of publishers' advertisements was commonplace and provided ample opportunity to promote forthcoming publications, particular those by the editors or their close acquaintances, the latter often contributors to that particular volume. At the back of *The Juvenile Forget-Me-Not* for 1829, there is just one page of advertisements, promoting her husband's annual *The Amulet*. Referring to the literary works in *The Amulet*, the advertisement echoes the oft-quoted refrain that 'their talents have been employed not merely to provide amusement, but to convey instruction'.[47] The 1830 annual has three pages of advertisements and the 1831 annual, four. Both of these highlight *The Amulet* but also *The British Magazine* which was edited by S.C. Hall and included numerous contributions by Mrs Hall. Apart from several short notices concerning other authors, the remaining pages include major coverage of Hall's second series of her *Sketches of Irish character* (1831) in addition to her *Chronicles of a school room* (1830). As was the practice with these advertisements, excerpts from reviews are quoted. The reviewer of the *Literary Gazette* notes that *Chronicles* is 'truly the task of a woman, and Mrs Hall has executed it delightfully'.[48] On the same page and in the same vein, *The Dublin Literary Gazette* states:

> There is no female writer of the present day, whose manner of com-
> position is more calculated to please than the lady whose names stands
> at the head of this review; there is a frankness and good nature in her
> style, a simplicity and feminine familiarity [...] to put her on good
> terms with her reader.[49]

47 Hall, *Forget-Me-Not* (1829), p. [240].   48 Hall, *Forget-Me-Not* (1831), p. [227].   49 Ibid.

No opportunity is lost in highlighting, through the advertisements, both the instructive nature of the publications and the undeniably feminine and womanly qualities of the editor.

CONCLUSION

Hall was a celebrated writer in the mid-nineteenth century and her unique position as the wife of the editor of an influential art magazine makes for a particularly interesting study on paratexts. Her connections in publishing and artistic circles equipped her with an extensive choice of artists, engravers and binders who contributed towards the adornment and ultimately the marketing of her publications. She had more control over the final product than many editors of the period due to her privileged connections and friendships.

Colleen Denney describes the need to examine how professional women in the Victorian world pictured themselves and how we perceive them today as a result of those representations. One way to come to a greater understanding of their multiple, often contradictory identities is, she acknowledges, to examine key portraits of them.[50] In doing precisely that with Hall, it can be shown that Hall used all the visual and verbal weaponry available in her repertoire to persuade, inform and entertain her readers – at all times mindful of negotiating the codes and protocols dictated by society. My initial quotation from Genette referred to the paratext as an influence on the public, facilitating 'a better reception for the text and a more pertinent reading of it'.[51] The portraits and paratexts in Hall's publications served to reinforce the didactic nature of her writing, not only for children but all her readers who might need reassurances that she did not step beyond acceptable boundaries for a woman writer.

50 Denney, *Women, portraiture*, pp 1–2.   51 Genette, *Paratexts*, p. 2.

Young women dealing with abuse: Catherine Breillat's cinematic perspective on *Bluebeard*

BRIGITTE LE JUEZ

Myths have given human societies the opportunity to reflect on the profound meaning of their existence and basic moral values. Myths have also allowed the formation of models according to which societies, communities, families, men and women may live in better harmony.[1] Like myths, as Jack Zipes reminds us, folk and fairy tales pervade the everyday world to such a degree that we are sometimes unaware of their enormous influence on our behaviour.[2] Folk and fairy tales are indeed the descendants of myths, and their combined corpus also offers many instances of universal stories about abandonment of children, rape, incest and other types of apparently unsolvable, brutal situations. If such narratives still contain mythic elements, however, they also present a substantial difference to myths insofar as they always 'provide the escape and consolation which the fearsome events in the fairy tale make necessary, to strengthen the child for meeting the vagaries of life'.[3] After a period of seemingly peaceful, if sometimes unhappy existence, young protagonists are suddenly placed in ominous circumstances which are too new not to seem extraordinary – hence the perception of both magical and monstrous elements around them. These considerations lay bare the basic elements that compose the tale in question, Charles Perrault's *La Barbe Bleue* (1697), or *Bluebeard* as it is known in the Anglophone world.

The influence that fairy tales have on ideologies and the politics behind them has evolved throughout history and via a variety of artistic spheres. They are widely used in mass media culture, whether they be films, animation, picturebooks, graphic novels or digital games. The tale of *Bluebeard* has undergone all these possible transformations and it has also been rewritten in a variety of literary genres and adapted to operatic and musical stages.[4] The

---

1 See G. Durand, *The anthropological structures of the imaginary* (Brisbane, 1999); M. Eliade, *Myth and reality*, trans. W.R. Trask (New York, 1963); and C. Lévi-Strauss, *Myth and meaning*, The 1977 Massey lectures (London, 1978). 2 J. Zipes, *Breaking the magic spell: radical theories of folk and fairy tales* (Austin, 1979). 3 B. Bettelheim, *The uses of enchantment* (London, 1991), p. 144. 4 Pantomime versions of the tale were staged at the Theatre Royal, Drury Lane, in London as early as 1798. Different versions over time include: William Makepeace Thackeray's short story *Bluebeard's ghost* (1843), Jacques

reason that *Bluebeard* has inspired so many artists in versions relating to different cultural and historical contexts, this essay argues, is to be found in the realistic overtones of its basic motif: the husband as serial abuser and killer of his young bride(s). Tellingly, in the last fifty years or so, *Bluebeard* has been modernized by an increasing number of women writers all over the world.[5] The version under scrutiny in this essay is a 2009 film, entitled *Barbe Bleue*, by French director Catherine Breillat. She is the first and only woman director to date to have given the tale the full feature-length treatment, in a long history of cinematic Bluebeards starting with George Méliès in 1901.[6] While most adaptations of *Bluebeard* have targeted either a child or an adult audience, Breillat brings the tale back where it belongs, as a text to be enjoyed by a family audience. In an interview attached to the DVD of her film, Breillat declares that *Bluebeard* is one of her seminal texts and that certain motifs from the tale can be found in some of her earlier films such as *A real young girl* (1976) or *Perfect love* (1996). Her adaptation of *Bluebeard* therefore presents her with opportunities to examine recurrent tropes and her own thematic preferences. To begin with, her choice of two parallel narratives is motivated by a wish to integrate her childhood memories into the film. Like other modern rewritings of *Bluebeard*, hers is a feminist approach that subverts many aspects of the traditional tale.[7] One such aspect is the personal development of her young protagonists, an interest developed in a number of her other films, namely *Virgin* (1988) and *Sleeping Beauty* (2010). Breillat admits to cinema critic, Maria Garcia, that the reason she is obsessed by young girls is that:

> [t]hey are individuals who exist but also do not yet exist. They are afraid, and they're strong and weak at the same time. They confront

Offenbach's 'opéra bouffe' *Barbe-Bleue* (1866), Béla Bartók's opera *Duke Bluebeard's castle* (1911), Edna St. Vincent Millay's poem *Bluebeard* (1917), Alfred Savoir's play *La huitième femme de Barbe-Bleue* (1921), Eudora Welty's novella *The robber bridegroom* (1942), Christian-Jaque's film *Barbe-Bleue* (1951), Pina Bausch' dance-theatre piece, *Barbe Bleue* (1977), Kurt Vonnegut's novel *Bluebeard* (1987), Alexandre Boubnov's animation film *La dernière femme de Barbe Bleue* (1996), Nina Kiriki Hoffman's short story *Chambers of the heart* (2003), Aimee Hertog's digital photography *Bluebeard the sociopath's stairwell* and sculpture *Bluebeard the sociopath's closet* (2012). 5 The latest of them is Belgian author Amélie Nothomb with her *Barbe Bleue* published in Paris, in September 2012. 6 The only other woman to have tackled the subject on screen is American director and writer Jessica Fox with her short film (15 minutes, silent) entitled *Bluebeard* (2008). Well-known film adaptations include, among many, Ernst Lubitsch, *Bluebeard's eighth wife* (1938), Edgar Ulmer, *Bluebeard* (1944), Edward Dmytryk, *Bluebeard* (1972) and Alain Ferrari, *La Barbe-Bleue* (1985). 7 Among many other rewritings by women are works by the following authors: Margaret Atwood (*Bluebeard's egg*), Angela Carter (*The bloody chamber*), Clarissa Estes (*Women who run with the wolves*), Pierrette Fleutiaux (*Les métamorphoses de la reine*), Suniti Namjoshi (*A room of his own*) and Sylvia Plath (*Bluebeard*).

life violently. They are weak because they do not know who they are going to become.[8]

In this essay, I will begin by discussing the universality of the *Bluebeard* tale. Underlying themes, such as marital abuse, male violence and forced marriage, but also female empowerment, will be considered. An exploration of Perrault's fairy tale and Breillat's filmic adaptation, in terms of social context, moral implications and narrative approaches will precede a more in-depth exploration of Breillat's treatment of the innocence of girlhood and the female protagonist's courage, maturation and ultimate self-actualization. Picturebook influences on the visual quality of Breillat's filmic treatment of the fairy tale will also be addressed. It is a fairy tale that may transcend epochs and genres but the central themes of psychological and sexual abuse do not change fundamentally and continue to be of concern in many societies today.

The plot of *Bluebeard* is well known. Bluebeard is a wealthy man, generally shunned due to the repulsive colour of his beard. Shortly after his latest marriage to a young woman, Bluebeard announces that he must leave to attend to important business. He gives his wife the keys of the castle, telling her that they open doors to rooms which contain all his riches. She is free to enjoy all of these while he is away but he also gives her a small key, stressing that she must not enter the room it opens, under any circumstances. She vows to obey him, and he sets off. Overcome by desire to see what the forbidden room holds, she discovers the room's ghastly secret: the slain bodies of her husband's former wives hanging from hooks on the walls and curdled blood all over the floor. Horrified, she drops the key, picks it up again and flees. However, the blood has stained the key, and she tries to clean it to no avail. That evening, Bluebeard returns home, discovers his wife's disobedience and sentences her to death. In the meantime, the young woman's sister Anne sends a sign to their brothers to come quickly and they arrive just in time to kill Bluebeard before he carries out his promise. His wife inherits his great fortune and puts it to good use, producing a dowry for her sister and securing captains' commissions for her brothers.

According to the Aarne-Thompson system of classifying folktale plots, the tale of *Bluebeard* is type 312, about women whose brothers rescue them from ruthless husbands or abductors.[9] It is closely related to type 311 in which the heroine rescues herself, and in some cases her sisters, from a ruthless husband or abductor. *Bluebeard* indeed belongs to these two types but also varies slightly from them: while the brothers do save their younger sister, she herself is instrumental in the rescue by cleverly delaying the moment of her

8 M. Garcia, 'Rewriting fairy tales, revisiting female identity: an interview with Catherine Breillat', *Cineaste*, 36:3 (2011), 32–5 at 34. 9 A. Aarne, *The types of the folktale: a classification and bibliography*, trans. and enlarged by Stith Thompson (Helsinki, 1961).

death; and Anne, the older sister, also contributes in her role as vigil. Anne is in fact the only character who has a proper name in the tale. Breillat's film, as we shall see, follows Perrault's original take on the two types, while adding historically factual background and also playing with the significance of women's first names. Although Breillat gives a name to the protagonist, she refuses to offer a patronym. This extends the premise of the original story, in which the father is absent, presumably deceased. Breillat begins the film with the imagined tragedy of his death and the dire consequences that might ensue for his wife and daughters, unless a strategic marriage is arranged to save them from penury. Breillat also removes the brothers, making *Bluebeard* more clearly a tale of female ability to survive, despite what may seem like insurmountable odds.

As is the case in many fairy tales, *Bluebeard* is about the rite of passage of a young girl into womanhood. For Breillat's heroine, this also means taking control of her destiny. Garcia confirms: '[Breillat's] protagonists take to the road and slay the dragons of girlhood confinement [...] Their reward is that they give birth to themselves.'[10] In other words, the heroine's triumph over death and her empowerment in the face of violence and abuse are important considerations in Breillat's film. As Catherine Wheatley states, 'marriage to the monster is not primarily a matter of romance so much as of survival'.[11]

Indeed, if *Bluebeard* has, over time, helped young women to reflect on questions of abuse, whether parental, sexual or societal, it is because it highlights realistic ordeals such as forced marriage due to poverty. Social acceptance of such practices and of their frequently devastating consequences may seem heinous in itself. Perrault's text clearly exposes the lack of ethical concerns of the times: while Bluebeard has had several wives who have disappeared under questionable circumstances, the fact that he is rich and therefore powerful has meant that he has never been held accountable or questioned about what happened to them. Breillat concurs with the commonly held belief that the character of Bluebeard was inspired by France's most notorious serial rapist and killer of young women, fifteenth-century nobleman Gilles de Rais, who was eventually hanged for his crimes.[12] This connection confirms that extreme use of violence against unprotected victims is at the heart of the tale.

The many versions that have been inspired by Perrault's tale all offer their own reading of the story. One of the interpretations of the text is that the forbidden room represents recently married young women who have died in

10 Garcia, 'Rewriting fairy tales', p. 32.   11 C. Wheatley, 'The new Eve: faith, femininity and the fairy tale in Catherine Breillat's *Barbe Bleue/Bluebeard* (2009)', *Studies in European Cinema* 10:1 (2013), 71–80 at 74.   12 See G. Bataille et P. Klossowski, *Procès de Gilles de Rais. Documents précédés d'une introduction de Georges Bataille* (Paris, 1959).

childbirth.[13] This view is not so much prompted by considerations about the poor medical conditions of the times as by revelations regarding the violence perpetrated against girls married at an early age: it indicates that Bluebeard's successive brides were too young to conceive or even have a sexual relationship. Our innocent heroine, not forewarned about the dangers of marrying a mature man with a shady past, has been used and betrayed by her elders. Indeed, Bluebeard did not court her, but rather her mother is partly to blame for her role in organizing lengthy matchmaking festivities. Her daughter's subsequent curiosity and disobedience, far from being flaws, can only seem legitimate as they allow her to discover not only who her husband really is but the dangers she will have to face.

A brief examination of the historical and sociological contexts of *Bluebeard* reveals that such viewpoints are not purely fictional. Courtship and marriage in seventeenth-century France followed precise rules and, until 1792, puberty remained the essential condition to allow marriages according to the legal age of consent, which was 12 for a girl.[14] Young women, in order to marry, usually had to have a dowry. Those without dowries might never get married at all, or they could be obliged to marry someone they disliked or dreaded. Families made it known to friends and relations that a daughter was marriageable and interested parties could send a representative to argue their case (there is such a scene in Breillat's film). Marriage was a political or social alliance, not a love match. After marriage, a husband could throw his wife out at any time if she displeased him. She had no legal rights to stop him from doing so. Perrault's *Bluebeard* is based on the understanding and acceptance of such injustices. Jack Zipes, in his study of filmic Bluebeards, confirms that under Louis XIV, the absolutist monarch, women had very few rights, were at the disposal of their fathers and husbands and 'had to learn to use cunning to cut into the laws and manners arranged to privilege white male power'.[15] As shall be shown, Breillat is interested in highlighting and extending the audience's understanding of these important areas.

Other aspects pertaining specifically to Perrault's *Bluebeard* are crucial to the presentation of ideological elements in and around the tale. While it has counterparts in the oral tradition of many cultures, the story as we know it, with its main character, title and gruesome details, first appeared in its written form in Perrault's collection *Mother Goose tales* (1697), alongside traditional folktales such as *Little Red Riding Hood, Cinderella* and *Sleeping Beauty.*

13 See dedicated page http://www.surlalunefairytales.com/bluebeard/history.html., accessed 7 Oct. 2013.   14 Jacques Houdaille and Louis Henry in 'Célibat et âge au mariage aux XVIIIe et XIXe siècles en France' note that, regrettably, the age of newlyweds was not systematically noted in marriage contracts until 1793, which makes it difficult to obtain satisfactory statistics. *Population* (1979).   15 J. Zipes, *The enchanted screen: the unknown history of fairy tale films* (New York, 2011), p. 159.

As an original text, and considering its rather unusual narrative structure, *Bluebeard* is often considered as one of the first 'modern' fairy tales.[16] Indeed, while most traditional fairy stories end with a marriage of love after which the characters live happily together, *Bluebeard* begins with a marriage of convenience that is about to go very wrong – albeit ultimately giving the heroine the opportunity to marry again and recover from her trauma. This departure from the traditional narrative structure of tales is not completely obvious, however, because, once the initial situation has been established, the text develops within the familiar narrative elements and functions usually found in tales, as identified by Vladimir Propp.[17] In this case, ambivalent questions remain in the end, allowing for perpetual re-interpretations.

The first question is one that Philip Lewis raises in his study of Perrault's *Bluebeard*.[18] It concerns the original motive for killing the first bride. The protagonist of the tale follows along after a number of other brides and it is implicitly stated that each of her predecessors made the same fatal mistake, disobediently using the magic key to open the door of the forbidden room, thus becoming witnesses to their husband's crimes. But it may be surmised that the very first wife did not find anything when she turned the key of the closet, that it was only an *empty* room, which she was then the first to inhabit. Why forbid someone to enter an empty room, if not to exercise excessive power? Lewis argues that Bluebeard kills his first bride, because she has realized that there is nothing to justify male domination. But it is not just that, as a wife, she was expected to obey unquestioningly or be punished; it is also that Bluebeard lied to the girl by saying he would be away for a long time, pretending he trusted her with everything he had, and then giving her the exact location of the small room as well as the key to enter it. He set her up, thus giving himself the perfect excuse to torture her psychologically, before killing her.

After offering his readers one of the most chilling fairy tales ever, Perrault concludes (somewhat disappointingly to a modern reader), with two equally glib comments:

> *Moral*
> Curiosity, in spite of its many charms,
> Can bring with it serious regrets;
> You can see a thousand examples of it every day.
> Women succumb, but it's a fleeting pleasure;
> As soon as you satisfy it, it ceases to be.
> And it always proves very, very costly.

16 C. Perrault, 'Bluebeard' in M. Tatar (ed.), *The classic fairy tales* (New York, 1999), pp 138–48.   17 V. Propp, *Morphology of the folktale*, trans. L. Scott (Austin, 1971).   18 P. Lewis, *Seeing through the Mother Goose tales* (Palo Alto, 1996).

Another Moral
If you just take a sensible point of view,
And study this grim little story,
You will understand that this tale
Is one that took place many years ago.
No longer are husbands so terrible,
Demanding the impossible,
Acting unhappy and jealous.
With their wives they toe the line;
And whatever color their beards might be,
It's not hard to tell which of the pair is master.[19]

On the one hand, Perrault scolds women for their inquisitiveness, a trait they have seemingly passed on to one another since Pandora and Eve. This is puzzling, as the story has just given the female protagonist the upper-hand and a happy prospect after her husband's death, thus justifying her curiosity. On the other hand, Perrault undermines the gravity of the husband's murderous intent by exonerating his male contemporaries of any possible inheritance of such sadistic traits. He even goes so far as to suggest that women actually always get their way with them anyway. This misogynistic and contradictory approach reflects the sensibilities prevalent during Perrault's times. However, the fact that such views still hold currency in many parts of the world today, may help to explain why *Bluebeard* continues to fascinate. The realistic overtones of Perrault's *Bluebeard* remain relevant to modern readers and auteurs, like Breillat. As Jack Zipes explains:

> No wonder this tale has taken root [...]. We are still perplexed and disturbed by the motives of serial killers [...]. It seems that we cannot put a stop to the raping and murdering of women even with all the laws and social codes established to prevent such actions. Not a day goes by without some husband striking out at his wife and killing her. [...] Women continue to live in a state of induced fear and are protected by the very men who may strike them down.[20]

In her filmic adaptation, Breillat offers us two narratives, both with their own central female protagonist. The first is a modern-day story-teller and the second the heroine in the tale being read, none other than *Bluebeard*. The story-teller is a fearless and quite bossy 5 or 6-year-old who insists on reading the frightening tale to her reluctant older sister (who appears to be 8 or 9), after having led her to a dusty attic, identified by the more obedient older sister as a forbidden room. Breillat reveals that, for her, the parallel narratives

19 Quoted in Tatar, *Classic fairy tales*, p. 148.   20 Zipes, *The enchanted screen*, p. 159.

serve as a mirror effect, adding to the interest of the tale. The attic is the other side of the mirror, reflecting modern times, which allows us to believe in the story and acknowledge its relevance today. The girls are in the attic without their parents' knowledge, which liberates them: they make all sorts of comments on and around the story, freely expressing their fears, beliefs and imagination. This emancipating situation may eventually lead to empowerment. That the younger girl should insist on reading aloud is, for instance, the first indication that she is taking control of the story, while at the same time learning to assert herself. Her babyish looks clash with the way she reads, without hesitation or fault, and with the way she forces her increasingly scared older sister to listen to the story to the end.

The two parallel yet connected narratives form the structure of the film: both take place in provincial France but, whereas one is set against a seventeenth-century background, with appropriate costumes, musketeers and stony castle, the other is set in the 1950s, the director's own childhood time (Breillat was born in 1948). The young reader, named Catherine (as is Breillat), reads the tale to a reluctant Marie-Anne.[21] The fact that their fairy-tale alter egos are called Marie-Catherine and Anne, although the cast is different (and slightly older) in the film within the film, also shows the identification of the girls with the characters of the story. In each case, the younger sister emerges as the stronger. The modern narrative is interrupted regularly as they discuss (and mostly argue about) related matters, such as marriage and love in their own childish terms.

Breillat revisits some of her recurrent themes, the tension between innocence and blooming adolescence, sisterhood and body images. Bluebeard, an older and seemingly wise and knowledgeable man, is both gloomy and obese: the archetypal physique of an ogre. His beard, and this is an innovative but significant change made by the director, grows blue only indoors. By way of contrast, his new wife is undeveloped: physically her body is still that of a child of approximately 12 years of age, and psychologically she is very innocent (but learning fast). However, she is given the same quality as her modern counterpart, a certain brazenness that comes from a sense of being unappreciated. She mentions that her sister is held in higher regard because she was born first – the typical complex of the second child and a complex which matches Bluebeard's own sense of otherness on their first meeting. It seems at this point that Breillat will give her film a meaning more complex and more ambiguous than that of the original tale. But she is only playing with Perrault's own ambivalence that he offered in his dual moralistic remarks. Breillat goes on to demonstrate unequivocally that Marie-Catherine is right to investigate the forbidden room and that she is also well able to survive the ordeal Bluebeard has in store for her.

21 The name of Breillat's sister, a well-known French actress, is Marie-Hélène.

Nonetheless, the ordeal had started before she even met Bluebeard. At the beginning of the film, adding a dimension absent from Perrault's narrative, Breillat brings in the sociological context of the tale.[22] Marie-Catherine and Anne first come to our attention when they learn from the Mother Superior of the convent school where they have been boarders that their father has died in an accident. The convent cannot keep them because their fees can no longer be paid. Their mother is devastated and insists that, unless they marry, they have no future. So, it is the absence of the father that brings about their awful and dangerous predicament. However, it is society at large that is to blame for allowing women to become totally vulnerable when the head of the family dies or disappears. Marie-Catherine's decision to marry Bluebeard is clearly seen as an attempt to save the family. Not realizing the menace that is looming, she is, at first, quite content with her new situation, which she feels is her own choice.

Breillat's young protagonist does not give in to male domination nor is she in a state of rebellion: she is kind to Bluebeard whom she willingly marries. She even appears to be quite fond of him. He is also kind and tender to her at first, not protesting when she refuses to sleep at the bottom of his bed, where he has installed a sort of cot for her to sleep in until she comes of age. Instead, she declares she wants her own room, the simplest and smallest there is in the castle, and one whose slim threshold, it turns out, Bluebeard cannot cross due his size. Not only does he not oppose her wishes, but it is the young girl who, a little later, sneakily passes her head through his bedroom door to watch him undress. Because she is small and softly spoken, Bluebeard does not suspect that she has reserves of inner strength.

Indeed, all could continue to go well if he did not put her to the usual test by giving her his magic key. Breillat does not play explicitly with any of these sexual metaphors nor with the obvious phallic symbol of the key, despite her reputation for erotic scenes in some of her other films.[23] This, as she explains, is because she wishes to address and include young viewers. However, she does not want to spare them fear, as she believes that children must be exposed to the attraction of evil in order, as with any disease, to be immunized against it. The particular quality of Marie-Catherine is precisely her ability to refuse to give in to fear, something modern Catherine feels her sister Marie-Anne is lacking.

At the end of the film, Marie-Anne, terrified by her young sister's narrative, is seen falling from the attic door, seemingly to her death, as she tries to

22 This is a privilege that authors of fairy-tale adaptations enjoy, according to Cristina Bacchilega: 'As a hybrid or transitional genre, the fairy tale also magically grants writers/tellers and readers/listeners [to which we add viewers here] access to the collective, if fictionalized past of social communing' in *Postmodern fairy tales: gender and narrative strategies* (Philadelphia, 1997), p. 5.   23 See *Romance* (1999) or *Anatomy of Hell* (2004).

flee the story. It may seem cruel of Breillat to give such a twist to the tale, but, in fact, it reflects the moral of the story as she sees it: if you are scared, so scared that you refuse to acknowledge the reality of a terrible situation, or refuse to fight it, then you may die. The 5-year-old seems better equipped to confront this harsh fact, hence her insistence on reading the story herself, and to the very end, defeating its demons in this way. Breillat's moral seems to be that only fearless girls survive heroic quests for self-actualization, even if it is at the expense of their husbands, and this does not seem unfair since it was the men who created and mastered the danger zone. Film critic, Peter Brunette, agrees on this point with Breillat and writes: 'it's the establishment through reversal of an imaginative paradigm in which little girls and, by implication, big girls in their turn conquer their fears by confronting them head on'.[24] Offering us, as a final shot, a painterly image of Marie-Catherine as a Judith-Salome figure, stroking Bluebeard's face as his severed head rests on a platter, Breillat emphasizes the fact that, contrary to her predecessors, Bluebeard's last bride has taken her destiny fully into her own hands.

As noted earlier, Breillat developed Perrault's ending to allow the young bride to take more credit for her rescue. Not only does Marie-Catherine show courage and, in the end, owes her life to her ability to remain cool and use her wits, but along with her sister Anne, she has made friends with young musketeers. These are the positive male figures who rush to help. The fact that women can have reliable and close male friends reflects the changing social values which have developed in the last century. Men and women have many relational possibilities which no longer lead to moral judgement on society's part. The film, in this way, although it reminds us that some things do not change but still need to be fought, offers positive insights about current mores. There is no indication at the end that Marie-Catherine remarries. None of this seems to bother the children who acted in the film and who saw it once it was completed. Breillat claims they were not shocked by any aspect and that, on the contrary, they liked it as much as she liked the tale in her youth – which for her was the best measure of having achieved her aim.

One reason why these children responded well to Breillat's *Bluebeard* may be that her production design reflects many qualities of Gustave Doré's illustrations in Perrault's *The complete fairy tales*.[25] According to Maria Garcia, the filmmaker and the illustrator share a common purpose, which is to portray the ways in which fairy tales can explain the adult world to children:

> Doré's drawings underscore scale and the relative power that oversized objects possess for children; the sets in [Breillat's] *Bluebeard* assume

24 P. Brunette, 'Film review: *Bluebeard*', *Film Journal International*, 113:5 (2010), p. 58.
25 G. Doré, *Illustrations des contes de Perrault* (Paris, 1867), pp 62–5. http://gallica.bnf.fr/ark:/12148/btv1b2200191h/f38.item, accessed 22 Mar. 2013.

•

the magnitude of childhood memory and emphasize the enormous obstacles the girls of the fairy tale must overcome if they are to survive.[26]

Indeed, there are several scenes where Marie-Catherine seems tiny compared to Bluebeard, starting with their wedding day. Breillat's spare design is also reminiscent of Doré's drawings as it calls attention to particular objects and confers upon them a symbolic stature they would not ordinarily possess. As Garcia also notes:

> [t]hese storybook qualities are augmented by Breillat's wonderful use of primary colours – the prism of childhood. Her inspired duplication of the same set for the forbidden attic and the bloody chamber accentuates the role that prohibition plays in the transition from childhood to adulthood and serves the narrative by linking the individuation of the two child heroes.[27]

Breillat, in her interview, confesses to having filmed the fairy tale as a picturebook, purposely adding more than just illustrations. As an example, she names the angels framing Bluebeard's fireplace, looming over Marie-Catherine, after she has visited the forbidden room, as she dips the small key into the ashes, hoping to remove the bloodstain. While her situation seems desperate, they may represent hope and, in a way, a protective presence in a fairy tale otherwise deprived of good fairies.

Perrault's fairy tale version is, for the most part, despite its (unorthodox) happy ending, far from reassuring. This deviation from the conventional fairy tale narrative was seen to be due, in no small measure, to the tale's starkly realized themes of domestic violence and arranged marriage. In particular, the morals he adds at the end were shown to be a reflection of the attitudes to women and marriage that prevailed in his time. Indeed, how could there be fairies in a tale, although progressively updated and enriched since the seventeenth century, transcending epochs and genres, whose very global success finally shows that its basic premise remains unchanged in many societies? For if the female protagonist has increased her share of power, as we have seen with Catherine Breillat's work, the tale's enduring message clearly states that psychological and sexual abuse of young women in intimate relationships with men continues, and that it is therefore a problem that societies still fail to address successfully.

---

26 M. Garcia, 'Film review: *Bluebeard*', *Cineaste*, 35:2 (2010), 61–3 at 63. 27 Ibid.

Sexual violence and rape myths in contemporary young adult fiction

MARION RANA

He just showed up, like the cavalry in one of those old movies.
Defending your honour.[1]

Sexual violence is a recurring topic in young adult literature. Problem-oriented novels like Laurie Halse Anderson's *Speak* (in which a teenage girl is raped at a high school party but dares not speak about it) or Alina Klein's *Rape girl* (in which rape victim Val's accusations turn her into a social out-cast) deal with issues such as rape and sexual abuse openly and provocatively. Such novels both contribute to and draw strength from the public discussion of sexual violence against girls and women.[2] At the same time, however, a considerable number of popular teen novels perpetuate a less problematized outlook on violence as a subcurrent of erotic desire, reinterpreting sexual violence as a particularly passionate way of expressing and acting upon sexual desire, or narratively reassigning responsibility for the sexual assault to the victim. Falling victim to an act of sexual violence may thus be presented as resulting in the loss of one's honour, as the above quote from *Vampire diaries* indicates, and does not leave the (intended) victim unduly traumatized. *Vampire diaries'* teen protagonist Elena thus confirms that even though she 'hurt all over', her attempted rape 'didn't matter anymore' because it led to her becoming an item with Stefan and, wonderfully: 'Nothing mattered except that Stefan loved her'.[3]

This essay will describe the presentation of rape and sexual violence in contemporary young adult fiction and the re-creation and perpetuation of rape myths that go along with them. It will do so, not only by analysing the vampire series *Twilight* and *Vampire diaries* in which, given the literary tradition they are building on, the appearance of sexual violence and patterns of its validation and negation are possibly not too surprising, but also by giving examples of other novels for young adults. The main thesis of this essay is that sexual violence is a recurrent theme in young adult fiction and that different rape myths are employed to justify sexual violence against women.

1 L.J. Smith, *Vampire diaries: the awakening* (New York, 1991; repr. London, 2009), p. 110. 2 L.H. Anderson, *Speak* (New York, 1999); A. Klein, *Rape girl* (New Hampshire, 2012). 3 L.J. Smith, *Awakening*, p. 108.

Sexual violence is violence that uses sexual actions or threats to punish women for perceived (sexual or non-sexual) transgressions, while rape myths can be defined as 'attitudes and beliefs that are generally false but are widely and persistently held, and that serve to deny and justify male sexual aggression against women'.[4] In the context of this paper, I use Martha R. Burt's definition of rape as:

> [p]enetration, however slight, of any bodily orifice, obtained against the victim's will by using force, or threat of force, of any part of the assailant's body or any object used by the assailant in the course of the assault.[5]

Burt argues that rape myths are part of our general culture, that they are linked to sex role stereotyping and acceptance of interpersonal violence.[6] Rape myths not only perpetuate and reinforce issues of sex role stereotyping and interpersonal violence, they also have a profound effect on future and past victims of sexual aggression, complicating victims' recovery as well as the prosecution of the offender, and creating an atmosphere in which sexual violence against women remains probable because the offender is likely to escape punishment while the victim is rendered responsible for the attack. Burt defines two categories of rape myths:[7]

1   Those that are focused on the victim and whose main aim is to remove an incident of sexual violence from the category of 'real' rape.
2   Those centred on the offender, either pointing to men's supposed inherently strong sexual drive and their helplessness in the face of sexual 'temptation', or supporting the idea of rapists as mentally deranged gender non-conformists.

My arguments will follow Burt's classification and give examples from young adult fiction to demonstrate the prevalence of these different myths. I will look at four categories of rape myths focused on the victim: Nothing happened; No harm was done; She wanted it; She deserved it. Following this, I will look at two categories of rape myths focused on the offender: Mentally disturbed; Ruled by natural predispositions.

---

4 K.A. Lonsway & L.F. Fitzgerald, 'Rape myths: a review', *Psychology of Women Quarterly*, 18:2 (1994), 133–64 at 134.   5 M.R. Burt, 'Rape myths' in M.E. Odem & J. Clay-Warner (eds), *Confronting rape and sexual assault* (Oxford, 1998), pp 129–61 at 129. 6 M.R. Burt, 'Cultural myths and support for rape', *Journal of Personality and Social Psychology*, 38:2 (1980), 217–30 at 218 and 229.   7 M.R. Burt, 'Rape myths', pp 130–1 (victim-centred myths) and pp 137–9 (offender-centred myths).

LIES AND DECEPTION! OR: NOTHING HAPPENED

The first group of myths focus on the offender's claim that nothing happened and assumes that for various reasons women blame innocent men without any sexual contact having occurred.[8] There is a very poignant example of this type of rape myth in *Vampire diaries* when Elena's antagonist, Caroline, falsely accuses Matt of having raped her.[9] The mental distress of rape victims is ridiculed in the narrative and put into question:

> Even if the adults saw Caroline's bizarre appearance and strange behaviour, they would dismiss it as being due to shock. Oh, poor Caroline, her whole personality has changed since that day. She's so frightened of Matt that she hides under her desk. She won't wash herself – maybe that's a common symptom after what she's been through.[10]

The false accusations of Caroline nearly result in Matt being sent to jail, and the court scenes in question are fraught with the idea that women can blame men for rape without any problem while men have no chance of getting a fair trial once this accusation has been made. Matt is thus not allowed to appoint an attorney of his choice and his public defender is informed of her appointment only thirty minutes before the trial starts, within hours of Matt having been arrested. He is beaten up by the interrogating officers and the judge dispenses with the opening arguments, robbing Matt of the chance to tell his side of the story. During the trial, Matt is restrained with duct tape to his chair and his mouth is taped.[11] At the conclusion of the trial, however, the power hierarchy is re-established: Elena and Stefan arrive with a huge dog, Saber, causing Caroline to transform into a werewolf, 'lick[ing] up at Saber's

---

8 Ibid.   9 L.J. Smith, *Vampire diaries: nightfall* (London, 2009), p. 446.   10 L.J. Smith, *Vampire diaries: shadow souls* (London, 2010), p. 55.   11 To counteract the inherent misogyny of portraying a rape case in such a light, the whole scene teems with references to the misogyny of the police and jurisdiction: Caroline's and Tyler's fathers belong to elitist 'no-women clubs with secret handshakes and stuff' (L.J. Smith, *Vampire diaries: midnight* (London, 2011), p. 211) and Matt is annoyed at one of the officers describing his confidante Dr Alpert as 'the black lady doctor': 'He tried the sound of "black lady doctor" on his tongue and found it tasted bad, sort of old-time-ish and just plain bad' (ibid., p. 213). Similarly, Matt wonders about the judge's use of the word 'pert' when scolding his lawyer: 'It was another of those words, he thought, that was never used towards males. A pert man was a joke. While a pert girl or woman sounded just fine. But why?' (ibid., p. 215). At the same time, the presentation of Matt as deeply respectful of women is reinforced, such as when he tells one of the officers that 'I've heard of mixed signals, but I've never seen them. I can hear "no" as well as you can, and I figure one "no" means "no"!' (Ibid., p. 214).

chops, rolling all the way on the floor to frolic around the huge animal, who was so obviously the alpha wolf':[12] the transgressive female is put into place by a dominant male whom she completely submits to and humiliates herself willingly.

IT CAN'T HAVE BEEN THAT BAD OR: NO HARM WAS DONE

The second category in Burt's classification of victim-centred rape myths acknowledges the fact that some sort of sexual encounter took place but denies that the victim has come to any harm through it, that is, the traumatizing effects of the attack are downplayed. Only under certain conditions, for instance if the victim was a virgin or married to another man, does this myth not necessarily hold anymore. Gerd Bohner explains:

> As an extension of these ideas, the 'no harm done' myth may comprise the fact that safety from sexual assault should only be extended to those women who put themselves under the exclusive protection of a single man while all other women are basically declared as legitimate victims. If only 'bad' women are raped, however, a woman who has been raped must have precipitated the attack.[13]

The credo of 'no harm was done' is a common rape myth, appearing frequently in young adult literature. It appears, for instance, in Sue Limb's *Girl, 15, charming but insane,* in which the reader witnesses no rape but several instances of sexual assault. The first is at a party where the protagonist Jess dances with a boy called Whizzer:

> Whizzer [...] put his arms round her and stuck his tongue down her throat. Jess was disgusted. He tasted of cigarettes. And Ben might be watching from somewhere nearby. She struggled slightly. It was hard to make a polite excuse and withdraw while a guy's tongue was down your throat [...] Jess tried to wriggle free, in a polite, nothing-personal kind of way, but there was no stopping Whizzer.[14]

Jess' first response is one of disgust. Tellingly, however, this feeling is not aimed at the actual attack but rather at Whizzer smelling of cigarettes and the false conclusions Ben, the boy Jess is in love with, might draw from the situation.

---

12 Ibid., p. 223.   13 G. Bohner, *Vergewaltigungsmythen: Soziologische Untersuchungen über täterentlastende und opferfeindliche Überzeugungen im Bereich sexueller Gewalt* (Landau, 1998), p. 15 (Marion Rana's translation).   14 S. Limb, *Girl, 15, charming but insane* (New York, 2004), pp 22–3.

Jess' second reaction is to attempt to free herself, her main aim, seemingly, being not to hurt Whizzer's feelings. The attack thus becomes trivialized and Jess' lack of outrage supports the idea that sexual assault is, in some sense, a peccadillo, or, as in the translation of the German term, a 'gentleman's offence'.

The second instance of sexual assault in *Girl, 15*, the installation of a video camera in the girls' bathroom at the above mentioned party, causes a greater stir. The narrative focus does not so much lie on the infringement of the girls' physical integrity than on the secrets revealed that way. The whole issue thus becomes problematic not because of the way the video was obtained or its inherent sexual aggression and invasive nature, but because of what Jess (and the other girls) did while being filmed. The only time Jess actually shows an appropriate reaction to the sexual aggression is when she is angry with her friend Flora for taking the boys' side in an argument on the video-taping. 'Videotaping girls in the bathroom wasn't a bit of fun, it was an invasion of their privacy',[15] the reader is told halfway through the novel. This attitude, however, is betrayed by the depiction of the incident as exactly that – a bit of fun – and by Jess actually watching the tape herself after a friend has retrieved it for her before it could be shown at the party.[16]

In the *Twilight* series, trivializations of sexual assault mainly centre on Jacob's sexual transgressions towards Bella. Not only does she always forgive him and in the end actually admits to her romantic feelings for him, thus legitimizing his assaults in retrospect, his attacks are also frequently endowed with humorous undertones (such as when Bella breaks her hand punching Jacob after he has kissed her against her will).[17]

'NO' MEANS 'NO' MEANS [...] 'YES'! OR: SHE WANTED IT

The third group of rape myths as defined by Burt, 'she wanted it', plays with the assumption that 'in reality', the victim wanted sexual intercourse after all. This myth finds its literary manifestation in the second novel of the *Vampire diaries* when Elena is forced into intercourse by Damon:

> Her memories of the last hours were confused and blurry [...] Damon's eyes looking down at her, filling her whole world. [...] He'd

15 S. Limb, *Girl*, p. 100.   16 It is not only Jess herself who trivializes the assault. When she does complain, her response is deemed inappropriate and disproportionate (Limb, *Girl*, p. 67). Even Jess' mother, who is repeatedly characterized as a 'radical feminist', has no stronger reaction to the video than exclaiming: 'Typical of the male concept of fun! Primitive and immature' (ibid., p. 91), and, after she has seen some of the video: 'If all the boys can come up with is this, it's a pretty poor show [...]. I've got sleazier stuff in the video department of the library' (ibid., p. 92).   17 S. Meyer, *Eclipse* (London, 2009), pp 293–301.

made her drink his blood then. If *made* was the right word. She didn't remember putting up any resistance or feeling any revulsion. By then, she had wanted it.[18]

This scene gives credence to James Twitchell's claim that 'as the vampire takes blood, he is also inseminating his victim with evil. A rape scene is played out through the gauze of fantasy'.[19] The fact that Damon does not use any physical force does not disqualify the assault from being rape. Rather, the assault follows a pattern frequently found in rape cases: 'In many cases, subjugation is accomplished without the actual use of physical violence. The assailant's threats and his apparent ability to carry them out may be the only means he uses to force compliance'.[20]

Similarly, Stefan and Damon's former partner Katherine's account of her transformation into a vampire is also fraught with sexual implications and rape myths:

I cried out to Gudren to save me, but she just stood there, watching. When he put his mouth to my neck, I thought he was going to kill me. [...] It was not so terrible after all. There was a little pain at first, but that quickly went away. And then the feeling was actually pleasant. When he gave me of his own blood to drink, I felt stronger than I had for months.[21]

Both Elena's account of Damon's assault and Katherine's recollection of her forced transformation bear a strong resemblance to the rape myth that rape victims are, in one way or the other, compliant and actually want sexual intercourse after all. Fittingly therefore, despite the psychological violence Damon uses against her and the sexual assaults she is subjected to, Elena does not bear any grudges against Damon and actually discovers tender and romantic feelings for him during the course of the next two novels. It seems that rape is just another form of courtship, then, and seemingly quite a successful one at that.

In *The hunger games*, the idea of the woman conceding to a previously unwanted sexual interaction is supported more subtly:

I was completely unprepared. I hadn't imagined how warm his lips would feel pressed against my own. Or how those hands, which could

18 L.J. Smith, *Vampire diaries: the struggle* (New York, 1991; repr. London, 2009), pp 347–8.   19 J.B. Twitchell, 'The vampire myth', *American Imago*, 37:1 (1980), 83–92 at 87.   20 Trauma Intervention Programs (TIP), 'Rape: reactions of the victims'. http://www.tip-national.org/ResourceMaterials/Rape%20Reactions%20of%20the%20Victim.pdf, accessed 16 Apr. 2013.   21 L.J. Smith, *Awakening*, p. 53.

set the most intricate of snares, could as easily entrap me. I think I made some sort of noise in the back of my throat, and I vaguely remember my fingers, curled tightly closed, resting on his chest. Then he let go and said 'I had to do that. At least once.' And he was gone. [...] I tried to decide how I felt about the kiss, if I had liked it or resented it, but all I really remembered was the pressure of Gale's lips and the scent of oranges that still lingered on his skin.[22]

Gale's kiss is a form of sexual assault and Katniss' reaction at first is one of reluctance – reluctance that she has made quite clear before. Gale's comment that he simply 'had to do that' supports the notion of the female body's constant availability to men. Nevertheless, the kiss seems to stir something inside Katniss: her fingers are tightly curled up, but merely resting on his chest in an intimate gesture, and she describes the kiss with a great number of sensual attributes (the feeling of his warm lips, the pressure of his hands, the scent of oranges). Since Katniss normally handles any kind of sexual arousal in a very detached manner or, rather, continuously tries to suppress her sexuality, this is quite a confession of sexual excitement for her, confirming the notion that a man just has to kiss a woman and she will most likely start liking it along the way.

NOBODY'S FAULT BUT HERS, OR: SHE DESERVED IT

Attribution of responsibility to the victim (who is either given the full blame or at least assumed to have precipitated the attack) is at the heart of the last victim-centred rape myth as classified by Burt, that is, She deserved it.[23] Indications for supposed victim precipitation may include 'risky' behaviour (such as hitchhiking or being alone on a dark street) or supposedly provocative behaviour (flirting, wearing tight or short clothing, or inviting a date into the flat). As Bohner argues, given the fact that a comparatively arbitrary number of factors constitute 'risky' behavior, women have to refrain from 'a multiplicity of (relatively vaguely outlined) patterns of behaviour if they do not want to become "legitimate victims"'.[24]

In the *Twilight* series, victim precipitation is particularly strong surrounding an incident not of sexual assault but of domestic violence. Sam, one of the werewolves in the novels, attacks his love-interest Emily in a fit of temper. This attack, in which she is severely disfigured (which can be read as an act of keeping her sexuality in check, especially considering that at the time of the attack, Emily was not yet interested in going out with Sam), is justified

22 S. Collins, *Catching fire* (New York, 2009), pp 32–3.   23 M.R. Burt, 'Rape myths', pp 134–6.   24 G. Bohner, *Vergewaltigungsmythen*, p. 16 (Marion Rana's translation).

through Sam's werewolf nature: 'Sam lost control of his temper for just one second [...] and she was standing too close'.[25] Sam is consumed with guilt after the assault but within the framework of werewolf fiction, his attack on Emily is not a moral dilemma; it is clear that he feels sorry, but it is equally clear that it was not in his power to spare Emily once he was outraged enough to turn into wolf-shape. Without explicitly stating it, Emily is held partly responsible for the attack. After all, 'she was standing too close'.[26]

As a consequence of rape victims being attributed (partial) responsibility, as explained by Gerd Bohner above, women have to follow certain patterns of behaviour, thus actively reattributing responsibility for their safety from sexual assault onto themselves rather than the possible attacker. In *Vampire diaries*, this pattern is a recurrent theme both in the protagonists' evaluation of other characters (such as when Bonnie assesses that Tami's provocative behaviour will likely result in her sexual violation)[27] and in Elena's control of her own sexual attraction in order to save her partners from unnecessary sexual arousal. As Stefan is unable to fully control his desire around Elena, she has to take precautions: 'Wear something with a high neck. A sweater'.[28] It thus becomes her responsibility not to ignite his desire and to keep herself safe, a logic that is repeated when she takes protective measures to keep herself from being noticed by passing vampires and arousing their sexual desire for her: 'Nowadays, my aura can make vampires want me ... the way human guys do. [...] So I have to practise keeping my aura hidden'.[29]

DANGEROUSLY DISTURBED OR RULED BY NATURAL PREDISPOSITIONS? OFFENDER-CENTRED RAPE MYTHS

Apart from her research on victim-centred rape myths, Burt has also classified two myths concerning rapists: while the first one of these assumes that rapists are mentally disturbed (which in reality is only true for a very small minority of rapists),[30] the second myth draws on biological assumptions about male sexuality and argues that men in general are not able to control their sexual urges. Thus, as soon as a man is even minimally aroused, he will try to have sex – even if he needs to use violence to achieve intercourse.[31]

---

25 S. Meyer, *New moon* (London, 2009), p. 304.   26 To be fair, when Bella retells the story in her head, she attributes the underlying blame differently: 'Sam had lost control just once when he was standing too close to her. Once was all it took [...]' (Myer, *Eclipse*, p. 155). In her rendering of the incident, Sam is the one standing too close to Emily. What stays the same, however, is the focus on Sam's lack of anger management – the attack is not really his fault.   27 L.J. Smith, *Nightfall*, p. 156.   28 L.J. Smith, *Struggle*, p. 260.   29 L.J. Smith, *Shadow souls*, p. 11.   30 H. Gordon & D. Grubin, 'Psychiatric aspects of the assessment and treatment of sex offenders', *Advances in Psychiatric Treatment*, 10 (2004), 73–80 at 77.   31 M.R. Burt, 'Rape Myths', pp 137–9.

Although these myths are partly contradictory, they can coexist because they are used to explain different types of rapes. Atypical cases of stranger rape, including extremely violent behaviour, can be explained with the help of the first myth, stressing the 'abnormality' of the offender. Myths of this type, supporting the idea that rape is committed by mentally defunct and perverted men, occur in most instances of narratively condemned rape in the novels analysed here, most prominently in the description of Rosalie's fatal gang rape in the *Twilight* series:

> Suddenly, Royce ripped my jacket from my shoulders [...] 'Show him what you look like, Rose!' He laughed again and then he tore my hat out of my hair. The pins wrenched my hair from the roots, and I cried out in pain. They seemed to enjoy that – the sound of my pain. They left me in the street, still laughing as they stumbled away.[32]

The rapists in this scene are described as monsters exerting excessive amounts of aggression and violence, as perverted and abnormal in their sexual behaviour and their deviant lack of any kind of moral code. Bella's near gang rape in *Twilight* does not explicate the perverted nature of her offenders as much but follows a similar pattern:

> 'There you are!' The booming voice of the stocky, dark-haired man shattered the intense quiet and made me jump. In the gathering darkness, it seemed like he was looking past me.
> 'Yeah,' a voice called loudly from behind me, making me jump again as I tried to hurry down the street. [...]
> 'Don't be like that, sugar,' he called, and the raucous laughter started again behind me.[33]

The idea of establishing or rearranging a power hierarchy is also the main reason behind many forms of sexual violence. In *The hunger games*, the fact that all the boys in the arena carry spears, which are phallic symbols, brings the issue of male sexual violence not exactly to the foreground, but makes the idea hover around the whole issue of violence in the arena. This is confirmed subtly in different scenes in which the antagonists of the main character, Katniss, plan to kill or hurt her in sadistic scenarios: Cato, her most dangerous and mentally disturbed opponent, exclaims: 'When we find her, I kill her in my own way, and no one interferes'.[34] Especially in the context of 'thrusting a spear into the hands' of another tribute as they walk off to find Katniss,[35] his threat becomes laced with sexual aggression. In the end, Cato

---

32 S. Myer, *Eclipse*, pp 142–3.   33 S. Myer, *Twilight*, pp 139–40.   34 S. Collins, *The hunger games* (New York, 2008), p. 284.   35 Ibid.

never actually battles Katniss hands-on, but leaves her killing to his partner Clove under the condition that she 'give[s] the audience a good show'.[36] Clove is contemplating cutting off Katniss' lips since Katniss will not 'have much use for [them] anymore. Want to blow Lover Boy one last kiss?'[37]

More typical cases, that of acquaintance rape, can be explained by the second myth, often used in conjunction with the final victim–centred example, explored above, where the victim is seen to deserve it or is somehow to blame for provoking the attack. The idea of the male's inherent biological inability to control sexual urges is particularly strong in the vampire series *Vampire diaries* and *Twilight*. Both Stefan and Edward have trouble restraining themselves when faced with the sexual allure of Elena and Bella:

> Stefan imagined how his lips would meet [her throat] with equal softness at first [...]. And how at last his lips would part, would draw back from aching teeth now sharp as little daggers, and – [...] He had no idea how he'd gotten away, only that some time later he was channelling his energy into hard exercise.[38]

Similarly, Edward explains about the first time he met Bella:

> The fragrance coming off your skin [...] I thought it would make me deranged that first day. In that one hour, I thought of a hundred different ways to lure you from the room with me, to get you alone. And I fought them each back.[39]

It is only due to Stefan's and Edward's tremendous self-control that they are able to suppress their physical urges at this point. The assumption is that 'normal' men would not have been able to withstand their desire and that Edward's and Stefan's ability to control themselves is exceptional.

SEXUALIZED VIOLENCE AND RAPE MYTHS IN YOUNG ADULT FICTION: CONCLUSIONS

In contrast to young adult fiction that thematizes and problematizes sexual violence consciously and is thus necessarily politically correct and highly didactic, mainstream young adult novels reproduce societal concepts of sexualized violence unreflectedly. Seemingly harmless instances of sexual violence such as the forced kiss and the invasive CCTV surveillance in the girls' bathroom in *Girl, 15* are cast as everyday occurrences for girls which they may

36 Ibid., p. 285.   37 Ibid., p. 286.   38 L.J. Smith, *Awakening*, p. 49.   39 S. Myer, *Twilight*, p. 236.

not like, but ultimately will have to live through as part of growing up. Girls that are cast as sexually deviant, such as Vickie or Caroline in *Vampire diaries*, are routinely blamed for the sexual aggression directed towards them. The idea that rapists are either lunatics or could not help their actions due to their biological hard-wiring is supported through the depiction of scenes of rape or sexualized violence as committed by mentally disturbed men such as Rosalie's fiancée Royce or Katniss' opponent Cato. Sexualized violence is thus trivialized and depicted as a necessary evil during the teenage years. The message is that in relationships, violence is always an issue, and if a girl decides to go to a party she has to reckon with having to defend herself against abusive class mates – either with or without success. While the victim's alternatives are to either trivialize the attacks and not prosecute the attacker or to become a social outcast, the offender succeeds in regaining or even strengthening his social position relatively quickly.

Vampire novels are known for their intermingling of sexuality and violence – the fact that the technical details of sucking blood and the accompanying ecstasy are so similar to sexual intercourse supports the (mostly female) protagonists' masochistic longing and the prevalence of rape myths. On the other hand, as we have seen, the occurrence of rape myths is not restricted to vampire fiction. Even romantic teenage novels such as *Girl, 15* harbour a surprising number of scenarios of sexualized violence and the congruent explanatory constructions. Thus, a broad segment of young adult fiction not only supports prevailing rape myths but also recreates traditional sexualized gender roles[40] (such as female passivity and male sexual dominance and aggression) and the acceptance of sexual violence as a rite of passage and initiation.

---

40 For further analysis of sexual gender roles in *Twilight* and *Vampire diaries*, see M. Rana, '"Killers are sort of romantic": the eroticization of sexual and domestic violence in *Vampire diaries* and *Twilight*', *Journal of Children's Literature Studies*, 8:1 (2011), 92–105.

Contributors

CLÉMENTINE BEAUVAIS is a junior research fellow at Homerton College, Cambridge. Her research interests include children's literature, the philosophy of childhood and educational thought. Her PhD thesis sought to work towards an existentialist theory of children's literature by analyzing adult-child power dynamics in radical children's picturebooks. She is currently converting this work into a book, which will be published by John Benjamins at the end of 2014.

JESSICA D'EATH was awarded a PhD in 2012 by the National University of Ireland, Galway. Her thesis examined representations of the Great War in Italian children's fiction from 1915 to the present. Her research interests include nineteenth- and twentieth-century children's literature and Italian literature and history, with a particular focus on the First World War.

VICTORIA DE RIJKE is reader in arts and education at Middlesex University, London, and co-editor of the journal *Children's Literature in Education*. She has engaged in political arts projects with children and has published widely on children's literature topics. Recent publications include *Duck* (London, 2008) and her co-produced picturebook *The A–Z of dangerous food* (London, 2012).

ELIZABETH A. GALWAY is associate professor of English at the University of Lethbridge, where she also serves on the directorate of the Institute for Child and Youth Studies (I-CYS). She is the author of *From nursery rhymes to nationhood: children's literature and the construction of Canadian identity* (London, 2008) and is currently working on a monograph on children's literature from the First World War.

ANNE MARIE HERRON is a former primary teacher and school principal. She is the author of language and literacy programmes for schools and has a number of publications aimed at emergent readers. She currently works as a freelance researcher. Her PhD thesis, 'The tyranny of the past? Revolution, retrospection and remembrance' (2011) focused on the work of Irish writer Eilís Dillon from the perspectives of memory and commemoration.

MARIAN THÉRÈSE KEYES is a senior executive librarian in Dún Laoghaire–Rathdown County Council Public Library Service, Dublin. While working at the National Art Library, London (1991–8), she spent several years cataloguing the Renier Collection of Children's Books. A former president of the Irish

Society for the Study of Children's Literature (2011–13), she completed her PhD in 2010 in St Patrick's College, Drumcondra. Her research interests include Victorian illustration and children's books published by Anna Maria Fielding Hall (1800–81).

BRIGITTE LE JUEZ is a senior lecturer in French and comparative literature in the School of Applied Language and Intercultural Studies at Dublin City University. She is currently president of the Comparative Literature Association of Ireland. Bluebeard has been one of her main topics of investigation and publication recently. Her latest article is: 'La réécriture des mythes comme lieu de passage: l'exemple de Barbe-Bleue', *La Revue de Littérature Comparée* (December 2013).

ÁINE MCGILLICUDDY lectures in German studies and children's literature studies at Dublin City University. Her research interests include politics and cultural identity in children's literature studies. A former vice-president of the International Board on Books for Young People (iBbY), Ireland, she is currently a committee member of the Irish Society for the Study of Children's Literature (ISSCL). She was awarded a three-month research fellowship at the International Youth Library in Munich in 2014.

CIARA NÍ BHROIN lectures in English literature in the Marino Institute of Education, Dublin. She is a founder member and former president of the Irish Society for the Study of Children's Literature. She has published a range of articles and book chapters on identity, ideology, mythology and the representation of the past in Irish children's fiction. Her most recent publication is a co-edited collection of essays *What do we tell the children? Critical essays on children's literature* (Cambridge, 2012).

EITHNE O'CONNELL is senior lecturer in translation studies at the Centre for Translation and Textual Studies in the School of Applied Language and Intercultural Studies at Dublin City University. In 2003, she published *Minority language dubbing for children* (Oxford). She is a founder member of ITIA (Irish Translators' and Interpreters' Association) and ESIST (European Association for Studies in Screen Translation) and she has published widely on aspects of audiovisual translation, texts for children and minority languages.

MARION RANA is chief editor of *interjuli* (www.interjuli.de), a scholarly magazine on international research in children's literature. She has just completed her PhD on 'Disruptive desire: sexuality in young adult fiction' at Johannes Gutenberg University, Mainz, and is currently working on a research project on deafness and cultural identity in literature. Recent publications dealt with (national and cultural) othering and otherness in the *Harry Potter* series, the *Twilight* films as ambiguous tales of sexuality and sexual awakening and the eroticization of sexual and domestic violence in *Twilight* and *Vampire diaries*.

OLGA SPRINGER worked as DAAD-Lektorin in the School of Applied Language and Intercultural Studies in Dublin City University between 2010 and 2012. She was awarded an MA in English literature and comparative literature in 2010 and she is currently completing her doctoral thesis on 'Ambiguity in Charlotte Brontë's *Villette*' in Tübingen University, Germany. Her research interests include Victorian literature, ambiguity in language and literature, detective fiction and the novels of Ngaio Marsh.

SUSAN SHAU MING TAN is a PhD student at the University of Cambridge. Her doctoral research focuses on violence as socio-historical initiation in young adult literature. Tan received her MPhil from the University of Cambridge and a BA in English literature from Williams College.

Index